.

Munsee Indian Trade in Ulster County, New York, 1712–1732

THE IROQUOIS AND THEIR NEIGHBORS

Christopher Vecsey, *Series Editor*

Munsee Indian Trade
in
Ulster County, New York, 1712–1732

Edited by
Kees-Jan Waterman *and* **J. Michael Smith**

Translated by Kees-Jan Waterman

Syracuse University Press

Munsee Indian Trade in Ulster County, New York, 1712–1732
A Section from the Anonymous "Account Book, 1711–1729" (in Dutch), Philip John Schuyler Papers
(Volume 11): A Manuscript in the Holdings of the Manuscripts and Archives Division, New York Public
Library, Astor, Lenox and Tilden Foundations

First Edition 2013
13   14   15   16   17   18   6   5   4   3   2   1

∞ The paper used in this publication meets the minimum requirements of the American National
Standard for Information Sciences—Permanence of Paper for Printed Library Materials, ANSI
Z39.48-1992.

For a listing of books published and distributed by Syracuse University Press, visit our website at
SyracuseUniversityPress.syr.edu.

The original manuscript is owned by the New York Public Library, Manuscripts and Archives Division,
Astor, Lenox and Tilden Foundations, 5th Avenue and 42nd Street, New York, NY 10018. It is cataloged
as *Account Book, 1711–1729 [in Dutch], Philip John Schuyler Papers, Volume 11*. A microfilm edition can be
ordered from the owner (Microfilm reel #30 of this set of papers).

This edition has been published with permission from the owner.

The translator has also produced a full transcription of the original Dutch manuscript. This document
is available at the publisher's website in .pdf format; if you do not have an Adobe Reader, it can be
downloaded for free from the Adobe website: http://www.adobe.com/products/acrobat/readstep2
.html.

Transcription citation: Waterman, Kees-Jan. Transcription, 2011. *Munsee Indian Trade in Ulster County,
New York, 1712–1732: A Section from The "Account Book, 1711–1729" [in Dutch], Philip John Schuyler
Papers, Volume 11*. Manuscripts and Archives Division, New York Public Library. Astor, Lenox
and Tilden Foundations. Internet publication, Syracuse, NY: Syracuse University Press.
www.syracuseuniversitypress.syr.edu/spring-2013/Munsee-Indian-Trade-section.pdf

Library of Congress Cataloging-in-Publication Data
Available upon request from the publisher.

Manufactured in the United States of America

To Karlijn

&

To Suzanne

Kees-Jan Waterman lives in Haarlem, the Netherlands. He received an MA from both the University of Amsterdam and the Catholic University of America, Washington, DC. He specializes in the history of initial contact and prolonged interactions between natives and settlers in New Netherland and early New York. Kees-Jan Waterman works at an institute of the Royal Netherlands Academy of Arts and Sciences. Among other publications, he has edited and translated *"To Do Justice to Him and Myself": Evert Wendell's Account Book of the Fur Trade with Indians in Albany, New York, 1695–1726.*

J. Michael Smith is a native of Dutchess County, New York, and a resident of Vermont. As an independent historian he has documented the cultural histories of Munsee-Delaware peoples and the lives of individual natives in the mid–Hudson River Valley. He is a contributing author to New York State Museum bulletins of the Native American Institute seminar papers, and has published various articles. J. Michael Smith is a Senior Media Specialist at Vermont Public Television.

Contents

Illustrations

Maps

Figure

Graphs

Plates

Photographs

Tables

Acknowledgments

DURING THE RESEARCH for this publication, we received gracious support from both individuals and organizations. People who shared their knowledge and expertise included Anne-Marie Cantwell, Shirley W. Dunn, Marc B. Fried, Charles Gehring, Robert S. Grumet, George R. Hamell, Laurence M. Hauptman, Jaap Jacobs, Eric J. Roth, Blair Rudes, and Janny Venema.

Among the organizations, we wish to express our gratitude to the staff of the New York Public Library, Manuscripts and Archives Division, in particular for the permission to publish this account book. In addition, we received assistance from the Ulster County Records Center, Ulster County Clerk's Office, where Ken Grey, Archivist, was especially helpful; the Bevier House Museum; and the Ulster County Historical Society, particularly Melinda J. Terpening, Director.

Portions of the introduction and sample pages of the translation were previously published in Kees-Jan Waterman and J. Michael Smith, "An Account Book of the Indian Trade in Ulster County, New York, 1712–1732," *Hudson River Valley Review* 21, no. 1 (Autumn 2007): 59–84. We wish to thank the editors of that journal for their permission to reproduce sections from that article. We are also indebted to the staffs of Mount Gulian Historic Site, Beacon, New York, and the Ulster County Clerk's Office, Kingston, New York, for their permission to reproduce photographs of Wappinger and Esopus artifacts.

We also express our gratitude to the D.U.T.C.H. Foundation for funding part of the publishing costs of this book.

Abbreviations

BMK   Roswell Randall Hoes, trans. and ed., *Baptismal and Marriage Registers of the Old Dutch Church of Kingston, Ulster County, New York, 1660–1809* (New York: De Vinne Press, 1891; repr. Baltimore, MD: Genealogical Publishing Co., 1980).

BSDC   Vassar Brothers Institute, *Book of the Supervisors of Dutchess County, NY* (Poughkeepsie, NY: Vassar Brothers Institute, 1911).

CFLP   Cockburn Family Land Papers, Manuscripts and Special Collections, New York State Library, Albany.

DHNY   Edmund B. O'Callaghan, ed., *Documentary History of the State of New York.* 4 vols. (Albany, NY: Weed, Parsons and Co., 1849–51.

GTM-PC   George Tappan Manuscripts. Transcriptions of records in the Ulster County Clerk's Office, 1847, Philhower Collection, Special Collections and University Archives, Rutgers University Libraries, New Brunswick, NJ.

MJC   Minutes, Justice Court, 1714–41, folders 1–3, Ulster County Clerk's Office, Kingston, NY.

MOA   Moravian Archives, Microfilm Series, New York State Library, Albany.

MPCP   Samuel Hazard, ed., *Minutes of the Provincial Council of Pennsylvania,* 16 vols. (Harrisburg, PA: Theopilus Fenn and Co., 1838–52).

NJHS   William A. Whitehead, ed., *The Papers of Lewis Morris, Governor of the Province of New Jersey from 1738 to 1746* (Newark: New Jersey Historical Society, 1852).

NYBP   New York Book of Patents and Deeds, Secretary of State, New York State Archives, Albany.

NYCD   Edmund B. O'Callaghan and Berthold Fernow, eds., *Documents Relative to the Colonial History of the State of New York*, 15 vols. (Albany, NY: Weed, Parsons and Co., 1856–87).

NYCM-LP New York Colonial Manuscripts, Indorsed Land Papers, New York State Archives, Albany.

NYHS   New-York Historical Society, New York.

NYSA   New York State Archives, Albany.

NYSL   New York State Library, Albany.

PGP   Philips-Governor Family Papers. Unpublished manuscripts on file at Rare Book and Manuscript Library, Columbia University, New York.

PWJ   James Sullivan et al., eds., *The Papers of Sir William Johnson*, 14 vols. (Albany: Univ. of the State of New York, 1921–65).

SCP   Julian P. Boyd and Robert J. Taylor, eds., *The Susquehannah Company Papers*, 11 vols. (Wilkes-Barre, PA: Wyoming Historical and Geological Society, 1930–71).

TDRK   Dutch Records Kingston. English translations of Dutch Records by Dingman Versteeg, 1896–99, Ulster County Clerk's Office, Kingston, NY.

UCCS   Minutes of the Ulster County Court of Sessions, Manuscripts, Ulster County Clerk's Office, Kingston, NY.

UCDB   Ulster County Deed Books, Ulster County Clerk's Office, Kingston, NY.

UCTAL   Ulster County Tax Assessment List, 1716–17, ICN 02-01657, Historic Records, 101 Box Collection, Ulster County Clerk's Office, Kingston, NY. (Also available at www.co.ulster.ny.us /archives/exhibits/burning/TaxAssessment.html.)

WAB   Kees-Jan Waterman, trans. and ed., *"To Do Justice to Him and Myself": Evert Wendell's Account Book of the Fur Trade with Indians in Albany, New York (1695–1726)*, Lightning Rod Press vol. 4 (Philadelphia, PA: American Philosophical Society, 2008).

Glossary

Dobelstin:	textiles, woven with a pattern of dice.
Dufel/duffel:	a coarse or thick woolen cloth.
Ell:	a standard Dutch linear measurement, used primarily for measuring cloth. Roughly equivalent to 68 centimeters, or 27 inches.
Eysersterck:	here probably also *eysen*. A type of fabric with slightly elevated figures. Also called *hakkebak* in Dutch.
f:	abbreviation of *florijn*, another word for guilder; see also there.
Floret:	silk ribbon.
Gall:	abbreviation of gallon.
Gemp:	also *gemt*. A fabric often used to hem the edges of a blanket, for decoration and reinforcement.
Guilder:	Dutch monetary unit, consisting of 20 stivers.
Hend:	also hendr. Abbreviated form of common first name in Dutch, Hendrik/Hendrick.
Kan:	Dutch liquid measure, equivalent to one quart.
Kno:	here also *know*; canoe.
Lap:	literally, a "cutting" or "remnant piece." The trader used this term predominantly to describe textiles. Where this is obviously intended, it has been translated as a "piece [of fabric]." In the single case where it refers to a pelt, the Dutch word has been maintained. Precise information on the size of a *lap* of peltry is not available.
lb:	pound.

Muts: also *mus*; liquid measure, 2.15 oz. Diminutive forms in-
                  clude *mutsie* and *musi(e)*.

Penneston: here also *pinneston*; a type of woolen cloth, named after
                  the place in England where it was produced.

Piece [of fabric]: see *lap*.

Oosburgh: Osnaburg; a kind of coarse, heavy cloth. Named after the
                  place in Germany where it was produced: Osnabrück.

pt: abbreviation of pint.

qt: abbreviation of quart.

sch: abbreviation of *schepel*; a dry measure, equivalent to 0.764
                  English bushels.

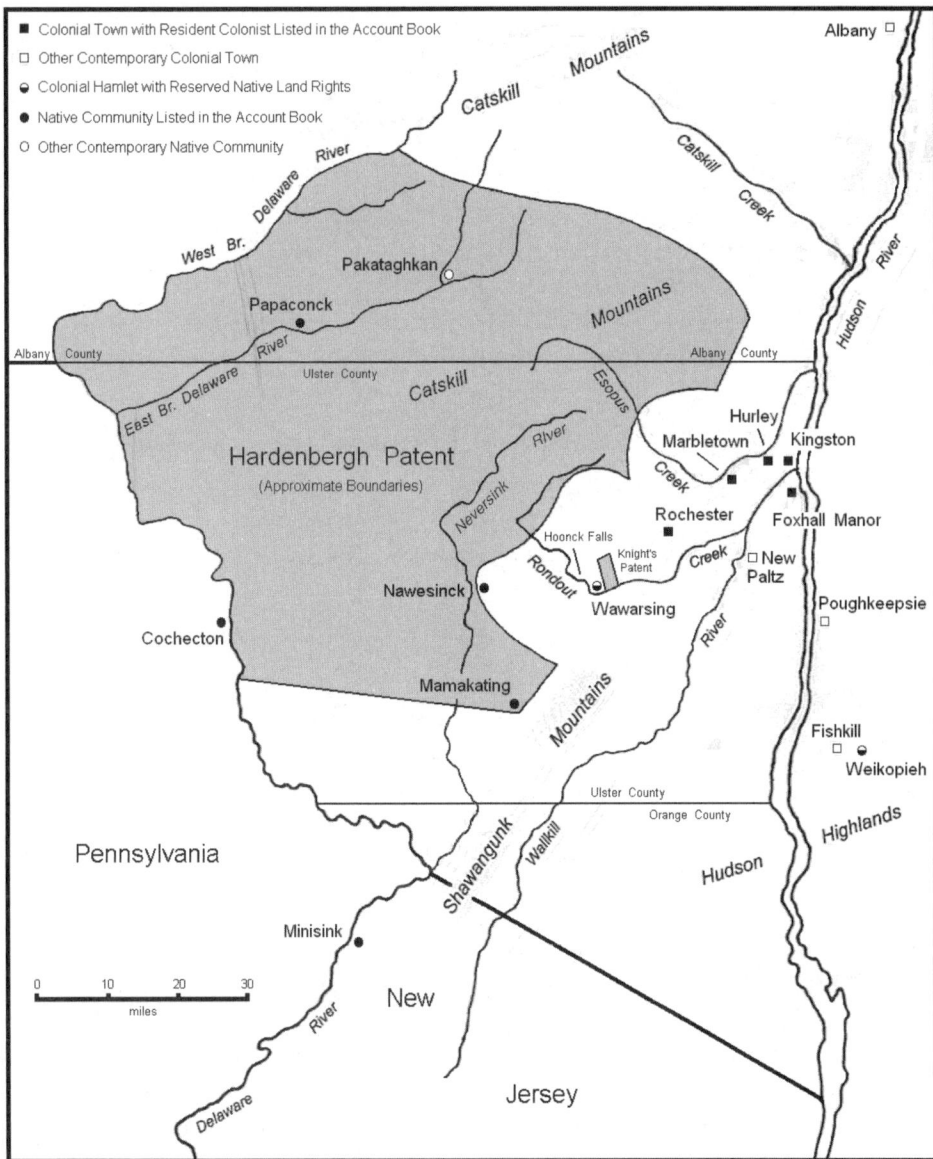

1. Places associated with the Indian Trade section (1712–32) of the Ulster County account book (1711–29). Created by J. Michael Smith.

2. Detail from a 1751 map depicting the lowlands along the Nawesinck (or present Neversink) River sold by the Esopus Indians in 1705. The island marked HH (shown at bottom) was the home of Old Abram or Kwakasagh, a man whose burial was recorded by the Ulster County trader in 1725 (Wilson Family Papers, Map Division, 3K-13, OCLC #248245876). Courtesy William L. Clements Library, Univ. of Michigan.

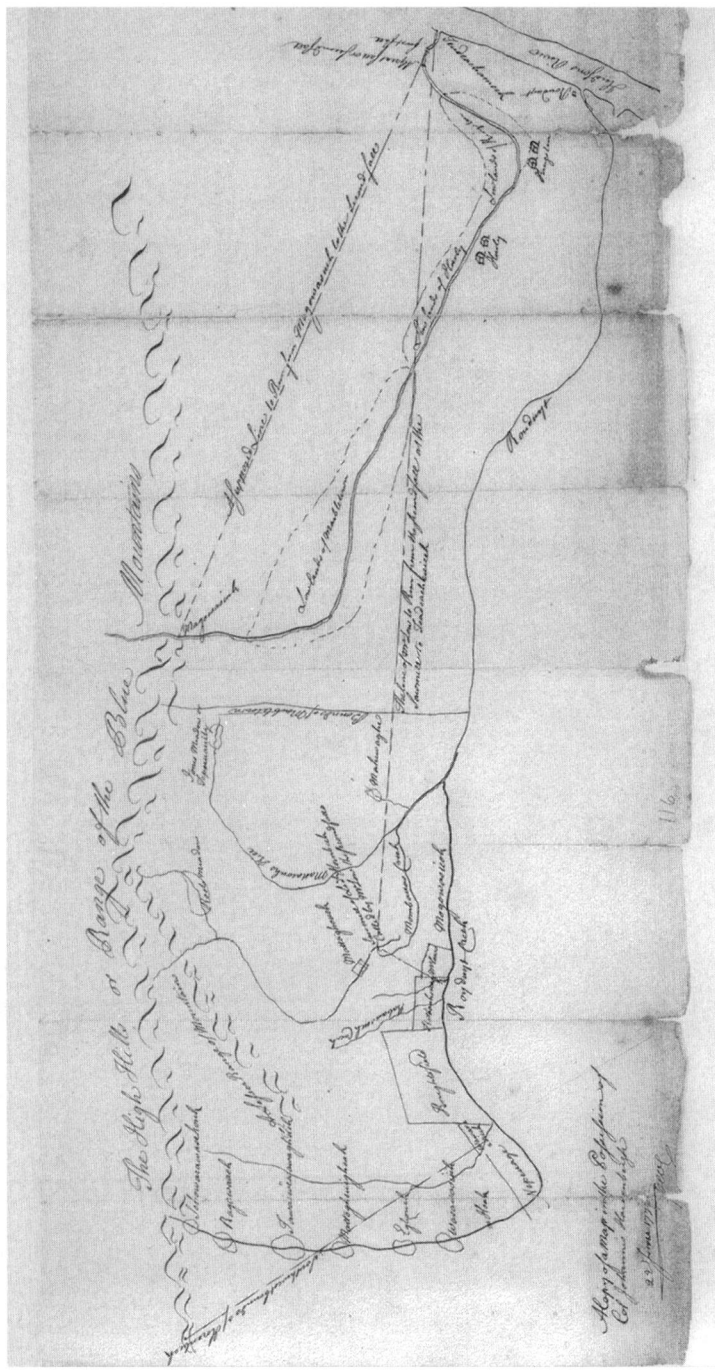

3. Copy of a map from 1772 depicting the heart of the Ulster County settlements in the early eighteenth century. Named Indian flats or meadow lands on the upper Rondout Creek (shown at far left) were sold by the Esopus Indians in 1703 and incorporated as part of the Rochester Patent that same year. Native individuals listed in the sale named Kattkies, Tautapagh, Kwakasagh, Pansogh, and Norman are all noted over a decade later as patrons of the anonymous Dutch trader (Cockburn Family Land Papers, box 9, folder 17, item 116). Courtesy of New York State Library, Manuscripts and Special Collections, Albany.

Munsee Indian Trade in Ulster County, New York, 1712–1732

Introduction

WORKING WITH SCATTERED and fragmentary primary sources forms one of the most serious challenges to students of European and Indian economic exchanges in northeastern America during the colonial period. Referring to the seventeenth-century fur trade in this region, one scholar has concluded that such exchanges are "known almost entirely through the archaeological record of the goods received by the native vendors."[1] This introduction examines several key aspects of a recently discovered Dutch account book recording trade with American Indians in Ulster County, New York, from 1712 to 1732. Throughout, comparisons are provided to a closely contemporaneous account book of the fur trade in Albany, New York, dating between 1695 and 1726.[2] The Ulster County account book is an important source for the study of intercultural trade in the mid–Hudson River Valley during the first decades of the eighteenth century. The account book is not mentioned in any secondary literature on commercial exchanges between Indians and Europeans in the American Northeast. Just over two thousand transactions with native individuals allow for detailed indexing and comparative analysis.

The manuscript is the only account book for the Indian trade in Ulster County that has so far been located.[3] It documents native women participating in commercial exchanges in numbers that are higher than reported or assumed in the existing historiography. Aggregated data from the transactions in the ledger provide information on the types of commodities and services that native customers acquired; the associated prices and conditions; the degree to which Indians paid off their debts with the trader; and the types of products and services they used in

1

doing so. The data indicate that in the exchanges in this region the deer-skin trade had replaced the declining beaver trade by the early decades of the eighteenth century.

The account book documents a substantial trade with a few hundred Indians who belonged to Algonquian-speaking groups in and around the mid–Hudson River Valley. Esopus and Wappinger Indians usually referred to collectively as the northernmost bands of the Munsee-Dela-wares or Munsees represent the most identifiable native peoples in these records.[4] The account book contains no evidence that the bookkeeper dealt with neighboring Mahican bands of the upper Hudson Valley. The manuscript lists a total of 243 accounts of Indians and reports on slightly more than two thousand transactions (see tables 1 and 2). During these exchanges, Indians acquired 2,057 products and services. In addition, they paid off all or part of their debts in 492 cases (see tables 3 and 4). The transactions can be organized into 580 grouped exchanges that occurred at or about the same moment in time. Eighty-five of these grouped trans-actions do not show the month and year in which goods or services were exchanged (see table 5).

The accounts contain data on commercial dealings with about two hundred Indians in Ulster County; slightly more than one hundred appear with their names listed. Careful tabulation and cross-referencing of all Indian individuals who appear in the accounts shows that about fifty of these natives were listed only with their name; they were not otherwise described, for instance as being connected to another Indian individual in the account book.[5] Besides this group of fifty natives, four Indians were identified by means of both their place of residence and their name.[6] Another fifty Indians appear with their names and, in addi-tion, the bookkeeper identified them through a connection with another named individual.

A large number of Indians make an appearance in the accounts with-out their name but with links to other named Indians—usually their close kin. This group consists of about ninety individuals. It includes one native man who was described by listing his place of residence and his relation to another individual. He appears as "the savage from kisechton[,] perraris['s] brother" in October 1725.[7] The largest subgroup within this pool of ninety natives consisted of women whom the bookkeeper described merely as the wives of named Indian men; at least twenty-seven such individuals can be discerned. Finally, a small number of Indians appear without their own name and without any described connection to another Indian in the account book. The appearances of such individuals are extremely difficult to distinguish from each other. This group seems to consist of between five and eleven individuals; one of them is identified only by his place of residence—or, rather, by a general description thereof.[8]

Description of the Manuscript

The account book is part of the holdings of the Manuscripts and Archives Division of the New York Public Library, Astor, Lenox and Tilden Foundations. It is cataloged as "Account Book, 1711–1729," volume 11 of the Philip John Schuyler Papers, 1684–1851. On the whole, the condition of the manuscript is excellent. Most pages are undamaged and the handwriting is clearly legible.[9] The volume was rebound in 1955, when a single restoration was made of the upper, outer corner of the last leaf of the manuscript. The bound manuscript contains no identifying statement, name, signature, initials, or other markings. According to documentation at the Manuscripts and Archives Division, the items in the Philip Schuyler Papers were acquired over various decades, starting in the early 1900s.

The volume contains 428 pages. With a few exceptions, all entries are in Dutch. The first 317 pages document trade between colonists in Ulster County. On page 318 it switches to records of commercial exchanges between a trader and his Indian clientele. The pages with accounts of colonists are numbered, showing the same page number for the left and right side of each double page, but the ones that record Indian trade are not. The transition from accounts that record trade between colonists to records of the Indian trade shows that the two sections were not kept in an entirely separate fashion. The final page of accounts with colonists (assigned page number 317) is on the recto side of a leaf, and the Indian accounts commence on the back side of the same leaf; also, accounts on pages 317 and 318 stem from around the year 1717. Page number 318 has been numbered [1] in the translation of the Indian section. The translator has applied numbers in between brackets, [1]–[111], to all pages in that section.[10] The pages that record commercial exchanges with native customers include three empty pages, reducing their total number to 108. Plates 1 through 5 provide samples of original account book pages.

The part that details the Indian trade is written in a different hand than the first section. Neither of the two handwritings has been identified. On a few occasions the bookkeeper of the Indian trade wrote brief entries in the section that details trade with colonists.[11] The section on trade with colonists clearly misses some pages; it starts with a leaf numbered '19,' being a credit page of accounts for which the debit page is lacking from the manuscript. A considerable number of pages in this part of the manuscript are badly torn and cut. But there are no indications that pages were removed from the Indian section, and none of the pages in that part shows signs of cutting or tearing. There are a few cases where an internal reference is made from an Indian's account to another account of the same person on a different page, and only some of such references have not been identified in the existing account book.

The manuscript contains evidence that the keeper of accounts of the trade with colonists was also involved in Indian affairs in the Ulster County region. An account on the left side of page 123 in the "European" section[12] shows entries on the account of "Mʳ William Nicols," recording two payments to Indians: in September 1699, the bookkeeper noted "to cash paid [to] the Indians[,] p[er] order—£ 63=6=0," and an otherwise undated entry from 1702–3 reports "To:d[ebit]:paid the Indians—£ 25=0=0." These entries are in English. The credit side of the same page has a single entry in Dutch, showing a "Contra Cr[e]d[it]" of £750 from May 1698, "for a piece of land Called Wawarsieneck."[13] A similarly named tract of land, "wawarasinck, . . . Lying and Being att Esopus" and later included as a part of the Rochester Patent had been sold by the "Indians Jochim and his Sister neraehanamon" to Wiliam Pieterse Rooks in September 1684. This tract was noted again in a 1699 lease for lands on the Rondout Creek as "Waarsinck or Knights field," and included reserved rights granted to the Indians "called Anckerops land running to a creek where the great wigwam now stands."[14]

Entries in the Indian trade section of the account book are dated between 1712 and 1732, with only isolated occurrences of entries for the years 1712, 1715, 1718, and 1732. No entries have been located for the years 1713, 1714, 1730, and 1731; the one entry that may be from the year 1716 is ambiguous.[15] The bulk of the Indian accounts shows entries dating from 1717 to 1729. As the description of the volume indicates, accounts in the section on trade with colonists cover the period from 1711 to 1729. The only references in this section to interactions with Indians have been listed in the previous paragraph.

The accounts are neatly kept; all verso sides contain accounts with entries that record purchases on credit by Indians. The recto sides always show payments by Indians. In a number of cases they are accompanied by entries with additional acquisitions on credit by indigenous customers. Most accounts are dated, and the debtor is usually identified either by name or by a reference to another Indian person—in most cases a relative of the customer. All accounts were kept in Dutch guilders, except a few totals and subtotals of accounts and some purchases of guns that were recorded in pounds. Horizontal lines on both the debit and the credit pages separate accounts associated with different individuals. However a closer reading of the various Indian accounts reveals there are some exceptions to this rule. When the trader received a payment, he crossed out the corresponding entries or accounts.

The bookkeeper recorded entries in the ledger, quite likely keeping track of transactions as he traded. This circumstance led him to jot down brief sentences and statements pertaining to individuals and their families conducting business with him. These entries include extensive kinship data and provide new and fresh insights into the lives of Munsee individuals that broaden our knowledge about native peoples from the region. In translating the document, the language style of the account book has been maintained as much as possible. Retaining the straightforward nature of the original text conveys the immediacy of the context in which it was written.

Context

All accounts in the Indian section and most in the part dealing with trade between colonists were kept in the Dutch language. For eighteenth-century Ulster County, this was not an aberration. In Kingston, the principal town and county seat, many official records were kept in Dutch until 1774. In the towns of Rochester and Marbletown, Dutch was regularly spoken through the early nineteenth century. Many private papers were written in Dutch, although English slowly became the dominant language during the late eighteenth and early nineteenth century. A number of eighteenth-century account books from the region were kept in Dutch, and in some cases both Dutch and French were used in a single account book of colonists in or around the New Paltz settlement.[16]

Although the first entry in the Indian section of the account book presents it as being kept in Kingston, New York, it is more plausible that after some years the account book was maintained in another location in Ulster County. An undated entry that can be placed in or around 1725 shows that the son of an Indian named "manonck" had part of his debt cancelled for "going to Kingston."[17] Another undated entry, one that can be placed in 1728, describes the debts of "Sar[,] hendreck hekan[']s wife" as deriving from "her old account in Kingston."[18] Two sections of the accounts of trade with colonists are clearly marked at the top of the page (in English) as "In Kingstoune," with the description "In the County of Ulster" added. The first one runs from pages 288 to 295; all entries are in English. The second section extends from pages 296 to 317; entries in this section are written in both Dutch and English.[19]

Nineteen colonists appear in the Indian section of the account book; all resided in various settlements within Ulster County. Of these, six or seven resided in Rochester and six are documented as living in Kingston.[20] This suggests that the account book was used for trade in and around Kingston and Rochester. The unidentified person who kept the Indian accounts recorded eight times the involvement of individuals whom he identified by their familial relationships to someone he refers to as "Your Honor." This person may have been the trader's employer. Without further evidence this man's identity and those of his relatives remain elusive.

Significance of the Manuscript

For most of the named Munsee Indians listed in the account book, an ethnic or band affiliation cannot be precisely determined. Biographical indexing of these names with additional data from Ulster County land deeds, treaty minutes, and other documents shows that thirty-three of the individuals mentioned can be identified as Esopus Indians.[21] Most of these are men; they are listed in the Esopus Cohort in the appendix. Moreover, seventeen of their named kin and an approximate number of twenty-two of their unnamed kin can be recognized as separate individuals.[22]

Another group of seven individuals listed by the trader are similarly identified as Wappinger Indians in administrative and land records from Dutchess County; they are listed in the Wappinger Cohort in the appendix. In addition, one named and eight unnamed members of their kinfolk can be recognized. Some of these Indian men were also reported in county records as the principal leaders ("sachems" or "chiefs") of the two groups, information not provided by the trader in the account book (see figure 1 and appendix). Furthermore, three individuals listed in the accounts can now be identified as principal men from other areas of Munsee territory ("tappose," "marinham" or "marenghan" and the latter man's son "Tabarhekan").[23]

The account book shows clearly that an active trade was conducted in Ulster County with a sizeable number of Indians. This trade is contrary to the general perception held by scholars examining relations between Indians and colonists in the region. Most authors have taken the view that local American Indians had retreated from Ulster County following the Esopus Wars fought with the Dutch settlers of New Netherland (1659–60 and 1663–64).[24] This interpretation maintains that Munsee Indians subsequently dispersed over the wide area inhabited by Algonquian-speaking Indians, a number of them settling in multiethnic villages in the Minisink region on the Upper Delaware River.[25] The fur trade, in this view, continued to be of some importance in relations between Indians and colonists during the 1660s and 1670s, but was quickly replaced by agriculture as the principal economic activity in Ulster County.[26]

While many Munsees did indeed migrate away from their traditional homelands, the pages in this manuscript contain evidence that they continued to journey to the lands on which they were once sovereign peoples. Alone or in small groups, Indians came to the trader in Ulster County on a regular basis to buy merchandise on credit up to the end of the third

Figure 1. Esopus Sachems recognizable in the Ulster County account book

Esopus individuals (plus known aliases) noted in Kingston court minutes as sachems (1709–45)	Individuals also identified in the Ulster County account book (1717–29)
- Ankerop II/Tackawaghkin	- Ankerop
- Crawamogh	- Krwamo or Karwamo
- Hendrick Hekan/Cacawalemin	- Hendrick Hekan
- Noundawagaeron/Renap	- Runup
- Sander/Nachnawachena	- Sander
- Shawanachkie/Jepthah	- Sawenakies or Sawanagkis
- Walengagkin/Mattakie	- Warangau/Matekie or
- Aramochtan/Hendrick	Hans Jacob
- Keatachkaugs	
- Maquarape	
- Moghweekaghkingh	
- Mamarhekemeck	
- Paijemhanck	
- Qualaghquninjou/Abel	

decade of the eighteenth century. They paid their debts with products that have always figured prominently in the intercultural trade in colonial America (see photos 1 and 2).

Information from the account book also shows that at least a number of Indian customers were originally from the area; in the second half of the 1720s they returned to their ancestral homelands to attend burials of other natives on at least six occasions. In addition, the Indian man "tatweu" purchased 8 "kan" of rum to "drink at his sister's grave" in 1727 (see table 6).[27] One of these accounts may contain a listing of goods that were to be buried with the deceased Indian named Mannonck in January 1727—a person of some consequence in the account book; he and his relatives developed the highest debt in the account book.[28] The listed items including rum are grave gifts that are consistent with those found in excavated burial sites from the colonial era in the Northeast.[29]

Munsee Indians who traveled to Ulster County to engage in trade and perform burial ceremonies acted within an existing framework established earlier with representatives of an expanding colonial society. Esopus leaders returned regularly to Kingston to ratify the Nicolls treaty. This tradition, begun by the first English governor of New York in 1665 after the seizure of the Dutch colony of New Netherland the year before, lasted until 1771 and resulted in twenty-three diplomatic encounters.[30]

During one of these conferences, on June 30, 1712, justices of the Kingston Court questioned Esopus sachems about "Rumors . . . spread in this County that the Indians would rise against the Christians." Their allegations were based on a letter sent earlier that month by officials from the town of Poughkeepsie to the New York Council, reporting that the neighboring "Katskill Indians had sent a belt of wampum to the Indians in Dutchess County warning them to prepare for Warr." Esopus sachems denied the charge that they were preparing for hostilities and two years later made incriminating accusations of their own before the justices, citing rumors from an African slave "that the Christians did intend to make warr against the Indians."[31] Clearly, native peoples of the region were still active players in the colonial and intertribal politics of the times. Wappinger Indians also met periodically from 1722 to 1743 with Dutchess County officials at Poughkeepsie, where disbursements of presents (mostly currency) were recorded for "Renewing articquils [sic] of Peace with them as Yearly."[32]

Until 1745, Esopus Indians continued to visit the area around Kingston to trade, though not always to their satisfaction. In May of that year, Esopus sachems complained to the authorities in Kingston that "their Produce is too Cheap and the Commodities which they want from the Christians Too Dear, and Therefore they Desire that their produce may be Dearer and the Christians Commodity Cheaper."[33]

Those sachems included "Sander, Chief Sachim of the Esopus" and the lesser sachems Hendrick Hekan and Renuade. Indians with the exact same names, "Sander" and "hendrick hekan," appear in this account book; the third man listed is likely to be the same individual described as "runup" in the trader's accounts.[34] Moreover, between 1720 and 1746, Dutchess County authorities recorded payments in twenty instances to fourteen named Indians—mostly Wappingers—who had collected bounties on wolves.[35] In addition, American Indians in many cases retained fishing and hunting rights after "land cessions" and thus returned to their original homeland to make use of these rights.[36]

There is incidental evidence that shows how parties of expatriate Indians reported as living at Cochecton during the French and Indian Wars had recently fled there from their homes in "the heart of the Ulster County settlements" in the winter of 1745–46 (see map 3).[37] New York agents sent to investigate reported the Indians had left the areas "where they usually traded & hunted" because "they were afraid of the people in the County . . . you are always under arms." After "renew[ing] their Covenant Chain" with the agents, these native groups returned to their homes near colonial settlements during the following year.[38] Later, on March 26, 1756, British Superintendent of Indian Affairs Sir William Johnson called off a group of forty to fifty "River Indians" who had gathered at Kingston for protection and settled them among the Mohawks.[39]

It is plausible that some of this trader's customers traveled only modest distances to reach the localities where he traded. Although Robert S. Grumet concludes that "Munsees . . . were forced to sell more than 82% of their lands by 1717," large portions of the interior sections of Ulster County were not sold until the mid-eighteenth century.[40] James D. Folts reports that while some Munsees were leaving their homelands in the early eighteenth century, various Munsee settlements remained, and a "few native communities persisted near colonial settlements in Orange and Ulster Counties (NY) and Warren County (NJ) until around 1750."[41]

Differences of interpretation over Indian land cessions were a "recurring matter of complaint" during the above-mentioned treaty conferences with the Esopus, suggesting that natives who dwelled there were asserting their rights to use the lands for their homes, gardens, and hunting grounds.[42] These disputes arose after some settlers purchasing small tracts of land claimed they had bought much more when applying for patent grants with colonial officials, and thereby creating vast estates that defrauded Indians of their remaining rights. Native people only gained knowledge about the size of such grants years later when patent holders attempted to survey and settle the unsold lands.[43]

These disputes were not uncommon in the mid–Hudson River Valley, and Munsee leaders were forced to defer to county and provincial authorities for resolution. In the early 1720s the then principal Esopus sachem young Ankerop—a man noted along with "his wife" and "his son" in the trader's accounts—lodged several complaints before county justices over settler encroachments in the Evans Patent south of New Paltz. Other complaints were made against settlers living near Coxsinck and on the little Esopus Creek, in the township of Marbletown.[44]

Esopus Indians also upheld long-standing grievances against the one-million-acre Hardenberg Patent straddling Albany and Ulster counties and demanded additional payments over several decades, before ultimately confirming the boundaries of the land grant in 1751 and forestalling for a time their removal.[45] Some Indians continued to live at or near their homelands in Ulster County after these sales well into the eighteenth century, or had reoccupied other lands that were deeded earlier to colonists but remained unsettled. The Esopus made their last known land sales in the region in 1767 and 1770, conveying two separate tracts lying in Marbletown and Rochester.[46] Moreover, after these closeout sales the Esopus continued to be numbered among the county's residents; in 1776 at the start of the American Revolution, Ulster County authorities were instructed to distribute gunpowder to the inhabitants of native communities there.[47]

Recurring Indian complaints over extravagant land grants were also not uncommon on the east side of the Hudson River, in Dutchess County. Wappinger territory had been entirely patented by 1706.[48] However, just as in Ulster County many of these patents exceeded the boundaries contained in the original Indian sales associated with the grants. Other patents were issued before the lands were even purchased from the Indians.

In 1721 and 1730, the Wappinger sachem Old Nimham, a man identified by the trader in the accounts of an unnamed "sister" and that of "his mother," demanded and received compensation for unsold lands contained within several patents. He was also successful in obtaining a certificate from the governor of New York confirming the tribe's remaining land rights in the county, including assurances of protection to improved lands at "Weikopieh" near the town of Fishkill where he and his family lived.[49] Additional evidence for a continued Wappinger presence on parts of their homeland is indicated by a letter from Sir William Johnson on

May 28, 1756, "To the Magistrates of the Precinct of Fish Kilns" in Dutchess County, concerning the removal of "River Indians whose families are at Fish Kilns" to settle among the Mohawks.[50]

The appearance of around two hundred Munsees trading in Ulster County becomes more understandable in light of the above-mentioned circumstances. Availability of this manuscript makes another significant contribution to our understanding of the fur trade. Recently it has been demonstrated that a respectable part of the fur trade between Indians and Evert and Harmanus Wendell in Albany, New York, from 1695 to 1726, was carried out by Indian women. They participated by maintaining accounts in their own name, or functioned as intermediaries in the trade with other Indians. In 20 percent of the cases in the Wendell brothers' account book women were the main account holder; but they were actively engaged in just less than half of all accounts—49.6 percent. Of all the individuals who accompanied Indians to the Wendells', 50 percent were women; for Indians acting as a guarantor for other customers, that figure stands at 37.5 percent. In addition, fully half of the natives whom the Wendells described as traveling to other Indian communities, sometimes as Evert's agents, were women, and they represented more than half (53%) of the individuals who engaged in transactions with the Wendells outside the town of Albany.[51]

Table 1 in this introduction relays almost exactly the same figures for the Indian trade in Ulster County: native women acted as main account holders on 22.2 percent of all accounts, and they engaged in trade on 50.6 percent of all accounts that witnessed active participation of Indians, other than the main account holder. Combining the number of women's own accounts (54) and those of men on which women actively participated (70), Indian women were represented on 51.4 percent of all accounts in the ledger. Three out of the nine cases that document the occurrences of escorting or accompanying other natives in this account book involved women (33.3%). Unlike the Wendell brothers, the trader in Ulster County did not describe any women traveling to other localities, and the only guarantor who appears in the exchanges listed in his accounts was a man. Moreover, it cannot be established if he recorded any significant trade as being conducted by native women on his behalf in or around the county apart from a 1725 entry noting that one woman had carried rum with her "to trade for me."

The three Indian women listed as escorting individuals to the anonymous Dutch trader all appear to be from areas outside of Ulster County, based on either their place of origin mentioned or their relations to men reported elsewhere in land sales. One of them "Ragel[, perhaps Rachel] the savage woman from Manesinck" was almost certainly associated with the Munsee ethnic group known as the Minisinks (proper) living in northern New Jersey. "Keghkenond['s] daughter" was likely from Wappinger territory, where her father is identified as "Kechkenond," a participant in a land sale in the Dutchess County highlands. The woman described only as "Tabarhekan['s] wife[']s sister" by the trader was probably from Orange County, where her brother-in-law is reported in land sales there as one of the principal men ("Taparnekan," noted earlier).[52] The above comparative analysis indicates that these women were traveling from differing Munsee territories beyond Ulster County to engage in trade. It cannot be determined if they did so on the trader's behalf as is indicated for some women in the Wendells' accounts.

Trading Practices

The information and aggregated data contained in the Ulster County trade book provide material for a detailed description and analysis of the contours and parameters that characterized the trading activities colonists and natives engaged in.

Occurrences of Trade

Although trade occurred in almost every year covered by the account book, the ledger also reveals unique patterns in time. As graph 1 shows, commercial exchanges with Indians were slow to take off when this trader initiated his activities in Ulster County. Between 1715 and 1723, the number of (groups of) transactions in 1719 stands out as an exception in this regard. The most promising years for this trader were between 1724 and 1726. The latter year represents the highest level of trade on credit recorded by this fur trader. Following that, activities clearly diminished and fell back to considerably lower levels in 1728. A small recovery occurred in 1729 with a few sizeable exchanges that constitute the last year in which the trader recorded transactions.[53] The sudden cessation of trade after 1729 coincides with the end of the account book. The account book contains no indication that the trader ceased to be active in trade with the Indians, but if he continued his operations beyond this point he recorded the Indians' debts and payments in another ledger.

Closer examination of the trade with Indians in Ulster County demonstrates the absence of an explicit trading season. A tabulation of all transactions that are recorded in the account book, arranged by month, shows that Indian customers visited the trader all year (see graph 2).[54] As stated earlier, the Indian trade events cover the years 1712 to 1732, yet most of the transactions are concentrated within a period of thirteen years, from 1717 to 1729. Every month witnessed trading activities in each year; not a single month shows fewer than thirteen (groups) of transactions during the given period. While the months of April and May, July, and September through November show a higher level of activity, only in February, June, and December did Indians trade considerably less than

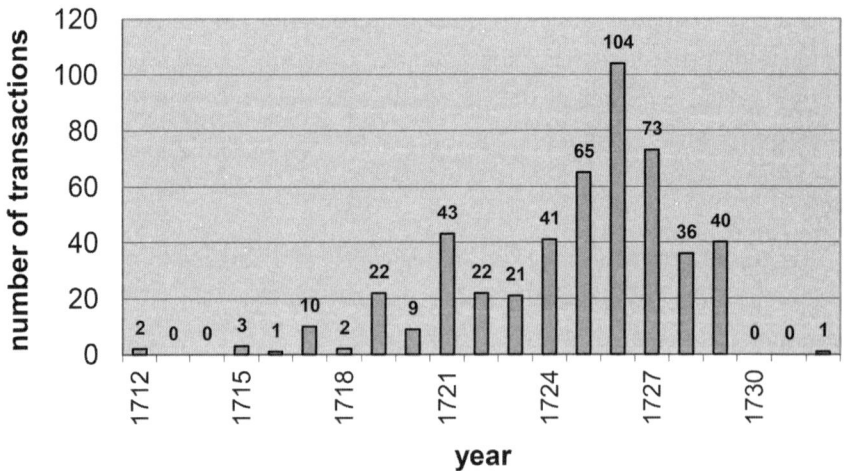

1. Distribution, (groups of) transactions, by year[a] [n=495].

[a]All transactions within one account that were entered in one year have been grouped together as one transaction.

the average of 32.4 (groups of) transactions in a given month. The turnout in April could be associated with fishing activities that coincided with the spawning season of two anadromous fish species, as has been described for Indians along the Delaware River. In a similar fashion, Esopus Indians may have returned to the Hudson River and tributary waterways like the Rondout Creek to catch these and other migratory fish during the annual spawning run.[55] Earlier it has been observed that Indians often retained fishing rights when signing lands over to colonists.

The contours of the Indian trade in Ulster County differed from that of the Wendells in Albany. While their account book also shows native customers engaged in trade on a year-round basis, a stronger seasonal pattern existed in the distribution of their trade over the various months of the year. The Wendells' trade was more robust between May and September, and showed a distinct peak in June. The stronger seasonal quality of commercial activity in Albany may have been caused by the fact that the Indians who traded there included representatives of groups who had to travel great distances to arrive in Albany.[56] The data for Ulster County suggest that this trader's customers were not as far removed from the marketplace and came to trade more frequently.

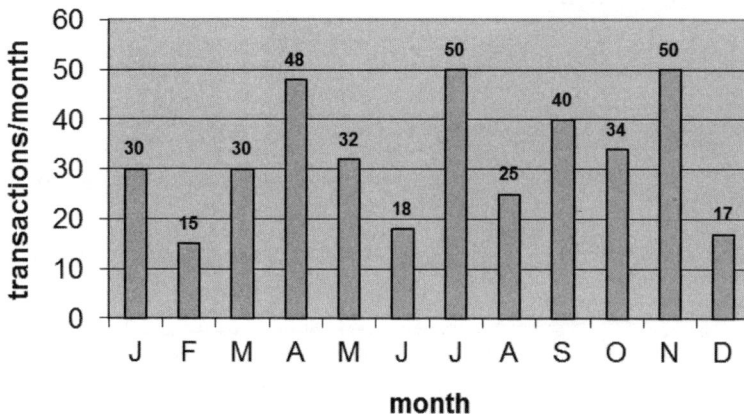

2. Distribution, (groups of) transactions, by month[a] [n=389].

[a]All transactions within one account that were entered in the same month have been grouped together as one appearance.

Categories of Goods Traded

Entries in this manuscript read as a virtual catalog of the types of products that Indians purchased during the seventeenth and eighteenth century from colonists in the American Northeast. A detailed listing of the commodities that the Ulster County trader sold on credit to native customers is presented in table 3. Data from that table have been summarized in graph 3.

It becomes evident that the Munsee Indians who traded in Ulster County had a strong preference for products of three types: textiles, alcoholic beverages, and ammunition. Together these categories constitute 87.85 percent of all merchandise that natives acquired on credit from this trader. The second largest group of transactions, 29.2 percent, involved the purchase of alcoholic beverages. As late as May 1745, the earlier mentioned Esopus sachem Sander complained to Kingston authorities that native people were buying liquor, beer, and cider too easily: "There are So Many Taverns, which is a great reason for their Poverty, and Desire That they may be Remedied."[57] The remaining types of goods are extremely

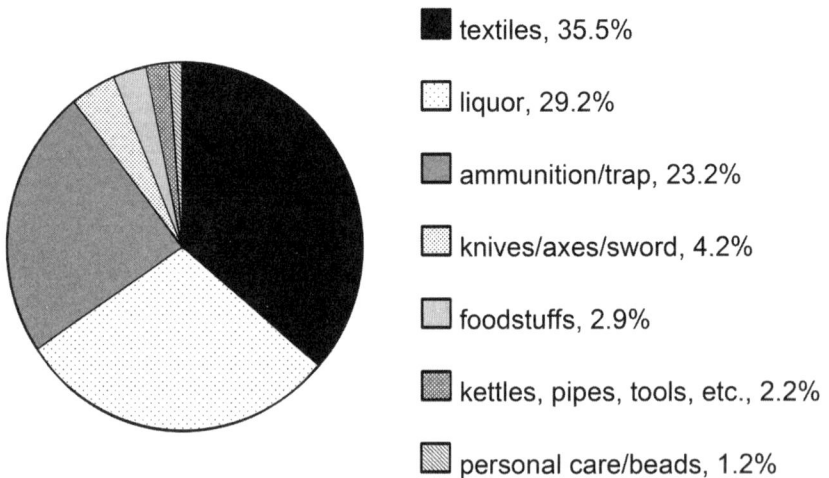

textiles, 35.5%

liquor, 29.2%

ammunition/trap, 23.2%

knives/axes/sword, 4.2%

foodstuffs, 2.9%

kettles, pipes, tools, etc., 2.2%

personal care/beads, 1.2%

3. Categories of trade goods; percentages.
Note: Categories of less than 0.5% have been excluded.

diverse (see table 3) but they represent a little more than 12 percent of the commodities that the Indians bought.

In terms of native preferences, analysis of the Wendells' trade with Indians in Albany shows some similarities with and differences from the account book from Ulster County. In both Ulster and Albany counties, sales of firearms were limited to a very small number of cases (0.5 and 1.4 percent, respectively). Native customers of the Ulster County trader and the Wendells' clientele both showed strong preferences for textiles, liquor, and ammunition—and in the same order. In fact, one scholar has observed that "cloth was the most universally desired and generally useful . . . of all trade goods craved by Native Americans in the Northeast."[58] But in Albany, native customers exhibited a more pronounced preference for manufactured textiles: clothing and woolens were sold on credit to Indians in the majority of all transactions (53.8 percent). In Ulster County, fabric and clothing were also the most sought-after types of commodity, but they were exchanged in just over one-third of the transactions (35.5 percent). Consequently, alcoholic beverages and ammunition feature more prominently in the trade in Ulster County than in Albany. In the Wendells' account book they constituted 19.9 and 12.9 percent of all transactions, whereas in Ulster County these categories were represented in 29.2 and 23.15 percent of all transactions.

In Albany, money was a trade item of some significance: it appeared in sixty-eight transactions on credit, or almost 4 percent of all transactions. In Ulster County this category was virtually absent from the trade, as Indians acquired it in merely 0.2 percent of all transactions. Conversely, foodstuffs appear with some regularity in the Ulster County account book, but are virtually absent from the Albany record: bread, molasses, corn, sugar, and other foodstuffs were purchased in Ulster County in fifty-eight transactions, or almost 3 percent of all recorded exchanges. In Albany, foodstuffs occur in only six transactions (0.3 percent of the total number of exchanges).

A number of the differences between these two nearly contemporary account books suggest possible economic disparities between the Wendells' clientele and the Ulster Country trader's patrons. Native customers

in Ulster County may have been less economically secure. Their purchasing patterns show that they bought far fewer items of clothing and
focused instead on small pieces of fabric; gunpowder was also purchased
in smaller quantities during transactions. Moreover, in a considerably
higher number of cases in Ulster County than in Albany, Indians bought
lesser amounts of rum during transactions, a more costly drink compared to beverages like beer and cider. In Albany, the Wendell brothers
sold almost no beer and cider was purchased on credit on only four occasions. In total, these latter beverages appear in just 0.8 percent of their
transactions; in Ulster County such purchases represented 4.3 percent of
all exchanges. In addition, the higher number of instances in which Indians bought foodstuffs on credit from the Ulster County trader indicates
they were perhaps not always capable of providing enough foodstuffs for
themselves and their families. The native peoples trading in Albany purchased far less food.[59] Whether this indicates a higher degree of depen-
dency on the Ulster County trader cannot be established.

Although they appear only very rarely, some items that were purchased by Indian customers are nonetheless interesting. Such instances
include the three cases in which Indian men bought a stack of playing
cards. Yet, between 1670 and 1680, travelers along the Hudson River
observed that card playing had become a regular form of entertainment
among the Munsees, adding that especially the young men were fond of
it.[60] It is even less expected to notice the purchase of a saddle by "peghtarend," an Indian man, in or after 1722. At around the same time he settled
his account by delivering two horses to the trader.[61] Finally, we do not
know if the native customers who acquired a bell and a silver cup intended
to use them for the purposes for which they were originally made.

Indians most often paid off their debts, or parts thereof, with peltry.
From the 492 recorded payments in which natives satisfied all or part of
their debts, 429 or 87 percent involved the delivery of peltry, meat, and
animals (see table 4). Within this category it is difficult to specify what
payments were in meat instead of peltries because the bookkeeper did
not always distinguish between the two products. But from the amount
of credit that the Indians received it becomes evident that almost all these
instances related to the delivery of peltry.[62] In Albany, beaver was the most

commonly used type of fur to compute debts and payments in the Wendells' accounts.[63] The Ulster County trader, however, listed beaver in only
10 percent of all cases where transactions were recorded as consisting of
peltry, meat, or animals. This may be an indication that his Munsee clients
were experiencing difficulties in obtaining beaver furs. In Ulster County
the largest number of debts and transactions were recorded in deerskins
and elk hides. Bear hides, marten furs, and raccoon skins also appear
with some frequency. The data clearly show that the deerskin trade had
replaced the declining beaver trade by the early decades of the eighteenth
century in this region.

In the remaining sixty-three recorded debit transactions by Indians
in Ulster County that did not involve peltry, most Indians provided labor
and services to the trader (thirty-eight cases). Primarily, Indians performed wage labor for credit against their debts (see table 7). Men were far
more likely to act in this fashion than women; twenty-six of the thirty-two
instances concerned men. Typically, these Indians' wages varied between
2 guilders for spinning and 9 guilders per day for doing fieldwork. On the
whole, Indian men earned more credit by providing labor than women
but "pitternel," "wife" of "kattias," earned 12 guilders per day for harvesting flax.[64] "Mack" and perhaps another one of "pansogh[']s son[s]"
worked on five occasions and earned a total credit of 181 guiders. And in
a total of four instances "Magh[,] hend[rick] hekan[']s son" decreased his
debt by 151 guilders for his work "on the farm."[65] One Indian man reduced
his debt by 12 guilders "for 1 day [of] shooting fire," perhaps indicating
that he shot burning arrows into the vegetation to prepare land for culti-
vation. The Indian named "tateu" received 16½ guilders worth of rum for
which he was not required to pay, provided he would point out a mine
in the following spring. An entry in another account shows a native man
earning a credit of 8 guilders for a "plain meal".[66] The Wendells' account
book contains only one instance of an Indian who offered to do manual
labor. On or before February 17, 1709, Evert recorded that an unnamed
Cayuga woman "wanted to cut my twigs with the axe," but no credit was
entered on her account.[67]

The other type of service that Indians in Ulster County provided with
some degree of regularity was to travel to various destinations (see table

8). Only Indian men traveled to localities in the region in order to earn credit against their debts. The Esopus sachem Sander was particularly involved in this type of service for the bookkeeper. In the 1720s he made three such trips, once in the company of a man named "herij" and twice by himself; his brother Lendert was also noted traveling to earn credit on his account to a place the trader called Nawesingh (i.e., Nawesinck). Two of Sander's journeys were directed to the Minisink region but the earnings differed considerably from each trip, ranging between 20 and 45 guilders. A relatively short trip to Kingston reduced the debt of "manonck's son" by 9 guilders. When compared to the findings from the Wendells' accounts at Albany, Indians who traveled for this bookkeeper from Ulster County operated within a smaller geographical range.[68]

Deferred Payments

As a result of the nature of purchases on credit, most of the Indians' payments were recorded after the transactions in which they incurred debts with the trader. Usually, at least one or two years passed between the moment debts were incurred and any subsequent payment by the customers. But it was not uncommon for native clients to pay all or part of their debts at a far later point in time. The account of a woman named "kisay," "wife" of the Indian "arent fynhout," acquired the debt of 12 guilders that her husband had developed exactly ten years earlier.[69] In twenty-two cases, the trader explicitly described natives' arrears as an "old debt," an "old account," or as deriving "from older times." In nine of these cases, the debtors were women.[70] Similar occurrences appear in the Wendells' account book. For example, the debt of one Canadian Mohawk man, started under Evert and Harmanus's father, was not paid until (at least) eleven years after the original transaction or transactions. Their account book lists seven additional cases of such arrears, described as being from older, or earlier, times.[71] In six of these cases, the debtors were women. Such asynchronous exchange of goods and services was also common among settlers in the Hudson Valley, and it persisted well into the eighteenth century.[72]

There are no remarks in the accounts to indicate that the trader urged his customers to pay off their debts in full within a certain period of time.

The same characteristic has been observed regarding the trade of the Wendell brothers in Albany with their Iroquois and Mahican patrons, but they nonetheless recorded a few instances in which they expected some customers to discharge part of their debts before a certain moment in time.[73] The overall debt performance of the Ulster County trader's patrons will be discussed in the "Prices, Values, Discharges, and Retention Rate" section of this introduction.

The Use of Dutch Guilders

The bookkeeper consistently used the Dutch currency, consisting of guilders and stivers, in almost all of the 243 accounts. Using guilders and stivers was fairly typical for account books in Ulster County during the early eighteenth century.[74] The accounts in the trade book of Evert and Harmanus Wendell at Albany in which money was used, 11.5 percent of all accounts, also showed the same characteristic.[75] The Ulster County trader's accounts with Indians recorded the use of English pounds in only nine instances, either to state the total debt of an Indian or to record the purchase of a gun. On one occasion, the debt that resulted from the purchase of a gun was recorded in Spanish pieces of eight (the "peso"), and three other accounts also feature the use of that currency (listed as "doller").

Escorters and Guarantors

Dating from the period between 1721 and 1727, the account book shows eight cases of Indians escorting other Indians to Ulster County to trade. In addition, there is one ambiguous case from May 1721 (see table 9). Indian men acted as escorters in most instances; five out eight cases are recorded by the trader. Men were escorted as often as women, reported in four cases each. Men usually escorted other men, and the same applied to women. However, considering the small amount of data it cannot be determined if the one case where a woman escorted "a boy" or the two cases where men escorted women constituted an aberration to an established pattern. One of the two men listed as escorting a woman, "quakeses[,] karwamo['s] son" may not have had to travel far to reach the trader; his father, identified under the name "Crawamogh," was a leading Esopus sachem signing numerous land sales in the Hudson Valley and noted at treaty conferences in Kingston. The only individual to act as an escorter more than once was the Indian called "the sawa(n)nos," but he did so for the same individual.

In addition, the Ulster County account book contains one entry showing an Indian man functioning as a guarantor, and he did so for another Indian man. This occurred on November 7, 1724, when "hendreck hekan" was guarantor for the purchase of a gun by an Indian man whose identity is difficult to ascertain.[76]

In the trade between Indians and this Dutch merchant, the need to deploy intermediaries was evidently not such a pressing matter as it was for the Wendells' trade with their customers visiting Albany, some of whom traveled long distances to get there. The Wendells recorded the appearance of escorters in thirty-seven, possibly thirty-eight cases; guarantors appeared sixteen times in their accounts.[77] Presumably the trade that was carried on in Ulster County involved native customers living within a closer proximity to the trader's locale, and a more intimate rapport may have already existed with the Indians who presented themselves at his store.

Securities

On eight instances during the period between 1720 and 1728 the bookkeeper required seven Indians to provide a security for the goods they acquired on credit. The only Indian to leave a security more than once was "abramhans['s] daughter, menckesonghua," but those instances occurred within the same month (see table 10). The practice was applied less than once a year. This average dwindles even further if one compares this number of cases with the complete period in which the bulk of transactions was recorded in the account book (1717–29; twelve years). Only two women had to leave a security, against five men. Of the four cases in which the customer had to leave a gun, three involved men; two out of three instances in which the security consisted of (a belt of) wampum involved women (see photos 3 and 4). Rum was the product for which Indians most often provided a security.

During a similar time period, the Wendells in Albany recorded eighteen instances of native customers' "putting down [a security]." The ratio between men and women appearing in such a fashion in their account book is almost exactly equal to the one reported for the Ulster County trade: fourteen to five—the cases included one couple.[78]

Borrowing by Indians

Indians borrowed items from the Ulster County trader on seven occasions in the period between 1723 and 1726 (see table 11). Men were more likely to do so than women, but no Indian was recorded as borrowing items more than once. European merchandise was loaned in only one instance; in all other cases, Indians borrowed peltry. Debts incurred in this fashion were small and in three cases the Indians were not charged at all—or, for some unknown reasons, the debts were not recorded.

The Wendells recorded slightly more cases of clients who borrowed commodities, twelve to be precise.[79] They included seven men, three of whom borrowed twice, and two women. Guns were borrowed on six occasions, all by men. Customers who borrowed from the Wendells were charged in seven cases; two customers borrowed without being charged. Of those charged, one man's debt was remitted, three customers paid their debt, and three did not—the other cases remain unclear.

Peddlers

The Wendells' account book from Albany contains twelve instances in which Indians functioned as peddlers in the trade with Indian groups outside of Albany. In addition, it documents a few dozen cases where such a role by Indians can be plausibly deduced from the accounts.[80] In the Ulster County account book, however, only one such instance is recorded. At an undisclosed time in 1725, an Indian woman "tatapagh['s] wife" purchased four "kan[s]" of rum on credit, and the bookkeeper remarked that "she carried [it] with her to trade for me."[81] She was charged the regular price for the rum. The ledger contains no information on how this Indian woman might have benefited from the arrangement.

Bills

Another significant difference apparent between the Ulster County account book and the Wendells' accounts in Albany relates to the use of written "bills." The Wendells supplied their customers with bills in eleven cases.[82] Hardly any such occurrences can be found in the Ulster County account book. The trader documents only one similar case in the accounts of "Mack, pansogh's son," from April 1725, in which he remarked that this Indian man had 21 guilders "coming to him on his bill," a debt the book-keeper "paid with 1 colored shirt."[83] Other cases are more ambiguous. For instance, an undated entry regarding the sachem Sander states that he had earned a credit of 48 guilders "for his note for moses du pri."[84] Also "wieijiekas's daughter," possibly "moskono . . . or margriet," received a credit of 12 guilders in November 1724, "for [a] note from klas roosa."[85] Although the exact nature of these entries remains unclear, it is evident that the practice of exchanging written bills or notes was less developed in the Ulster County trade than in the economic exchanges between the Wendells and their clientele in Albany.

Indian Debts Paid by the Trader

Both the Ulster County account book and the Wendells' accounts in Albany contain unique references reporting payments on some of their customers' debts with other nearby merchants. The Wendell brothers listed eight such cases in their account book.[86] However, the Ulster County account book contains more conflicted evidence in this regard. While the merchant lists Indians' debts with other traders in Ulster County nine times in the period from 1719 to 1729 (see table 12), the ledger presents no direct indications that the trader was involved in payments to the merchants. All but one of the Indian debtors were men; two of the seven creditors were women. Indians' debts with only one colonist were recorded more than once, those with the unnamed man described as "the smith."

Entries of this kind were usually concerned with small debts; typically the Indians' arrears were between 2 and 6 guilders. Two debts clearly stand out in this regard. The account keeper's mother stood to receive 280 guilders (also recorded as £6:10) for a gun she sold to "Winhas[,] sawagonck hend[rick's] son," and "pitter tappen" expected the Indian "Mack[,] pansogh['s] son" to pay 240 guilders (no amount in pounds given)—also for a gun. But the account book provides no indications that the book-keeper ever paid these Indians' debts.

On the other hand, the Ulster County account book shows that a larger number of colonists were actively involved in this bookkeeper's intercultural trade than in Albany. A total of twenty colonists either fetched goods for Indians or delivered payments that were counted as a credit toward the latter's debts. All instances are listed in tables 13 and 14. Such involvement could be on a modest scale, as was the case in or after November 1719, when "benyamen du pri" paid a debt of 5 guilders that the sachem Sander owed to the bookkeeper. Other more substantial dealings were also carried out through such channels. Jan van Kampen, for instance, settled the debt of a female relative of the Indian Manonck in December 1718; this woman's arrears amounted to 120 guilders. In this case, as in all others, the European settler paid only a part of a native's debts with the bookkeeper.

Tables 13 and 14 show twenty-seven cases in which European individuals either fetched goods for Indians or paid part of the Indians' debts for them. Among the twenty Europeans who acted in this fashion, the group of relatives associated with the person whom the trader referred to as "Your Honor" played a pronounced role. In total, that person's mother, brother, sister, and daughter appear eight times in such capacities. The mother of "Your Honor" fetched goods for native clients on four occasions, twice for "mattiso, mannonck['s] son," once in 1725 and then again in 1728. The unidentified man's brother picked up merchandise for Indians twice, on one occasion for the same son of Mannonck, in 1726. Another European appearing more than once in such a role was "klas roosa," who paid part of the debts of two different natives in November 1724. Between 1723 and 1726, "Jors/Jores[,] hester['s] son" had his debts paid by colonists on three occasions; "pitt[er] van Cornel[i]s" provided this service twice for him, and another man named "a: stenberge" did so once.[87] These intercultural services were a predominantly male affair. Only seven or eight women are among the forty or forty-one individuals who provided or received these services for or from one another.

Parts of Larger Debts and Shared Accounts

The Ulster County account book contains information on another aspect that differs from the accounts of the Wendells in Albany. On four occasions the Ulster County bookkeeper described transactions for which an individual Indian's payments or debts were recorded as that individual's "part" of a larger quantity. Such occurrences are absent from the Wendells' account book.

Payments described as one particular Indian's "part" of a larger transaction are recorded on pages [6], [40], and [50]. The customers delivered "skin," meat, and deer meat. Two of these occurred on the same day, August 6, 1728.[88] A description relating to part of a debt appears on [91]. Two Indian men and two women were involved in these transactions. This brief overview excludes the case on [106], in which it is uncertain if the reference to "kisay['s] daughter annatie['s] part" recorded a debt or a payment. That entry is undated and the word "part" has been crossed out.

Accounts that were evidently shared between Indians appear rarely in this account book. The occurrences of such accounts with multiple main account holders are listed in table 1. Only one account had two main account holders, documenting one man and one woman in that fashion; three holders were noted in three accounts, and all of these concerned a man, a woman, and a son.[89] Taken together, accounts with multiple main holders constitute 1.6 percent of all accounts.

Prices, Values, Discharges, and Retention Rate

The wide array of exchanged goods and services that are listed in the Ulster County account book provides data for a discussion about prices, values of traded commodities, and labor. The natives' debt performance can also be gauged and an indication of the trader's success in retaining his customers can be presented.

Prices of European Merchandise

An overview of the prices Indians paid for commodities that they bought from the trader in Ulster County is provided in table 15. This overview also includes one type of service for which natives developed a debt: repairs to guns. It should be noted that these price levels showed no tendency to change over time; no substantial shifts are recognizable during the years in which the bulk of the transactions were recorded, 1717–29.

Some types of merchandise that appear in table 3 (categories of trade goods) have been excluded from table 15. In many cases, the bookkeeper neglected to specify the exact quantity that a native customer purchased of a certain product. For example, entries documenting the sale of molasses suffer from this limitation. In addition, for some products the number of occurrences is too limited to contain any informative value. Finally, transactions involving clothing have been all but excluded because of the wide variety of qualities and textiles in which they were offered and sold. Stockings, for instance, were recorded in pairs and by measure (in "ells"); they could be made of baize, strouds, and "seyette," and were listed in various sizes. The same situation occurs with the numerous sales of shirts.

Since alcohol was sold in standard measurements,[90] establishing the range of prices at which it changed hands presents fewer difficulties. The same applies to the prices of gunpowder and lead. Various types of textiles were measured by reasonably set standards, as well; "ells" of various types of cloth and "blankets" have been included in table 15.

Value of Indian Goods

Tabulating the goods and labor that Indians applied to ease or pay off their debts presents us with similar complications. In establishing the value of a pelt, weight and quality are paramount. But the bookkeeper recorded such characteristics only on a few occasions. Elk skins, for instance, earned Indians credit in a range between 12 and 30 guilders. The same situation applies to cases in which a customer delivered "one deer" or "one deerskin" to the bookkeeper. Lacking any indications of the size or weight of the animal, its meat, or its skin, the credit that was listed cannot be rated in table 16. Finally, several accounts contain entries that recorded receipt of various types of peltry but report only the total credit for that transaction, without specifying the value of the specific furs. More clearly defined amounts of the credit natives earned by offering their labor to the trader have already been listed in tables 7 and 8.

The exchange rates that can be derived from tables 15 and 16 allow for a brief analysis of the Indians' purchasing power in their dealings with the Ulster County trader. Evidently a native customer was expected to deliver one otter skin for one pound of gunpowder, three bars of lead, or six pounds of lead. One fisher fur would fetch him or her one ell of duffels or slightly more than one gallon of rum. To purchase one stroud blanket on credit left the Indian customer with a debt that was equivalent to between two and four bear hides, or about five pounds of beaver fur. One raccoon would pay off the debt for one bottle or one "kan" of rum; one pound of deer or elk skin covered the debt for one pint of rum. One pound of grease or rendered animal fat was equivalent to the debt for one "kan" of cider or beer. The purchase of a gun on credit presented the customer with a considerable debt of several hundred guilders. To settle that type of debt, a customer would have to deliver around two-dozen pounds of beaver fur, or more.

Debt Performances by Natives

The account book enables us to determine to what degree Indians paid off their arrears with the trader. In total, 175 of all 243 accounts carry entries in which Indians developed a debt with the bookkeeper. Since the bookkeeper crossed out debts when they were settled, it is possible to arrive at a reconstruction of the Indians' aggregated debit performance.

These percentages show no signs of variation over the years. Accounts of prominent natives and their relatives, and their transactions on other natives' accounts, closely follow the general pattern shown on table 17. In all, 52 percent of Indian leaders' accounts and transactions were paid in full, 11 percent were paid in part, and 37 percent were left unpaid.[91] Although in general they acted no different than other Indians, relatives of native leaders could develop substantial accounts. Lendert, a brother of the Esopus sachem Sander, paid off one of the largest debts listed in this account book, 486 guilders, but the last page shows his being indebted to the further amount of 474 guilders.[92]

From the data in table 5 another indicator of the Indians' performance in this regard can be obtained. The total number of 2,005 transactions in this account book can be organized into 580 grouped exchanges that occurred at or about the same moment in time. Of this total, 200 grouped exchanges document payments by native customers. This amounts to 34.5 percent of all grouped transactions.

Indians in this account book performed better than the Mahican and Iroquois customers of Evert and Harmanus Wendell in early eighteenth-century Albany. There, Indians from various ethnic groups fully paid only between 20 and 29.5 percent of their debts. While the number of debit accounts that were paid in part was considerably higher (21.3–47.8 percent), Iroquois and Mahican customers of the Wendell brothers left more accounts fully unpaid. On the whole, Mahicans refrained from making discharges on 46.2 percent of their debit accounts. In some years, the Iroquois performed better in this regard (28.4–36.9 percent) and paid off more than the Indians in the Ulster County account book, but aggregated data from the Wendells' account book show that in one grouping of eighty accounts they made no discharges on 58.8 percent of their debit accounts.[93]

The Trader's Retention Rate

Detailed knowledge of the types of merchandise that the trader made available to Indians, the quality and pricing of the goods, and the conditions under which such items were traded leads to questions regarding the trader's success rate at attracting native clients. While it cannot be established how his Indian customers viewed the above-mentioned prices or the quality and conditions offered, the rate at which they returned to trade with the bookkeeper constitutes a significant indication of this trader's ability to generate additional traffic in his store.

From the account book, we can collect information about the number of first transactions with native traders on all accounts, grouped by year. Plotting those data into graph 4, where they appear as line 1, and combining these with the total number of transactions in a given year allow us to make several observations. Data on the total number of transactions per year are derived from the data in graph 1.[94] Variance in graph 4 between the two lines constitutes the subsequent activity on existing and newly opened accounts.

It becomes apparent that during the first years of his business the trader saw only limited numbers of customers return to engage in commercial exchanges. Between 1718 and 1723, the total volume of transactions per year was only slightly larger than the number of first exchanges that were recorded in accounts during those years. Yet the customer base that he had developed between 1712 and 1723 started to yield considerably more transactions in the years between 1724 and 1729. Particularly

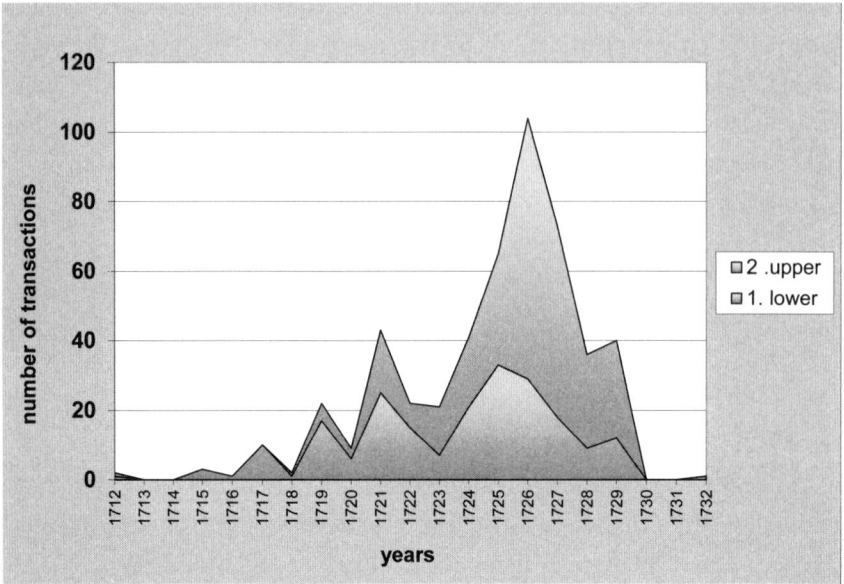

4. Correlation between (1) number of first transactions on all accounts, by year; and (2) number of (groups of) transactions,[a] by year.

Line 1: Data assembled from account book. Line 2: Data from graph 1.

[a]All transactions within one account that were entered in one year have been grouped together as one transaction.

productive, from the point of view of the trader, were the years 1725–27, with 1726 clearly representing a peak year.

Descriptions and Identification of the Native Patrons

Besides containing detailed information on the activities of native men and women trading in Ulster County, the account book also provides varying degrees of insight into the methods that the trader used to identify and describe his Munsee patrons.

Some descriptions of individuals noted in the accounts present almost insurmountable obstacles for a thorough identification of every person involved. Occasionally the author described native individuals in circular ways. For instance, after noting the name of the main account holder Andries in 1726, he further commented on an unnamed male customer's appearance in the same account, reporting that the latter was the "brother" of the main account holder's "wife."[95] In most cases, wives of Indian customers were not otherwise identified, let alone one man's sister-in-law.[96] Women are often referred to simply as an Indian man's wife, a practice occurring in at least twenty-seven cases. Only one male customer is described just as a woman's "husband." He is the unnamed husband of "Keg(h)kenond's daughter."[97]

In describing his customers, the trader often listed their kin relations. At times he showed quite detailed knowledge of his clients' private circumstances. In several accounts he described a woman's "niece," a man's "old wife," and a woman's "former husband."[98] On one instance in August 1725, however, the trader was unable to determine the exact relationship of "debora[,] maggel[']s wife or wido[w]."[99] The bookkeeper also made occasional remarks on the physical appearance of his customers. On May 1, 1722, for instance, he recorded a small transaction with "the lame savage." Similarly, in 1725 he listed purchases made by "arrons with the lame arms."[100] Two Indian men were described as deaf; one of them appears as "nanset the deaf savage."[101] Another Indian man was reported as a "small fellow[,] or sansis Rennos."[102] It is difficult to determine whether the appearances of "Jacob the big savage" and "the big savage woman" are indicative of their physical stature or signal their status within native society.[103]

In identifying his native customers, the trader used Dutch names in approximately forty-one to forty-four cases.[104] This represents around 22 percent of his clientele. Remarkable in this regard are the five individuals who appear in the account book with a Dutch given name and surname. They were recorded as "arent fynhout," "Jan van gelder," "Willam Krom," "Jan Palin," and "Jan Roos." If "Roos" is a reference to Roosa, then all Dutch surnames associated with these individuals are the equivalents of surnames belonging to settlers living in Ulster County.[105] The last name of one Indian man listed as "antonij frinses" is not directly recognizable as being of Dutch origins.[106] Two of the Indian men noted with full Dutch names, Jan van Gelder and Willam Krom, are identified in land records under their native names Tawanout and Allamaaseeit, both of whom are now known to be the sons of Wappinger and Esopus leaders respectively.[107] The Indian Jan Palin (or John Pauling) is additionally noted in land records and in this account book as the son of Nanisinos (or "nenison"), an individual himself reported in deeds founding the Marbletown and Hardenbergh patents as one of two sons of the Esopus woman and "Sachimests" Doesto.[108]

One Indian man was described in the account book with his native name and what appear to be two Dutch first names, "Matekie or hans Jacob."[109] This individual was almost certainly the same man identified in county court records as "Werangagh" or "Walengaghkin alias Mattakie," a minor sachem of the Esopus. This is also the same man listed in the trader's ledger as "Warangau," first mentioned in a transaction recorded four years earlier from that of Matekie's appearance, who then closed out the account.[110] Although the trader made no direct entry linking these two native names with a single individual, this sachem's many aliases were nonetheless well known to the bookkeeper.

The trader also recorded the identity of one Indian woman with her native name, her father's native name, and her Dutch given name, "moskono[,] or wiyiekas['s] daughter margriet"; only one Indian was directly identified with a double native name, "Keman the savage[,] or watschap."[111] All other double names that were documented combined native and Dutch names: hend[rick] hekan, hend[rick] sawagonck (or sawagonck hend[rick][112]), hans or kwatten, Abraham (also Abram) or kwakasagh, kosoes or kobes, watpotgau or pitter [Pieter], and jacob or nockkehan. The largest number of Indians who appear with Dutch names in the pages of the account book are recorded only with a given name; in most cases a native name is not discernible in the accounts. This group consists of twenty-six to twenty-nine individuals.[113]

Throughout the account book the trader never identifies any individuals in their capacity as leaders, although clearly some must have been known to him. Seven of the fourteen Esopus men mentioned in Kingston court minutes as "Sachems" from 1709 to 1745 are listed in the accounts along with their kinfolk (see figure 1). Instead, many of the trader's entries in the ledger focus on the identification of his customers in terms of their immediate and extended family relations. The kinship data as documented by the trader point to the egalitarian nature of Munsee sociopolitical life first described by seventeenth-century Dutch observers such as Adriaen van der Donck, who reported that "[t]he oldest and foremost of the households and families, together with the supreme chief, represent the whole [leadership of that] nation."[114] Such individuals made up the council of elders that governed group decision making of the tribe.

Several of the Indian men mentioned in the accounts but not recognized in Kingston court records as leaders were probably also sachems, prominent elders of their respective kin groups. A few individuals and their kinfolk listed by the trader including Tautapagh (an Esopus man noted elsewhere as a shaman[115]) and Mannonck almost certainly fall into this category; Tautapagh's daughter Pitternel is noted as the "wife" of Mannonck's son Kattias, making the two elder men fathers-in-law. Tautapagh's son Willam Krom (already noted) would have been Kattias's brother-in-law.[116]

Finally, the account book documents the activities of one intriguing individual who was probably not a Munsee Indian. This man, who was identified as fetching goods for other customers, escorting an Indian man to the trader, and having dealings with some of the prominent Esopus individuals mentioned in the ledger, appears ten times under many variations of "(the) sawanoss(i)e."[117] The trader's use of an article before the man's name (or title) suggests that he personified a leadership role of some sort, yet he is clearly identified in the accounts as a single person. Perhaps the trader perceived this Indian man as a representative of the Shawnees, an Algonquian group known to have settled in the Minisink region in the early 1690s.[118] One Shawnee man traded in Albany with Harmanus Wendell in 1699 and once again at an undated moment; Harmanus referred to him as a "sounos" and a "souwenos."[119] Kingston treaty minutes and provincial records from 1712 note a request made by Esopus leaders to resettle an unnamed "Sachime" and a group of up to fifty "Shawonnos" or "Shawanoes" from Minisink territory to lands in Ulster County.[120] It is possible that this "Sachime" is the same man identified by the Ulster

County trader beginning in 1724, and whom he sometimes described as a representative of the Shawnees, perhaps in the capacity of a sachem, and in other instances as an ordinary individual.

Concluding Remarks

From an inventory of all transactions on credit in this account book, it becomes apparent that Indian clients of the Ulster County trader purchased large quantities of textiles, followed by alcohol and ammunition. In this respect, the findings from this trade ledger are similar to conclusions drawn from a study of the Wendell brothers' account book of the fur trade in Albany in the last years of the seventeenth and the first decades of the eighteenth century.[121] However, the array of trade goods that native clients bought in Albany was considerably more diverse.

Both account books document native women participating in commercial exchanges in numbers that are higher than has been discussed in the existing literature. Other similarities between the Albany and the Ulster County account books are apparent in the large percentage of default rates of the native customers. In Albany, between 28.4 and 58.8 percent of the debts were only partially paid or not paid at all; this default rate varied over time and between groups of native customers from different ethnicities. In Ulster County the default rates of the Indians amounted to at least 48 percent.

A close study of the Wendells' account book from Albany has suggested that "by moving from a macro- to a micro-level, and by observing and interpreting the almost daily exchanges described in [it], the conclusion of another historian can be confirmed; the effects of native participation in the fur trade 'cannot be applied as a formulaic constant.' Individual Indians, like those in any other society, discerned possibilities and opportunities in participating in commercial exchanges."[122]

Analysis of the intercultural exchanges in Ulster County does not yield a comparable impression. The Wendell brothers developed close commercial relations with a select group of Iroquois traders and a few Mahican intermediaries. Such agents provided a disproportionate share of the Wendells' revenues. In Ulster County, however, native mediators did not play such a role. The Ulster County account book documents larger numbers of colonial settlers that were directly involved in exchanges between that trader and his native customers.

In general, when compared to the Wendells' native clientele in Albany, Munsee customers trading in Ulster County appear to have been more limited in the amounts and diversity of goods they were able to acquire. Munsee groups had far less access to the beaver resources coveted by European traders. In their exchanges with the Ulster County trader they redeemed most of their debts with deerskins and elk hides, whereas the Wendells still predominantly computed their customers' accounts in terms of beavers. Moreover, the Wendell brothers never hired native people to reduce their debts through labor. Munsee customers in the Ulster County trade, on the other hand, exchanged their labor and services for the purpose of debt reduction in thirty-eight cases. Most of these instances document Indians performing fieldwork for the trader.

The data from this ledger strongly suggest that in bringing their products and services to the colonial marketplace, the Esopus, Wappinger, and other Munsee Indians who came to trade in Ulster County were experiencing the long-term effects of European capitalistic relationships on native societies and economies—more so than the Indians who were catered to by Evert and Harmanus Wendell in Albany just to the north along the Hudson River.

Notes to the Introduction

1. Marshall J. Becker, "Matchcoats: Cultural Conservatism and Change in One Aspect of Native American Clothing," *Ethnohistory* 52 (2005): 729.

2. Published as Kees-Jan Waterman, trans. and ed., *"To Do Justice to Him and Myself": Evert Wendell's Account Book of the Fur Trade with Indians in Albany, New York, 1695–1726,* Lightning Rod Press vol. 4 (Philadelphia: American Philosophical Society, 2008).

3. The Cottin Ledgers, 1707–21, in the Old Dutch Church Heritage Museum in Kingston, New York, have records of the bartering of "wheat and peltries" between the French merchant Jean Cottin and "local farmers, hunters and trappers," but such exchanges occurred after colonists had obtained the peltries by hunting or trapping or through trade with Indians; Sally M. Schultz and Joan Hollister, "Jean Cottin, Eighteenth-Century Huguenot Merchant," *New York History* 86 (Spring 2005): 134, 145.

4. The historic term *Munsee*, first recorded in 1727 among Pennsylvanian Indian refugees, has acquired a number of applications over time. It has been used to describe a ceramic style (Munsee-incised wares) and a linguistic dialect (Munsee-Delaware), and as a reference to a culture group (Proto-Munsee) indigenous to the Lower Hudson and Upper Delaware River valleys in southern New York, northern New Jersey, and northeastern Pennsylvania at first contact. This present work follows Grumet and others in acknowledging and promoting the term's general modern acceptance as a description of a cultural group distinctive from the historic "Delawares" in southern New Jersey and southeastern Pennsylvania (speakers of the Unami and Unalachtigo dialects) with whom they are related linguistically. Grumet's contributions include "Strangely Decreast by the Hand of God: A Documentary Appearance-Disappearance Model for Munsee Demography, 1630–1801," *Journal of Middle Atlantic Archaeology* 5 (1989): 129–45; "The Minisink Settlements: Native American Identity and Society in the Munsee Heartland, 1650–1778," in *The People of the Minisink: Papers from the 1989 Delaware Water Gap Symposium,* ed. David G. Orr and Douglas V. Campana (Philadelphia: National Park Service, 1991), 175–250; *Historic Contact: Indian People and Colonists in Today's Northeastern United States in the Sixteenth through Eighteenth Centuries* (Norman: Univ. of Oklahoma Press, 1995). Supporting literature includes Ives Goddard, "The Historical Phonology of Munsee," *International Journal of American Linguistics* 48 (1982):

16–48; William A. Hunter, "Documented Subdivisions of the Delaware Indians," *Bulletin of the Archaeological Society of New Jersey* 35 (1978): 20–40; Paul Otto, *The Dutch-Munsee Encounter in America: The Struggle for Sovereignty in the Hudson Valley* (New York: Oxford Univ. Press, 2006); J. Michael Smith, "The Seventeenth Century Sachems of the Wapping Country: Ethnic Identity and Interaction in the Hudson River Valley," in *The Journey: An Algonquian Peoples Seminar, Selected Research Papers, 2003–2004,* ed. Shirley W. Dunn (Albany: New York State Museum, 2009), 39–67.

Marshall J. Becker advocates a differing interpretation of the identities of Munsees and other Algonquian-speaking bands in the Hudson and Delaware River valleys; see, for instance, "Lenopi; Or, What's in a Name? Interpreting the Evidence for Cultural Boundaries in the Lower Delaware Valley," *Bulletin of the Archaeological Society of New Jersey,* no. 63 (2008): 11–32.

5. This tentative figure derives from the difficulties in establishing unique identities of some Indians. For example, the account book shows trade by an Indian man named "jacob," but it also contains entries of a man described as "Jacob the big savage"; in cases like this, it is problematic to conclude that such occurrences refer to one and the same individual.

6. For these individuals, see accounts on [77], [97], [98], and [103].

7. For this instance, see the account on [79]. Kisechton was Cochecton, a native, multi-ethnic village along the Delaware River. See also map 1.

8. For this instance, see the account on [45].

9. Images on the microfilm of the manuscript that one can order from the New York Public Library (Philip John Schuyler Papers, reel 30) show a number of smudges on the pages, and almost every image creates the impression that the upper edges of all pages suffer from damage by fire and/or water. This constitutes a distorted impression of the quality of the original.

10. The page numbers in the translation will be in brackets and those in the transcription in parentheses.

11. See for instance on the page numbered 64 in the first section of the manuscript, assigned page number 86.

12. Assigned page number 196.

13. Around present-day Wawarsing, New York.

14. UCDB, AA:2–3, Sept. 10, 1684. The Indian Jochim identified here appears in other land sales in Ulster County from the same time period as "Keghgekapowett alias Joghem" or "Kagakapou alias Jochem" and earlier in 1677 as "Kugakapo," a spokesman "for the Mahow [or Maheuw] family"—one of four known kin groups associated with the Esopus Indians (NYBP, 5:82–84; TDRK, book 3:240; *NYCD,* 13:505). He made his last appearance in a deed record in 1705 (as "Keggekapewet alyas Joghim") selling lands in the Rochester Patent of Ulster County near "nawesinck," a place coincidently also noted by the Dutch trader in his accounts as "nawesingh," to which some of his Indian clients traveled and where others possibly lived (UCDB, AA:352). The Indian Jochim above is not to be confused with the individual listed in the trader's account book as "Joghem, Sawanagh's son" on [53]; they

are in fact two different men. For the reference pertaining to the Indians' reserved tract at "Waarsinck" called "Anckerop's Land" see UCDB, AA:206, May 29, 1699. The native community called Nawesingh by the trader is the same place identified as "Nawesinck" or "Neawesinks," located near "the southwest bounds of the pattant [sic] of Rochester" on a 1751 map of lands sold in the 1705 deed above; map by Jacob Hoornbeck of lands belonging to Henry Beekman Sr., in the township of Rochester, Ulster County: Wilson Family Papers, Map Division, William L. Clements Library, University of Michigan (map 2 of this book. See also map 1 of this book).

15. See the last account on page [7].

16. Thomas S. Wermuth, *Rip Van Winkle's Neighbors: The Transformation of a Rural Society in the Hudson River Valley, 1720–1850* (Albany: State Univ. of New York Press, 2001), 15, 43. As part of a translation project, Kees-Jan Waterman provides translations of eighteenth-century Dutch records from the holdings of the Huguenot Historical Society, New Paltz, New York. A number of these are being brought online through the Hudson River Valley Heritage project (www.hrvh.org). For the use of French and Dutch in one account book from New Paltz (Roggen Ledger, 1750, 1795), see Hollister, "Account Books and Economic Life in Early New Paltz," www.hhs-newpaltz.org/library_archives/exhibits_research/early_newpaltz_history/hollister.html (accessed May 25, 2007).

17. See the second account on [68]. The Indian Manonck is also referred to by the trader as Mannonck or Mannock and appears often in the account book beginning in 1717: [2], [5], [67], [69], [73], [99], and [107]. References to his burial in 1727 are on [83] and [101]. He was also likely identified many years after his death in a 1771 deposition as "Menonck," an Indian noted along with Hendrick Hekan as having lived on the Upper Delaware River at "Kishiston" or Cochecton (NYCM-LP, 28:71). This town, also mentioned by the trader, is probably where he and others lived during the events recorded in the account book.

18. See the second account on [91].

19. Pages from the first section bear the numbers 173–79; those from the second section, 180–90.

20. Colonists referred to with generic names ("the smith") or listed with only their first name or surname have not been identified. In addition, the racial identity of at least one individual remains uncertain ("rutsen"). Excluding the above-mentioned persons, a group of nineteen individuals remains. Besides the residents of Rochester and Kingston, one or two lived in Marbletown, one in Hurley, and one at Foxhall manor. Three colonists lived in Ulster County, but the records do not specify their hometown.

21. This supersedes the number of identified Esopus Indians that we reported earlier; Kees-Jan Waterman and J. Michael Smith, "An Account Book of the Indian Trade in Ulster County, New York, 1712–1732," *Hudson River Valley Review* 24 (Autumn 2007): 61.

22. The number of identified unnamed kin depends, for instance, on whether the sister of "Tatteu"/"tateu"/"taweu," who is described as "andris['s] wife" on [75], is the same individual as the woman who is generically listed as his "sister" on [75] and [76].

23. These are "tappose," listed to identify his son "Kattis" on [29], "marinham"/ "marenghan" on [27] and [43], and the latter man's son "Tabarhekan" on [49]. For the iden- tification of the first, see Robert S. Grumet, "Taphow: The Forgotten 'Sakemau and Com- mander in Chief of All Those Indians Inhabiting Northern New Jersey,'" *Bulletin of the Archaeological Society of New Jersey* 43 (1988): 23–28. For a profile of the second individual, listed as "Marringgamahhan," see Grumet, "Minisink Settlements," 210. For data on the third man, noted as "Taparnekan" during land sales in colonial Orange County, New York, in 1696 and 1704, see Edward J. Lenik, *Indians in the Ramapos: Survival, Persistence and Pres- ence* (Ringwood: North Jersey Highlands Historical Society, 1999), 42.

24. Most recently this view was expressed by Paul Otto. Although he did not specifi- cally date his observation, he remarked that "most Munsees eventually retreated from the region [along the Hudson] altogether . . . and their leaving was a means to protect their worldview and cultural identity." Otto, *Dutch-Munsee Encounter*, 18, 176.

25. Herbert C. Kraft, *The Lenape-Delaware Indian Heritage: 10,000 BC to AD 2000* (Stan- hope, NJ: Lenape Books, 2001), 428–29, 440. James D. Folts somewhat qualifies this inter- pretation, but asserts that "around 1700, the Upper Delaware watershed became the new home of Minisink Indians . . . and of Esopus Indians moving west from the mid–Hudson Valley," and "by 1712, the Esopus Indians were reported to have moved to the East (Pepac- ton) Branch of the Delaware River." "The Westward Migration of the Munsee Indians in the Eighteenth Century," in *The Challenge: An Algonquian Peoples Seminar*, ed. Shirley W. Dunn (Albany: New York State Museum, 2005), 34.

26. For the fur trade in and around Kingston in the 1660s and 1670s, already described as "no longer a major economic factor," see Allen W. Trelease, *Indian Affairs in Colonial New York: The Seventeenth Century* (Ithaca, NY: Cornell Univ. Press, 1960); repr., with an introduc- tion by William A. Starna (Lincoln: Univ. of Nebraska Press, 1997), 186–88, quotation on 186. Wermuth asserts that "by the late seventeenth century, the fur trade was moving north and west" from Ulster County and concludes that the fur trade continued in Kingston and other localities in that county as a "by-industry" only until the end of that century (*Rip Van Winkle's Neighbors*, 13–14).

27. The bookkeeper described such instances using the preposition *op* (at), indicating that the recorded transactions occurred during or just before or after the actual burial. Based on travelers' journals and archeological evidence, Otto has concluded that the Mun- sees continued native funeral practices well into the eighteenth century (*Dutch-Munsee Encounter*, 173). Evidence from this account book indicates that such ongoing practices also applied to the location of at least some burials.

28. See the account on [67], amounting to 586 guilders and 10 stivers.

29. For the possible list of items to be buried with "manonck," see the account of "kampo['s] son" on [83]; for examples of Delaware Indian burial practices that included grave gifts like the ones listed there, see Kraft, *Lenape-Delaware Indian Heritage*, 343, 347, 380–81, 390–97. In *Unearthing Gotham: The Archaeology of New York City* (New Haven: Yale

Univ. Press, 2003), Anne-Marie Cantwell and Diana diZerega Wall present similar evidence for Munsee burial sites in the Lower Hudson River Valley, 129, 139.

30. Kenneth Scott and Charles E. Baker, "Renewals of Governor Nicolls' Treaty of 1665 with the Esopus Indians at Kingston, N.Y.," *New-York Historical Society Quarterly* 37 (1953): 251–72; Robert S. Grumet and Herbert C. Kraft, "Munsee," in *The Encyclopedia of New York State*, ed. Peter Eisenstadt (Syracuse, NY: Syracuse Univ. Press, 2005), 1023–25.

31. UCCS, 1712–20; New York Executive Council Minutes, NYSA, 11:103; MJC, Aug. 5–6, 1714, folder 1.

32. BSDC, 52, 122, 211, 257.

33. UCCS, 1737–50.

34. For the latter, see the first account on [59] and the note there.

35. See table 2 on 52–73 in J. Michael Smith, "The Highland King Nimhammaw and the Native Indian Proprietors of Land in Dutchess County, New York: 1712–1765," in *The Continuance: An Algonquian Peoples Seminar*, ed. Shirley W. Dunn (Albany: New York State Museum, 2004), 39–76. A handful of similar cases, where the names of the Indians were not recorded, are excluded from the total of twenty cases.

36. See, for instance, the New Paltz purchase of May 26, 1677, stating that "the Indians shall also have fully as much liberty and license to hunt all kinds of wild animal[s] and to fish, as the Christians," *NYCD*, 13:506; and also a conveyance from the Esopus to John Knight near Wawarsing on May 25, 1688, noting that "ye Indians must [be allowed to] plant half of ye Land [for] 6 years" (UCDB, AA:74). A conditional sale made on September 27, 1677, by the Esopus sachem (Old) Ankerop stipulated he would have planting rights "for as long as he shall live"—later language in a 1680 lease for these lands further reported that "the lessee shall, during the lease, permit Anckerop to plant four sch. of maize, and shall plow for him two days in the year" (NYCM-LP, 1:124–25; TDRK, book 2:283). Some Indian rights extended after land sales were based solely on verbal agreements. In 1762 during a dispute over a land patent in Dutchess County, the Wappinger sachem Daniel Nimham stated that "when Mr. Rumbout bought Rumbout Precinct from the Wappingoes, this Tract [at Weikopieh] was reserved for the Indians and not sold, which the Complainant says Mrs. Brett well knows having confirmed that Reservation, and procured from the Father of the Complainant a promise that whenever it was sold she should have the first offer" (J. Michael Smith, "Wappinger Kinship Associations: Daniel Nimham's Family Tree," *Hudson River Valley Review* 26 (Spring 2010): 87. See also Kraft, *Lenape-Delaware Indian Heritage*, 426. We are indebted to Dr. L. Hauptman for providing this observation.

37. Robert S. Grumet, "That Their Issue Be Not Spurious: An Inquiry into Munsee Matriliny," *Bulletin of the Archaeological Society of New Jersey* 45 (1990): 22; these were allegedly not war parties, returning from a campaign during King George's War. For Cochecton, see note 7.

38. New York Executive Council Minutes, NYSA, 21:71–72. Also note that the New York Colonial Council desired "them to be Faithful to this Government and to come and reside amongst the English like Brethren *as usual*" (italics added).

39. *NYCD*, 7:94, 96, 99–100.

40. Grumet, "Minisink Settlements," 185 and the map on 177. See also Grumet, "Esopus," in Eisenstadt, *Encyclopedia of New York State*, 527.

41. Folts, "Westward Migration of the Munsee Indians," 31, 33.

42. Scott and Baker, "Renewals of Governor Nicolls' Treaty of 1665," 261.

43. Stuart Banner, *How the Indians Lost Their Land: Law and Power on the Frontier* (Cambridge, MA: Belknap Press of Harvard Univ. Press, 2005), 64–65; Smith, "Highland King Nimhammaw and the Native Indian Proprietors," 46.

44. GTM-PC, box P26, folder 14.

45. Deed mss., 1726 and 1751, Kingston Senate House; 1746 deed, UCDB, EE:63–65; second 1751 deed, Jay Gould, *History of Delaware County and Border Wars of New York* (Roxbury, NY: Keeny and Gould, 1856), 242.

46. UCDB, GG:8–9; *Olde Ulster Magazine* 9:213–15.

47. Scott and Baker, "Renewals of Governor Nicolls' Treaty of 1665," 271. For the Esopus as a horticultural people, see Marshall J. Becker, "The Lenape and Other 'Delawarean' Peoples at the Time of European Contact: Population Estimates Derived from Archaeological and Historical Sources," *Bulletin of the New York Archaeological Association* 105 (1993): 16–25.

48. Smith, "Highland King Nimhammaw and the Native Indian Proprietors," 43.

49. Smith, "Wappinger Kinship Associations," 76–77.

50. *PWJ*, 2:477–78.

51. *WAB*, 17–18, 26–33, tables 4, 6, 7, 12, and 19.

52. Lenik, *Indians in the Ramapos*, 42; PGP, pocket 14, #56.

53. For a full listing of the data, see table 5.

54. For a full listing of the data, see table 5.

55. Marshall J. Becker, "Anadromous Fish and the Lenape," *Pennsylvania Archaeologist* 76 (Fall 2006): 31–32. Also see Amy C. Schutt, *Peoples of the River Valleys: The Odyssey of the Delaware Indians* (Philadelphia: Univ. of Pennsylvania Press, 2007), 19.

56. *WAB*, 19–21.

57. Scott and Baker, "Renewals of Governor Nicolls' Treaty of 1665," 269.

58. Becker, "Matchcoats," 727. See also his observation that "the cloth matchcoat . . . had completely replaced skin mantles by 1700" (748), and that "imported fabric was one of the most valued aspects of the European economy sought by the cultures of the northeastern zone of the New World" (764).

59. For instance, the Wendells in Albany recorded only three acquisitions of corn by their customers; in two cases, the patron was a man. See *WAB*, 22–23, tables 5 and 8. The Ulster County account book shows seven instances of natives buying Indian corn; all of these customers were men.

60. Transactions involving playing cards appear on [81], [95], and [97]. For the travelers' observations, see Otto, *Dutch-Munsee Encounter*, citing Daniel Denton (1670) and Jasper Danckaerts (1679–80), 170, 172. A Moravian visitor of the village of Shamokin on the

Susquehanna River noticed in 1745 that, to his chagrin, Delawares there were more interested in their card game than in his mission: James H. Merrell, *Into the American Woods: Negotiators on the Pennsylvania Frontier* (New York: W. W. Norton, 1999), 86.

61. See the debit and credit accounts on [51] and [52].

62. For a fuller discussion of the value of the products that Indians used to reduce or pay off their debts, see section "Prices, Values, Discharges, and Retention Rate" of this introduction and table 15.

63. *WAB*, 23, table 9.

64. See the account on [70].

65. See the instances in table 7. Internal references in the account book clearly suggest that Pansogh's unnamed son is identical to his son called "Mack."

66. For these three cases, see [108], [76], and [44].

67. *WAB*, 196.

68. Compare to *WAB*, 12–16 and table 12.

69. See the last account on [71].

70. Those cases appear on [5], [9], [13], [23], [25], [29], [43], [45], [47], [52], [54], [62], [71], [72], [81], [89] (twice), [91], [97], [98], [106], and [111].

71. For the Canadian Mohawk's account, see *WAB*, 180. The other cases appear on 116, 137, 138, 140, 161, 163, and 166.

72. For an example from the seventeenth century, see *WAB*, 81n124. In 1783, Marytie Rosa balanced her ten-year outstanding debts with North Kingston storekeeper Ben Snyder by spinning and weaving: Wermuth, *Rip Van Winkle's Neighbors*, 64. For asynchronous commercial exchanges as "prevalent" in the Hudson Valley and "in colonial and early America" in general, see Joan Hollister and Sally M. Schultz, "From Emancipation to Representation: John Hasbrouck and His Account Books," *Hudson Valley Historical Review* 20 (Spring 2004): 1–24, esp. 21. The same authors state elsewhere that in the eighteenth century, merchants in colonial America "typically kept an account for an individual running for a number of years before it would be balanced and settled," and that "there was no specified time for repayment" (see Schultz and Hollister, "Jean Cottin, Eighteenth-Century Huguenot Merchant," 146.

73. *WAB*, 25–26.

74. See the second section of this introduction, "Context," and various account books in the archives of the Huguenot Historical Society, New Paltz, New York (such as the Roggen account book, 1751–95; account book, Johan Jacob Roggen, 1751–71; account book, Jannetje DuBois, 1773–96), and Schultz and Hollister, "Jean Cottin, Eighteenth-Century Huguenot Merchant," 147.

75. *WAB*, 32.

76. See the account on [61].

77. *WAB*, 26–27 and tables 6 and 7.

78. *WAB*, 28–29 and table 15.

79. These cases were not listed separately in *WAB*; some appear in tables 16 and 17 therein. For specific cases, see *WAB*, 111, 121, 150, 160, 176 (twice), 177, 183, 190, 191, 196, and 208. The instance on 121 is incorporated into table 16; table 17 includes the cases on 111, 150, 160, one from 176, and the one on 190. Those instances occurred between 1700 and 1710.

80. *WAB*, 27–31 and tables 13 and 12. Such cases appeared throughout the entire account book of the Wendells.

81. See [23].

82. *WAB*, 28 and table 14. Those instances occurred between 1699 and 1718.

83. See [64].

84. See [18].

85. See [60].

86. For such activities of the Wendells, see *WAB*, 31 and table 18. Those instances occurred between 1705 and 1709.

87. See the note with this "stenberge" on [56], identifying him as a man.

88. See the accounts on [40] and [50].

89. The account with two main holders appears on [35]; the ones with three on [63], [64], and [67].

90. See also the glossary.

91. These percentages are based on a tabulation of seventy-one accounts and transactions of the following prominent individuals and their relatives: the Esopus leaders Hendrick Hekan, Sander, Ankerop, Nanoghquarij, Karwamo, Runup, Warangau, Sawis, and Sawanaghki; the Wappinger Indians Keghkenond, Peghtarend, Nackarend, Nemham, Jan van Gelder, and Wappenack; and the leaders Marinham and Tappose from the southern areas of Munsee territory. See the appendix for their profiles and variants of their names.

92. His name was also spelled as "Lendart." For his accounts, see [21]–[22] and [111]. The balance of his payments and crossed-out entries on [21] is 486 guilders.

93. *WAB*, 25–26 and table 11.

94. For a tabulation, see table 5.

95. See the account of "andris" on [57]. On [75] it becomes apparent that this Indian's brother-in-law is "Tatteu."

96. See the accounts of "tabarhekan['s]" and "pansogh['s]" "wife['s] sister" on [39] and [63].

97. See the accounts on [13] and [35].

98. See entries pertaining to "Ja[s]mijn" on [27] and "abraham" on [75], and the account of "wieijiekas" on [59].

99. See the account on [73].

100. See the accounts on [49] and [73]. This "arrons" later appears in another customer's account, without any remarks about his arms; see [84].

101. See the account on [27]. The other deaf man appears as "the small deaf savage" on [25].

102. See the account on [89].

103. See the account on [43].

104. Establishing the exact number is complicated by the fact that the trader mixed the use of Dutch and Indian names and because it remains unclear if all entries of an individual recorded as, for instance, "jacob" refer to the same person.

105. For their accounts and appearances, see: "arent fynhout," [71], [81], [89], and [103]–[104]; "Willam Krom," [47]; "Jan Palin," [15]; "Jan roos," [4] and [70] (also listed as "Jan Roos[,] domeni[']s son," on [63]); and "Jan van gelder" [22] and [29]. Another man with a Dutch name mentioned by the trader, who appears in the accounts of the Indian "arent fynhout" on [104] as "johanes vernoy" (but not directly identified as being native), may refer to the Esopus Indian "Pecghakagharin alias Hans Vernoy" noted in a 1746 deed for lands in the Hardenbergh Patent; see UCDB, EE:63–65.

106. He is listed with an account on [19].

107. For the identification of "Tawanout or John van Gelder" as the son of Awansous, a Wappinger chief active from 1680 to 1707, see Smith, "Wappinger Kinship Associations," 90–91. The Indian man Willam Krom is noted by the trader as the son of "Tatepagh" on [47]. For "William Crom" listed under variants of his native alias Allamaaseeit, see UCDB, EE:61–65. For Tautapagh, an Esopus Indian noted in Ulster County land sales between 1683 and 1705, see UCDB, AA:74, 336 and 352. See also the appendix: Wappinger, "John van Gelder," and Esopus, "Allamaaseeit" and "Tautapagh."

108. Jan Palin is identified by the trader on [15] as the son of "nenison," a likely spelling variant referring to the Esopus sachem Nanisinos or Nenechonoas (NYCM-LP, 4:92 and 2B:276), active in land sales from 1700 to 1734. For Doesto's documented genealogy see CFLP, box 6, folder 6, #94, where she is described in a 1785 memorandum written many years after her death as "Dosto an old squa[w] the Daughter [of] Ameltas & mother of Nisinas who was the father [of] John Pauling." For a reference during her lifetime indicating that Doesto had two sons, see UCDB, BB:380–81. Doesto also appears in the account book under a phonetic variant of her name on [25] in the exchanges of "Sawis[,] dorso[']s son" (and possibly "his mother" on [26]), a man likely noted as one of her two sons "Ochperawim" (UCDB, BB:380), and later in a 1746 deed as "Achpalawamin alias Suwies" (see UCDB, EE:63–65). Unfortunately, the trader made no entry in the account book describing the relationship between Doesto and Nanisinos that is documented in other records. See also the appendix: Esopus, "John Pauling," "Nanisinos," "Doesto," and "Achpalawamin/(Old) Suwies."

109. In Dutch, Jacob was and is a common first name, but Jacobs is a common surname; see his account on [19]. It remains uncertain whether he is the same individual as the man who was used to describe the account of "pamberoch quet[,] hans's wife" on [11] or the "hans or kwatten" on [13].

110. BSDC, book 1:47–48, GTM-PC, box P26, folder 14; see the trader's entry for Matekie on [19] "at balancing the account" totalling 38 guilders in 1721 and Warangau's entry on [7]–[8] opening this account in 1717 and his remaining debt of 38 guilders. The man listed to

describe the account of "pamberoch quet[,] hans's wife" on [11] and the Indian man "hans or kwatten" on [13] likely refer to a different individual or individuals. See also the appendix: Esopus, "Walengaghkin."

111. For the appearances of "moskono" and "keman," see [59] and [65].

112. We take these inverted names to represent the same person. On [65] and [85], the Indian man "Kobes" appears in accounts from 1725 as "Kobes[,] sawagonck hendreck['s] son," and as "kobes[,] hendreck sawagonck['s] son." In both cases he is described as being married to one of daughters of the Indian woman "kesay" or "kisa." The chances are very slim that there would be two different Kobes in the same year with different fathers who had such similar names and who would both be married to a daughter of the same woman. Such inversions of first and given name do not otherwise occur in the account book.

113. In alphabetical order, they are: Abraham/Abram (perhaps identical in all cases to the Indian who was also identified as kwakasagh/quakesas/kwakesas), young Abraham, Andris, Antony, Arent (perhaps identical to Arent Fynhout), Blandina, Catharina/Catrijn/ Catryn, Cornelis, Debora, Eijsack (Isaac), Gertie, Hanna, Hester, Jacob, possibly Jamijn (for Jasmijn?), Joghem, Jores, Juren, Kryn, Lendert, Martie (a woman), Maycke, Norman, Pitternel, Ragel (for Rachel?), Salomon, Sammetie, Sander, Sar, Sett, Symon, and Willam (Sander's younger brother, a separate individual from Willam Krom).

114. Adriaen van der Donck, *A Description of New Netherland*, ed. Charles T. Gehring and William A. Starna, trans. Diederik Willam Goedhuys, foreword by Russell Shorto (Lincoln: Univ. of Nebraska press, 2008), 100. Van der Donck further qualifies his observations on the nature of Indian leadership in the Hudson Valley, writing that "[t]hose of one tribe or nation tend to keep together and have a particular chief and their own form of government. There are also higher chiefs, to whom the others submit. . . . Just as tribes, settlements, and places have their chiefs, so has every house. He who is the most prominent and respectable of each such community has the authority and eminence" (93).

This account is also published in Kees-Jan Waterman, Jaap Jacobs, and Charles Gehring, eds., *Indianenverhalen: De eerste beschrijvingen van Indianen langs de Hudsonrivier, 1609– 1680* (Zutphen, the Netherlands: Walburg Pers, 2009), 113–46, see 134–35 and 130.

115. For a reference to the Esopus Indian "Tautapagh, a medicine man" (i.e., shaman), see *Olde Ulster Magazine* 3:175–76).

116. The Indian Mannonck and his family (including his unnamed wife and at least three sons, Jacob, Kattias, and Mattiso) are noted by the trader as frequent visitors with substantial accounts. He and some of his family members also appear with some regularity in the accounts of other Indian customers. Mannonck is mentioned about a dozen times by the trader from 1717 until Mannonck's death in 1727. One reference can be directly attributed to him outside of the account book and is found in a deposition from 1771, reporting that "Menonck" and Hendrick Hekan had once been residents of Cochecton on the Upper Delaware River (NYCM-LP, 28:71). It is possible that the names Mannonck or Menonck are abbreviated spelling variants of a longer formal name that could refer to an earlier

individual called "Waskamennick," a signer to a 1684 land sale at "Wawarasinck" (UCDB, AA:2–3). This interpretation would make Mannonck a contemporary of other Esopus elders such as Tautapagh, Kattkies, and the sachem Crawamogh identified in the account book and who first appear in Ulster County land sales beginning in the 1680s. See also the appendix: Esopus, "Mannonck."

117. For these appearances, see various accounts on [61], [62], [67], [77], [89], [91] (two times), and [93] (three times). The man appears with a bewildering array of variants of his name: the sawonossie, sawanos (once with "the," once without), sawanosse (once with "the," once without), sawannes, sawannos (three times, once with "the"), and sawonnos.

118. Trelease, *Indian Affairs in Colonial New York*, 325.

119. For the accounts of the Shawnee man "tackkarores," or "Tankarores," see *WAB*, 97–98.

120. UCCS, June 2 and 30; Berthold Fernow, comp., *Calendar of Council Minutes, 1668–1783* (Albany: State Univ. of New York Press, 1902), 248 (July 3), New York Council minutes reporting "Treaty with the Esopus Indians renewed. Shawanoes. Tuscaroras may conditionally settle beyond the Blue Hills [Catskill Mountains]"; Scott and Baker, "Renewals of Governor Nicolls' Treaty of 1665," 259–61, 264n17. See also the appendix: Esopus, "Ankerop II/Tackawaghkin." Robert S. Grumet maintains that these immigrants were Tuscarora Iroquois, not Shawnees: *The Munsee Indians: A History* (Norman: Univ. of Oklahoma Press, 2009).

121. See *WAB*.

122. *WAB*, 44, quoting William L. Ramsey, "'Something Cloudy in Their Looks': The Origins of the Yamasee War Reconsidered," *Journal of American History* 91 (2003): 55.

Table 1. Number of Accounts

		Numbers	Percentages
Total *n* of debit and credit accounts:		243	
Main account holders:	men	194	79.8
	women	54	22.2
	unknown	2[a]	0.8[b]
Accounts with active involvement by Indians other than main holders:		164	
	active involvement by men	80	48.8
	active involvement by women	83	50.6
	unknown	1	0.6
Accounts with active involvement by Indians other than main holders (164), compared to total n *of accounts*			
	men involved	80	32.9
	women involved	83	34.2
	unknown	1	0.4[c]
Shared account, two holders			
	(1 man, 1 woman):	1	0.4
Shared account, three holders			
	(1 man, 1 woman, 1 son):	3	1.2

[a] Total not equal to 243 because of shared accounts with multiple main account holders.

[b] Total not equal to 100.0% because of shared accounts with multiple main account holders.

[c] Total not equal to 100.0% because *n* of accounts with other individuals actively involved is smaller than the total *n* of accounts.

Table 2. Number of Transactions

Total n of transactions:	2,005	
Consists of:		
Debit:	1,562	
Additions:	1,	woman takes rum to sell for bookkeeper; she is charged
	1,	seems to be a purchase, an unknown item
Total:	1,564	
Credit:	398	
Additions:	32,	labor performed as payment
	5,	trip made as payment
	1,	expected to provide another service (show a mine)
	1,	unclear
Total:	436	
Unknown/uncertain:	5	

Table 3. Categories of Trade Goods and Services Acquired in Transactions on Credit by Indians, Absolute Figures and Percentages (*n*=2,057)

Category	Items	n *of acquisitions*	% *of total* n
1. Textiles		**730**	**35.5**
1.a Fabric		536	26.1
	1.a.1 ells	240	11.7
	1.a.2 blankets	193	9.4
	1.a.3 pieces; unknown	103	5.0
1.b Clothing		194	9.4
	1.b.1 shirts	124	6.0
	1.b.2 stockings	31	1.5
	1.b.3 ribbons, garters	17	.8
	1.b.4 headgear	8	.4
	1.b.5 coats, frocks	8	.4
	1.b.6 girdles	6	.3
2. Alcohol		**600**	**29.2**
	2.a rum	504	24.5
	2.b cider	52	2.5
	2.c beer	36	1.8
	2.d wine	4	.2
	2.e "barrel"	3	.15
	2.f glass bottle	1	.05
3. Ammunition/trap		**476**	**23.15**
	3.a gunpowder	222	10.8
	3.b lead	199	9.7
	3.c flintstones	44	2.1
	3.d shot	10	.5
	3.e trap	1	.05
4. Knives/axes/sword		**86**	**4.2**
	4.a knives[a]	72	3.5
	4.b axes	12	.6
	4.c sword	2	.1

(continued)

Table 3 (*Continued*)

Category	Items	n *of acquisitions*	% *of total* n
5. Foodstuffs		**58**	**2.85**
	5.a bread	18	.9
	5.b molasses	11	.5
	5.c corn	7	.35
	5.d sugar	6	.3
	5.e bran	4	.2
	5.f meat	2	.1
	5.g wheat	2	.1
	5.h flour	2	.1
	5.i juice	2	.1
	5.j turkey	1	.05
	5.k peas	1	.05
	5.l pepper	1	.05
	5.m pig(?)[b]	1	.05
6. Kettles/pipes/tools/pot/pan/bell		**45**	**2.2**
	6.a kettles	20	1.0
	6.b pipes	13	.6
	6.c tools[c]	9	.45
	6.d copper pot	1	.05
	6.e frying pan	1	.05
	6.f bell	1	.05
7. Personal care/beads/combs		**24**	**1.2**
	7.a personal care[d]	14	.7
	7.b beads	10	.5
8. Guns		**10**	**.5**
9. Repairs		**9**	**.45**
	9.a repairs to guns	7	.35
	9.b repairs to axes	2	.1
10. Cards, Jew's-harp		**4**	**.2**
	10.a stacks of cards	3	.15
	10.b Jew's-harp	1	.05
11. Money		**4**	**.2**

Table 3 *(Continued)*

Category	Items	n *of acquisitions*	% *of total* n
12. Silver, silverware		**3**	**.15**
	12.a silver gorget[e]	1	.05
	12.b silver cup	1	.05
	12.c piece of silver	1	.05
13. Goat skins		**3**	**.15**
14. Peltry		**2**	**.1**
	14.a raccoons	1	.05
	14.b skins	1	.05
15. Shoes		**2**	**.1**
16. Tobacco		**1**	**.05**
		2,057 (2x)	100.2[f] (2x)

[a] Knives includes the occurrence of specific knives (2 types).

[b] This instance is ambiguous; see the introduction.

[c] Tools includes: awls (7 transactions); scissors (2); and "beversteker" (1).

[d] Personal care includes: paint (6 transactions); buttons (3); combs (2); small looking glass (1); buckles (1).

[e] For this likely translation of the Dutch *schulp*, see note 321 to the translation.

[f] The deviation from 100.0% is caused by the small number of some of the types of goods, and their effect on rounding off the percentages.

Note: The purchase of a saddle has been excluded from this table. It is difficult to assign to one of the categories, and it occurs only once.

Table 4. Labor and Products of Indians to Pay off Debts, Total Number of Occurrences[a]

Peltry, meat, and animals:

Skins	125
Skins	*95*
Dressed	*25*
Raw	*5*
Deer	64[b]
Martens	58
Beavers	43
"Lap"	*1*
Bears	41
Elks	28
Parchment	*1*
Raccoons	20
Pigs	11
Fishers	8
Otters	6
Wolves	6
Meat	4
Foxes	4
Minks	3
Turkeys	3
Horses	1
Cats	1
Cuts of hare	1
"Katlos"	1
"Wateratten"	1
Subtotal:	429

Other animal products:

Grease and fat	9
Feathers	1
Subtotal:	10

Table 4. *(Continued)*

Labor:

In agriculture	26
Travel elsewhere	5
Dressing skins	3
Spinning	2
Show a mine	1
Shooting fire	1
Subtotal:	38

Money: 6[c]

Canoes: 4[d]

Foodstuffs:

Beans	1
Grits	1
Cranberries	1
Hops	1
A "plain meal"	1
Subtotal:	5

Total: 492

[a] Data do not reflect actual volumes or numbers of furs, products, and services; they constitute the *number of times* they were used in describing transactions.

[b] The category consists of deerskins (26), "deer" (20), deer meat (13), and deer quarters (5).

[c] Includes two instances where payments by Indians were recorded in "guilders." It is not certain that coinage was exchanged in these transactions.

[d] This excludes one occurrence, where it remains uncertain if the transaction was concluded; no credit was entered.

Table 5. Number of Debit and Credit Transactions, per Year (Grouped)

Not specified by month:			Specified by month:			Total n of (grouped) trans/yr:		
1712	2	[Db 2, Cr 0]	1712	0		1712	2	[Db 2, Cr 0]
1713	0		1713	0		1713	0	
1714	0		1714	0		1714	0	
1715	2	[Db 2, Cr 0]	1715	1	[Db 1, Cr 0]	1715	3	[Db 3, Cr 0]
1716[a]	1?	[Db 1?, Cr 0]	1716	0		1716	1?	[Db 1?, Cr 0]
1717[a]	4+1?	[Db 3+1?, Cr 1]	1717	6	[Db 6, Cr 0]	1717	10+1?	[Db 9+1?, Cr 1]
1718	0		1718	2	[Db 1, Cr 1]	1718	2	[Db 1, Cr 1]
1719	7	[Db 5, Cr 2]	1719	15	[Db 12, Cr 3]	1719	22	[Db 17, Cr 5]
1720	4	[Db 4, Cr 0]	1720	5	[Db 5, Cr 0]	1720	9	[Db 9, Cr 0]
1721	3	[Db 3, Cr 0]	1721	40	[Db 34, Cr 6]	1721	43	[Db 37, Cr 6]
1722	1	[Db 0, Cr 1]	1722	21	[Db 16, Cr 5]	1722	22	[Db 16, Cr 6]
1723	2	[Db 2, Cr 0]	1723	19	[Db 9, Cr 10]	1723	21	[Db 11, Cr 10]
1724	3	[Db 3, Cr 0]	1724	38	[Db 28, Cr 10]	1724	41	[Db 31, Cr 10]
1725	17	[Db 10, Cr 7]	1725	48	[Db 38, Cr 10]	1725	65	[Db 48, Cr 17]
1726	12	[Db 8, Cr 4]	1726	92	[Db 60, Cr 32]	1726	104	[Db 68, Cr 36]
1727	28	[Db 21, Cr 7]	1727	45	[Db 20, Cr 25]	1727	73	[Db 41, Cr 32]
1728	8	[Db 4, Cr 4]	1728	28	[Db 20, Cr 8]	1728	36	[Db 24, Cr 12]
1729	11	[Db 6, Cr 5]	1729	29	[Db 22, Cr 7]	1729	40	[Db 28, Cr 12]
1730	0		1730	0		1730	0	
1731	0		1731	0		1731	0	
1732	1	[Db 1, Cr 0]	1732	0		1732	1	[Db 1, Cr 0]

Total: 106   Total: 389   Total: 495
[Db 75, Cr 31]   [Db 272, Cr 117]   [Db 347, Cr 148]

No month or year stated: 85 [Db 33, Cr 52]

Total n *of (grouped) debit and credit transactions: 580* [Db 380, Cr 200]

[a] For the purpose of plotting the results in graphs 1 and 2, the uncertain debit account from 1716 or 1717 (no month given) has been placed under 1716.

Table 6. Indian Burials Mentioned in Accounts, by Date

Page	Date: month/year	Description	In the account of	Sex	Merchandise bought for the occasion	Remarks
[67]	9/1725	abram[']s burial	manonck	m	7 "kan" of rum	
[73]	9/1725	abram[']s burial	mattiso[,] mannonck['s] son	m	4 "kan" of rum	
[87]	[in/before] 5/1726	kettene[']s dead child	pony [or his wife, Catrin?]	m?	1½ ell of cotton	Conflicting information on burials relating to "kettene"/"K/kattener" and his daughter/child on [5], [73], and [87]; see the translation.
[69]	7/1726	the burial	kattias[,] manonck['s] son	m	1 pint of rum	
[73]	7/1726	burial of kattener	mattiso[,] mannonck['s] son	m	1 pint of rum	
[5]	7/1726	the burial	Kattener	m	4 "kan" of rum	

(continued)

Table 6. (*Continued*)

Page	Date: month/year	Description	In the account of	Sex	Merchandise bought for the occasion	Remarks
[5]	9/1726	his daughter's burial	Kattener	m	1 stroud blanket	
[83]	1/1727	manonck['s] burial	kampo['s] son	m	?; either a list of goods, or only 2¼ gallons of rum	
[101]	1/1727	manonck['s] burial	andris the savage	m	½ a gallon of rum	
[101]	1/1727	the burial	makwas	m	1 gallon of rum	manonck's burial
[76]	?/1727	[to] drink at his sister's grave	tatweu	m	8 "kan" of rum	
[91]	10/1728	bur[ial] of andries['s] child	Sar or hendrick hekan	f/m	1 "kan" of rum	
[99]	11/1726?	Abraham[']s burial	manonck	m	Rum	Date is different from cases on [67] and [73]; see the translation.

[a]The ? indicates that data have not been conclusively ascertained.

Table 7. Indians Paying off Debts with Labor, by date

Page	Date: month/year	Name, description	Sex	Type of labor	Credit, guilders	Wages, per day, guilders
[64]	5/1725	pansogh's son	m	Harvesting flax	9	?ª
[58]	7/1725	pooni/ponij	m	Days on the farm	?	?
[62]	4/1726	the sawanossie	m	Preparing skins	1 lb of gunpowder, 1 *kan* rom	n.a.
[61]	>4/1726	gasrit the savage	m	Working on the farm	35	7
[74]	7/1726	mattiso[,] mannock[']s son	m	Days on the farm	18	6
[80]	7/1726	mack[,] pansogh['s] son	m	Days on the farm	48	6
[80]	1/1727?	" "	m	Days on the farm	42	6
[70]	3/1727	abraham or kwakasagh	m	Mowing	36	8
[94]	4/1727	sawannos's daughter	f	Days on the farm	51	6
[104]	7/1727	arent fynhout the savage	m	Days on the farm	12	6
[88]	7/1727	Pony	m	Days on the farm	30	6
[90]	?/1727	gertie	f	Harvesting flax	12	?
[76]	3?/1728	tateu	m	Pointing out a mine	16, 10 stivers	?
[64]	?/1727	pansogh's son	m	Harvesting flax	12	?
[106]	>7/1728	arronshagkie[,] or anckerop[']s son	m	Days on the farm	27	6, 15 stivers

(continued)

Table 7. (*Continued*)

Page	Date: month/year	Name, description	Sex	Type of labor	Credit, guilders	Wages, per day, guilders
[108]	1/1729	matisso[,] mannonck[']s son	m	Shooting fire	9	9
[106]	>3/1729	Kisay	f	Harvesting flax	18	?
[42]	7/1729	Sander[']s brother[,] Willam	m	Mowing	90	9
[42]	7/1729	" "	m	Cutting the meadow	20	?
[100]	?/1729	mack[,] pansogh[']s son	m	Days on the farm	70	7
[22]	?	Lendert the savage[,] Sander's brother	m	Preparing skins	45	?
[22]	?	" "	m	Mowing	44	8, 16 stivers
[24]	?	Jacob the savage	m	Mowing	4	8
[24]	?	tatapagh[']s wife	f	Cutting twigs	16	4
[36]	?	[Juren and?] hanna; their daughter?	?	Spinning [twice]	36; 10	?; 2
[42]	?	Sander the savage	m	Preparing skins	57	?
[42]	?	" "	m	Working at [the] "southfield"	26	4, 10 stivers
[70]	?	pitternel[,] kattias[']s wife	f	Harvesting flax	12	12
[110]	?	magh[,] hend[rick] hekan[']s son	m	Binding [sheaves]	51	6
[110]	?	" "	m	Binding on the farm	66	6, 12 stivers
[110]	?	" "	m	Cutting in the meadow	27	?
[110]	?	" "	m	Cutting in the meadow	7	?

[a]The ? indicates that data have not been conclusively ascertained.

Table 8. Indians Paying off Debts with Travels, by Date

Page	Date: month/year	Name, description	Sex	Destination	Payment, guilders
[18]	5/1721	Sander the savage	m	manesenck	45
[18]	in/before 1721?[a]	Sander the savage, with herij	m	namesinck	20
[22]	in/before 1727?	Lendert the savage, Sander's brother	m	nawesingh	20
[42]	1720s?	Sander the savage	m	menisenck	20
[68]	1720s?	manonck's son [Jacob?]	m	kingston	9

[a] The ? indicates that data have not been conclusively ascertained.

Table 9. Occurrences of Practice of Escorting, by Date

Page	Date: month/year	Escorter	Sex	Escorted	Sex	Remarks
[31]	5/1721	norman	m	meckek	?[a]	The entry is left incomplete, but "meckek" was escorted by "norman."
[35]	8/1721	Keghkenond['s] daughter	f	A savage woman	f	
[40]	>11/1721	tabarhekan['s] wife's sister	f	A boy	m	
[15]	3/1722	quakesas[,] karwamo['s] son	m	A savage woman	f	
[85]	12/1725	kosoes or kobes[,] hendreck sawagonck['s] son	m	A savage boy	m	
[97]	<4/1727	parraris from kasegton	m	A savage woman	f	
[62]	>4/1726	the sawanos	m	towis	m	
[103]	4/1727	Ragel[,] the savage woman from manesinck	f	saij	f	
[93]	?	the sawannos	m	touwas	m	

[a]The ? indicates that data have not been conclusively ascertained.

Table 10. Occurrences of Securities Provided by Indians, by Date

Page	Date: month/year	Provider	Sex	Security	Merchandise; value	Remarks
[25]	5/1720	the small deaf savage	m	His gun	Rum and a small cask; ?[a]	
[29]	3/1721	tappose[']s son[,] Kattis	m	His trap	Goods and rum; 58 guilders	
[47]	3/1722	abramhans[s] daughter[,] menckesonghua	f	Gun	Rum; 30 guilders	The account contains indications that she took out additional credit, with the same gun as a security.
[47]	" "	" "	f	Wampum belt	1 ell of strouds; 18 guilders	
[49]	5/1722	the lame savage	m	His gun	Rum and a small cask; 82 guilders	
[65]	7/1725	Keman the savage[,] or watschap	m	His gun	Rum and a small cask; 24 guilders	This entry is repeated on [83], in an entry dating from 1725.
[103]	4/1727	Ragel[,] the savage woman from manisenck	f	Wampum	1 lb gunpowder; 7 guilders	
[90]	4/1728	small fellow[,] or sansis Rennos	m	His wampum belt	A small looking glass; 7 guilders	

[a]The ? indicates that data have not been conclusively ascertained.

Table 11. Occurrences of Indians Borrowing Peltry and Merchandise, by Date

Page	Date: month/year	Name	Sex	Items(s) borrowed	Remarks
[53]	?ª/1723	symon the savage	m	The bookkeeper's gun	No charge recorded
[61]	11/1725	the sawanossie	m	1 skin, weighing 1¼ lb	No charge recorded
[93]	11/1726	sawannos['s] daughter[,] gasris['s wife]	f	1 skin, weighing 1¼ lb, at 8½ guilders	Charged. Full account was paid.
[71]	3/1727	Winhas[,] sawagonck hendr['s] son	m	1 skin, at 6 guilders	Charged. Full account was paid.
[87]	3/1727	pony	m	1 skin, weighing 1½ lb	No charge recorded
[85]	?/1727	Cattrijn, wife of kosoes or kobes[,] hendreck sawagonck['s] son	f	1 skin	Charged, unknown debt in guilders. Full account was paid.
[92]	?/1729	hend hekan	m	1 skin, weighing 1 lb, at 6–7 guilders	Charged

ªThe ? indicates that data have not been conclusively ascertained.

Table 12. Indians' Debts with Other Colonists, by Date

Page	Date: month/year	Indian with debt with other trader	Sex	Nature and amount of debt	Other trader/ colonist, name	Sex
[19]	12/1719	antonij frinses	m	?; 3 guilders	willam douty	m
[13]	?ª/1719	Keghkenond	m	The axe; 2 guilders	the smith	m
[35]	8/1721	keghkenond['s] daughter	f	An axe; 2 guilders	the smith	m
[51]	11/1722	peghtarend	m	?; 12 guilders	mary stenbergen	f
[63]	1/1724	Eijsack[,] Abraham['s] son	m	2 goat skins; 35.5 guilders	barent niewkerck	m
[85]	12/1725	kosoes or kobes[,] hendreck sawagonck['s] son	m	?; 6 guilders	tobyas hornbeck	m
[71]	4/1727	Winhas[,] sawagonck hendr['s] son	m	1 gun; £6:10/280 guilders	"mother"	f
[95]	2/1728	mattason	m	1 gun; 240 guilders	pitter tappen	m
[99]	3/1729	mack[,] pansogh['s] son	m	1 small skin; 3 guilders	the smith	m

ªThe ? indicates that data have not been conclusively ascertained.

Table 13. Colonists Paying Indians' Debts with Bookkeeper, by Date

Page	Date: month/year	Colonist, paying Indian's debt	Sex	Debt with bookkeeper paid	Indian, debt paid	Sex
[2]	12/1718	Jan van Kampen	m	120 guilders	A female relative of manonck the savage [his wife?a]	f
[18]	>11/1719	benyamen du pri	m	5 guilders	Sander the savage	m
[14]	7/1720	y[our] H[onor's] daughter	f	6 guilders	keghkenond	m
[22]	11/1723	pitt van Cornels	m	1 skin @ 24 guilders	Jores[,] hester's son	m
[56]	12/1723	p:v:C	m	1 deerskin @ 26 guilders	Jors[,] hester[']s son	m
[60]	11/1724	Klas Roosa	m	12 guilders, "a note"	wieijiekas['s] daughter	f
[62]	11/1724	klas roosa	m	8 guilders	gasrit the savage/ weghtagkarin	m
[56]	5/1726	a: stenberge	m	98 guilders	Jors[,] hester[']s son	m
[104]	7/1727	johanes vernoy	m	38.5 guilders	arent fynhout the savage	m
[60]	?/1728	teunus meddagh	m	33 guilders	Moskono or wiyiekas['s] daughter margriet	f
[32]	7/1729	derck westbroek	m	26 guilders	Norman	m
[98]	10/1729	pit lou	m	13 guilders	kewessie[, a] keseton savage	m
[18]	?	moses du pri	m	48 guildersb	Sander the savage	m
[30]	?	Coll gasbeek	m	10 guilders	Jan van gelder['s] sister	f
[24]	?	nicklas mayer	m	33 guilders	Jacob the savage	m
[26]	?	jores meddagh	m	1 Elk skin @ 20 guilders	Sawis[,] dorsol[']s son	m

aThe ? indicates that data have not been conclusively ascertained.

bThe exact nature of this transaction remains obscure.

Table 14. Colonists Fetching Merchandise for Indians, by Date

Page	Date: month/year	Colonist, fetching goods	Sex	Fetched goods; charges	Goods fetched for	Sex
[43]	12/1721	t: tapes	m	1 coarse blanket ("combars"); 2.5 guilders remain	marenghan['s] son[,] barnat	m
[45]	9/1723	nicklas hofman	m	Small axe; 6 guilders	sawangh['s] son	m
[73]	9/1725	y[our] H[onor's] mother	f	1 stroud blanket; 28 guilders remain	mattisol[,] mannonck['s] son	m
[65]	6/1725	westbroek	m	Rum; 3 guilders	Kobes sawagonck[,] hendreck['s] son	m
[81]	11/1725	y[our] H[onor's] mother	f	1 "schepel" Indian corn; 5 guilders	Wappaneck[,] kisay['s] son	m
[73]	7/1726	y[our] H[onor's] brother	m	Rum; 1.5 guilders	mattisol[,] mannonck[']s son	m
[47]	9/1726	y[our] H[onor's] mother	f	Gunpowder and lead; 8 guilders	Willam Krom[,] tatepagh's son	m
[78]	1/1727	y[our] H[onor's] brother	m	Cotton; 3 guilders remain	hend hekan, or one of his sons	m
[107]	9/1728	y[our] H[onor's] mother	f	1 ell of strouds; 16 guilders	matissol[,] manonck['s] son	m
[91]	9/1728	mary pawling	f	Gunpowder; 35 guilders	hend hekan	m
[99]	3/1729	y[our] H[onor's] sister	f	½ "schepel" bran, ½ ell of cotton; 12 guilders	mack[,] pansogh['s] son	m

Table 15. Prices of Merchandise and Services Purchased by Indians

Main type, merchandise and services	Subgroup, merchandise	Price range, guilders	Most common price, guilders	Remarks
A. Textiles				
- Fabric				"Pieces," excl.
Ells	Strouds	16–20	16–18	Once: 12; 15
	Duffels	11	11	
	Baize	6–8	6	
	Penneston	6–7	7	
	Linen	4–5	5	
	"Gemp"	1–2	1	
Blankets	Strouds	40–50	45	Once: 27; 34
	Coarse blanket; "Combars"	25–36	36	
	Duffels	20–30	24–28	
	Cotton	6–10	6/8–10	Straight/colored
- Clothing				
Headgear	Hat	9–14	–	
	Cap	6	6	
B. Alcohol	Rum, gallon	10–12	10	
	Rum, quart	3	3	Once: 4.5
	Rum, bottle	2.5–3	3	
	Rum, "kan"	2.5–3	3	Once: 1.75; 4.5
	Rum, pint	1.5–2.25	1.5	
	Rum, "muts"	0.5	0.5	
	Cider, bucket	5–6	5	
	Cider, "kan"	1–1.5	1	
	Beer, bucket	3–5	–	
	Beer, "kan"	0.5–1	1	
C. Ammunition	Gunpowder, lb	6–7	6	
	Lead, bar	2–3	2	
	Lead, lb	1–1.25	1	

(continued)

Table 15. *(Continued)*

Main type, merchandise and services	Subgroup, merchandise	Price range, guilders	Most common price, guilders	Remarks
D. Knives/axes	Axes, large	9	9	
	Knives	1.5–3	–	Jackknives: 2.5–3
	Axes, small	4–6	6	
E. Foodstuffs	Corn, "sch"	4–5	4	
	Bread	1.5–2	2	
	Sugar, lb	1–1.5	–	
F. Guns	Gun	240–320	240	Once: 60; 120
G. Repairs	Repairs, guns	5–12	–	
H. Shoes	Shoes	15–16	–	

Note: The types of goods are listed as they appear in table 3 (Categories of Trade Goods), with a different subdivision in the types "Fabric" and "Clothing."

Table 16. Prices of Goods Exchanged by Indians for Credit

Main type, goods	Subgroup, goods	Credit range, guilders	Most common credit, guilders	Remarks[a]
Peltry	Bear hide	8–20	10–12	
	Fisher	9–12	11	
	Beaver, lb	3.5–11.25	8–10	
	Marten	6–8	7	
	Otter	5–6	6	Only 3 occurrences
	Fox	5	–	Only 2 occurrences
	Raccoon	3–4	3	
	Mink	1.5–2	–	Only 2 occurrences; 1.5, "small mink"
	Deerskin, lb	1–2	1.5–1.75	Incl. raw skins
	"Prepared skins"	6.45–8	7	
	Elk skin, lb	1–1.4	1.25	
	Prepared, lb	5	5	Specified only once
	Wolf	18	–	
	Pelt and head	25–30	–	
	Head	24	–	
	Pelt	3.5–6	–	
Animals	Pig	33–80	60	Once: 112
Animal products	Feathers, lb	3	–	Only 1 occurrence, see [98]
	Grease / fat, lb	1	–	
Foodstuffs	Cranberries, "sch"	6	–	Only 1 occurrence, [20]
	Beans, "sch"	4.5	–	"Small beans"; only 1 occurrence, [48]
	Grits, "sch"	4.5	–	Only 1 occurrence, [48]
Other	Canoe	27–63	–	

[a] For other earnings by Indians, see tables 7 and 8.

Table 17. Discharges on Debit Accounts, per Account

Number of accounts with debit transactions	175	(100.0%)
Debit transactions, fully paid	91	(52.0%)
Debit transactions, paid in part	17	(9.7%)
Debit transactions, not paid	67	(38.3%)

1. Sample page [15], showing entries from 1719 to 1725. The lower account is of the Indian man named Jan Palin, described as "nenison[']s son." Palin's unnamed brother and an Indian man identified as "son of sawis" were also active on the account. All other accounts on the page were crossed out, indicating that they had been satisfied. For Jan Palin and "sawis," see the appendix. Courtesy of Manuscripts and Archives Division, New York Public Library, Astor, Lenox and Tilden Foundations.

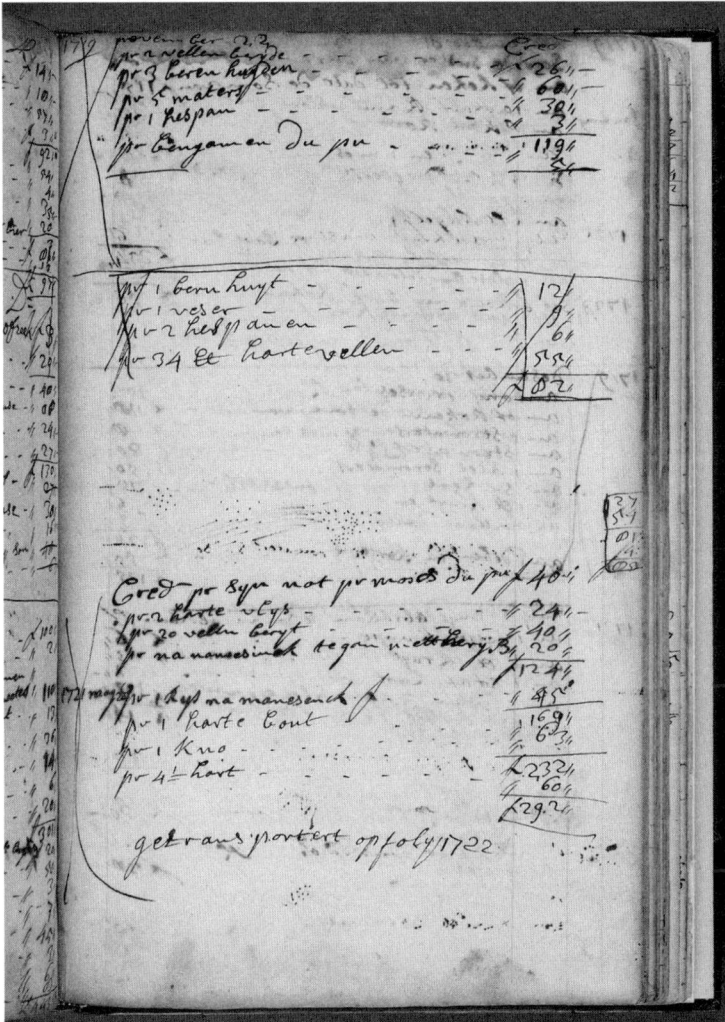

2. Sample page [18]. One of the more disorderly pages in the account book. Documents payments or services rendered by native customers from 1719 to 1721 to reduce their debts. The trader records trips by "Sander the savage" to namesinck (Nawesinck, at the Neversink River) and manesenck (Minisink); see also map 1. The same man also delivered a *kno* (canoe). For a profile of Sander, see the appendix. Accounts show payments by two settlers (benyamen and moses du pri) on Indians' accounts. A number of accounts were crossed out, indicating that they had been settled. Courtesy of Manuscripts and Archives Division, New York Public Library, Astor, Lenox and Tilden Foundations.

3. Sample page [67]. Contains the largest amount of debt recorded in the account book; the first account on the page lists a total debt of almost 600 guilders. It was developed by the Indian man "manonck" and his relatives. This man and his kin occur frequently in the ledger. Remarkably, we have not been able to identify this individual. Note the reference to a purchase of rum "at abram['s] burial." Courtesy of Manuscripts and Archives Division, New York Public Library, Astor, Lenox and Tilden Foundations.

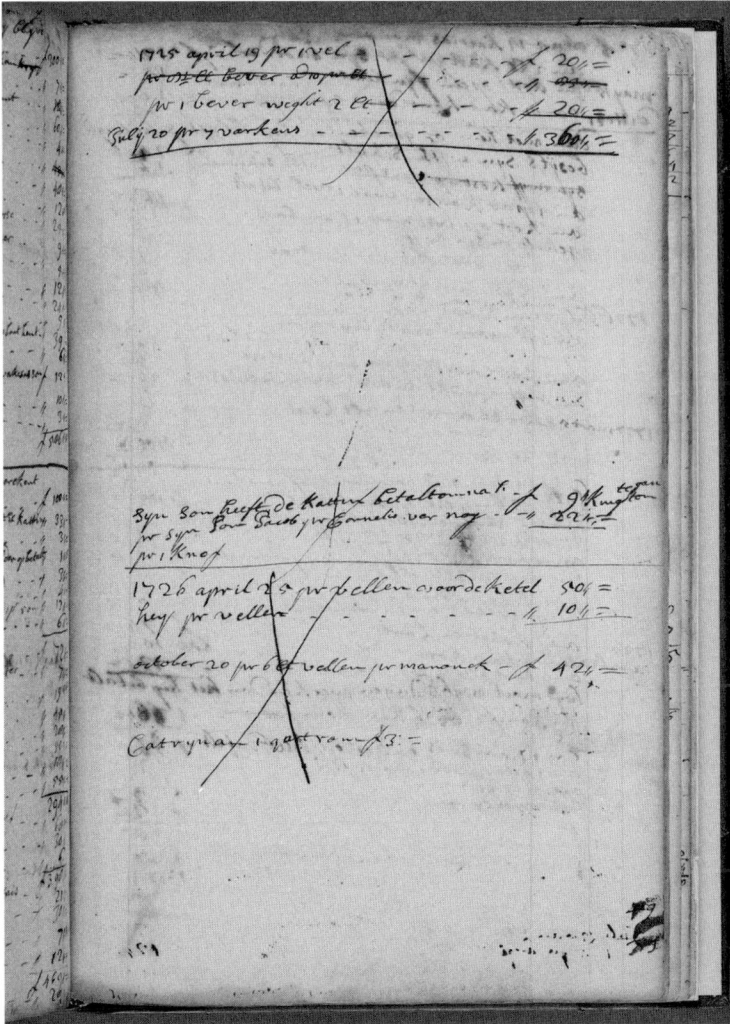

4. Sample page [68]. Shows payments and services by "manonck" and his relatives to reduce their debt. The first cluster of transactions on the page includes the delivery of seven pigs and amounts to more than 300 guilders; the second contains a reference to a trip by an unnamed son of "manonck" to Kingston. Although the payment of a canoe is mentioned, it remains unclear if the Indian was debited as no amount was entered. Courtesy of Manuscripts and Archives Division, New York Public Library, Astor, Lenox and Tilden Foundations.

5. Final page of the account book, [111]. Shows damage to upper left-hand corner. Contains sizable accounts with goods acquired on credit. "Lendart the savage" and the Indian man listed as "waddie" developed debts with the trader amounting to hundreds of guilders. The man named "waddie" was a son of the Esopus leader Hendrick Hekan (see appendix). Courtesy of Manuscripts and Archives Division, New York Public Library, Astor, Lenox and Tilden Foundations.

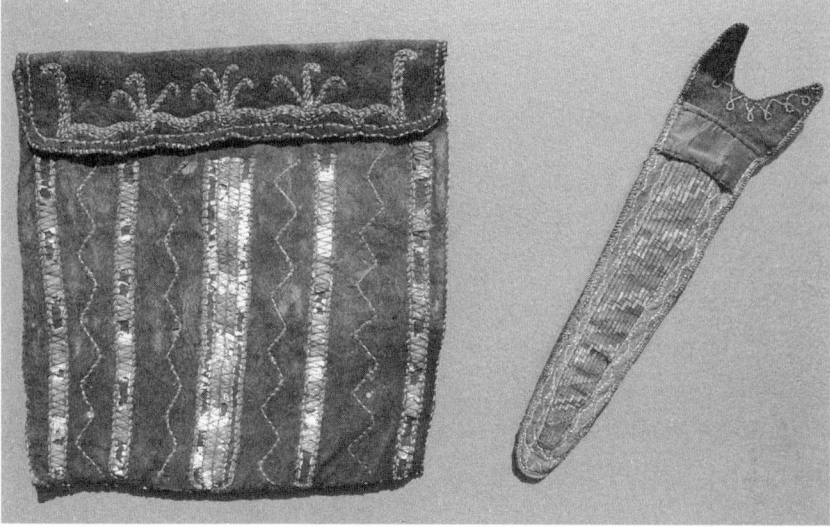

1. Wappinger cultural items consisting of a tobacco pouch and knife sheath that were given by the Indians to the Ver Plank family in Dutchess County. Courtesy, Mount Gulian Historic Site, Beacon, NY.

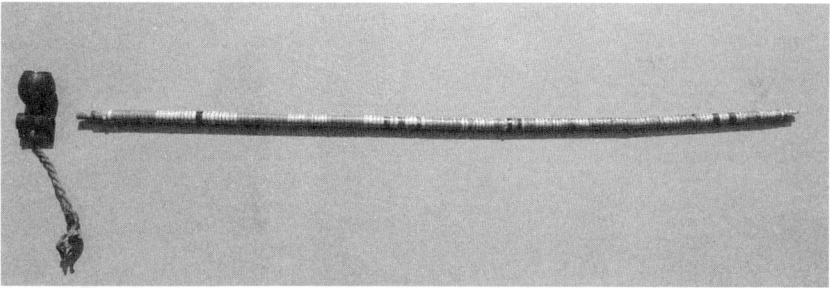

2. A Wappinger pipe that was given by the Indians to the Ver Plank family in Dutchess County. Courtesy, Mount Gulian Historic Site, Beacon, NY.

3. Esopus treaty belt, 1664/1665. Courtesy of the Ulster County Clerk's Office, Kingston, NY, Nina Postupack, Ulster County Clerk.

4. Esopus treaty belt, 1664/1665; detail. Courtesy of the Ulster County Clerk's Office, Kingston, NY, Nina Postupack, Ulster County Clerk.

Munsee Indian Trade in Ulster County, New York, 1712–1732;
A Section from the Anonymous "Account Book, 1711–1729"
[in Dutch],
Philip John Schuyler Papers (Volume 11)

A Manuscript in the Holdings of the
Manuscripts and Archives Division
New York Public Library
Astor, Lenox and Tilden Foundations

ANNOTATED TRANSLATION

Translated by Kees-Jan Waterman
Edited by Kees-Jan Waterman and J. Michael Smith

Editorial Method

THE LAYOUT of the pages in the manuscript has been retained as much as possible. The text represents a direct transcription of words in the original manuscript.

cr: crossed out.

[ ]: text between brackets could not be transcribed.

[text]: remarks between brackets reflect editorial comments on, for instance, the layout of the original text. On occasion, the brackets contain additions to the original text.

[text?]: an editorial suggestion.

~~text~~: words or entries scratched out in the manuscript.

Annotated Translation

[1]

(318) --Debit-side--

<u>1717</u>

Kingston August 21	
manonck[1] the savage	
on remainder on strouds	f 8/
on 1 knife f3 1 Piece [of fabric]	
1 pair of stockings	" 27/
on beads f4: 2 lb gunpowder	" 16/
on 1 pair of children's stockings	" 3/
on 1 duffel blanket	" 28/

on 1 bottle of rum 1 p^t of rum	" 4/
on 1 gun for 5 pieces of eight[2]	" 60/-
if he keeps it	
on 4 ells of strouds	" 60/
on 1½ ell of dufels	" 17/
on 9 lb of lead	" 9/
	f231/[3]

[entries on the remainder of page, from 1718 down, are cr=satisfied]
1718 december 15 balanced account with manonck

	and they [sic] remain indebted in all	f111/-
1719	on 2 ells of blue textiles	" 16/
	on 4 p^t rum f8 on 2 small axes	" 20/
	on 2 stroud blankets	" 90/
	on 1 lb gunpowder	" 6/
	on 1 pair of stockings	" 6/
		f249/

june 28 on remainder on rum consumed		" 9/
1721	on 3 ells of silver ribbon	" 33/-
	to his son 2 *kan* rum	" 5/
	on 28 kan rum	" 70/-
	on 4 kan rum	" 10/
	on 2 boxes with paint	" 5/
	on 1 *tromp*[4]	" 1/-
	on 1 shirt and 2 pairs of buttons	" 30/-
	to his son 1 coat	"[empty]
	on 1 coarse blanket f34 on[5]	" 34/
	on 2 kan rum that the other savage[6]	" 6/-
september 27		452/
1721	on 4 gall rum	40/
		f492/
	his son on 1 qt rum	" 3/
	on 1 ell of strouds by his son	" 20/
	on slices of meat	" 12/
1722	on 1 coarse blanket	" 33/

sept. 20 on 2 qt rum on 2 occasions	" 6/
[last date is repeated at	f566/-7
the left side of the page: sept. 20]	

[2]

(319) --Credit-side, but also contains some debts--8

1718	december 15	
	Cred[it] by Jan van Kampen9	f120/-
	have paid them for their other wares	
	+ balanced account up to then	

[entries on the remainder of the page, from 1719 down, are cr]

1719	september 4	Cred[it]
	by debora10 in addition	f 12/-
	for 7 ½ lb beaver	" 42/
	for 7 deerskins	" 54/-
		108/-
	his son still has 1 stroud blanket coming to him	
	that he has paid	
1721	sept. 27 for 11 lb dressed skins	f 71/-
	for 3 skins	" 14/
		f193/
	1722 for 1 pig	f112
		f305/-
	her oldest son for 4 lb beavers	" 28/-
		f333/-
1724	sept 2 on remainder on white baize	f 14/-
	on 1 knife f2:10 his wife	" 2/10
	on 1 lb gunpowder f6 on 4 lb lead	" 10/-
	manonck11 on 1 coarse blanket	" 28/-
January 10 on 1 shirt for his son Jacob12		" 12/-
	on remainder on white baize	" 4/-
		f 70/10/
	their son Jacob Cred[it] for beaver	" 10/-

on 2 lb gunpowder and lead	" 16/
on 1 axe + rum *gelyt*[13]	" 3/-
in addition see after 49[14]	
hend hekan's[15] son on gunpowder and lead	" 7/-
their oldest son on 2 ells of baize	" 12/-

[3]
(320) --Debit-side--
[all accounts on this page, cr=satisfied]

1717	august 20 Sammetie[,] Sametie's[16] son	
	At balancing the Account	f 15/
	on 14 kan rum f40 on 1 ell of strouds	f 58/

1717	august 21 annondo's[17] daughter Catrijn[18]	
	on various goods	f 50/
	on 8 kan rum	" 24/
1719	august 17 on 5 kan rum again	" 15
january	on 20 kan rum	" 60/-
	on pair of stockings	" 5/-
	on 1 lb gunpowder	" 6/-
	on 11 kan rum	" 33/
	on 12 kan rum	" 36/
		f155/
	on 1 shirt and 1 frock	" 16/
	on 16 kan rum	" 39/-
		210/
1721	sep[t] on 6 kan rum	" 15/-
	on 10 kan rum	" 25/-
		250/
1724	on 6 kan rum	f 12/
		f262/
1724	January 10 on 11½ kan rum	" 23/-
	ditto 31 on 10 kan rum	" 20

on 1 p^t rum f1:10	" <u>1/10</u>
f306/10	
1725 august 5 on 23 kan rum	"[40, cr]
on remainder on 1 dufels blanket	" <u>10/</u>
	"316/10
on 1 stroud blanket	" <u>45/</u>

[4]

(321) --Credit-side--

[empty upper half]

   [the entire account, cr]

Cred[it] for 1 *doller*[19] 1 mink[20]	[empty]
for 1 pig[,] settling the account	

———————

Cred[it] for 1 pig	f 60/
1719 for 6 martens	" 36/
[Se]p^t for 1 raccoon	" 4/
for 1 beaver	" <u>12/</u>
	f112/
for 1 fox	" <u>5/</u>
	f117/
for 1 deerskin	" <u>16/</u>
	f133/
<u>1724</u> January 10 for grease and skins	" <u>20/-</u>
	"153/-
January 31 for 4 lb dressed skins	" 32/-
by Jan roos — the savage[21]	" <u>12/-</u>
	f197/
<u>1725/6</u> march 13 for 11 lb dressed skins	" 77/-
for 9 lb deerskin	" <u>9/-</u> 250
	283/- <u>133</u>
	117

361	
<u>283</u>	
78	262
	<u>153</u>
	109

[5]
(322) --Debit-side--

<u>1717</u> august tiet the savage woman's Daughter

on 1 stroud blanket	f 50/
on 1 blanket that her mother owes	f 50/

<u>1717</u>
august nanoghqaurij[22]

at balancing the account	f 67/
on 1 kettle f40 on 5 ells of penneston	" 75/
his wife from older times	" 13/
on 2 ½ ells of penneston	<u>" 17/10</u>
	172/10

[remainder of the page, from 1719 down, cr=satisfied]

1719 september 16 Kattener[23]	
on 1 knife and shot	f 0[24]/-
1724 sep[t] 12 on 4 kan rum by manonck's son[25]	f 10/-
on remainder on 1 bottle f4 on remainder	f 4/-
on his wife's stockings	f 1/-
1725 on 4 lb lead	" 4/-
on 1 pint rum f1:10 another pint rum	" 3/-
on 1 pt rum f1:10	" 1/10
his wife on 1 colored shirt	<u>" 24/-</u>
	f 47/10

on 1 lb gunpowder	" 6/-
on 4 lb lead	" 4/-
may 15 to his wife 6 kan rum that he has paid[26]	" 18/-
	[empty]/10
1726 July 22[27] ~~on 1 stroud blanket~~	~~f 45/-~~
on 4 kan rum at the burial[28]	" 12/-
Remains f85:-	f085/-
1726 sep[t] 10 then balanced accounts with him and he	
and his wife and 33 guilders	f 90
on 1 stroud blanket at his daughter's	
burial[29]	" 40/-
on 3/4 of one ell of strouds f14 on 2 ½ ells	
of colored textiles f20	" 34/-
	f164/-
april 20 on 1 p[t] rum f1:10	" 1/10
	f165/10

[6]
(323) --Credit-side--

[upper part of page is empty]

1717[30]	
Cred[it] for various	f 91/-
for 2 bear hides	" 28/
	119/

54

[the following entry, cr]

1719[31] Cred[it] for skins to [sic]	
comes his part of the skin	f 6/-

[7]
(324) --Debit-side--
1717 august 21 warangau[32][,] samtie[33][']s daughter's husband

on remainder on strouds	f 36/-
on rum and beer f 4 on 1 lb gunpowder and lead	f 12/-

[empty half page]

171[6/7][34] ankerop[35]

on remainder on textiles f 3 on 1 bar of lead	f 5/
on remainder on strouds	f 13/
to his wife on wine and beer	f 6/7
on ditto 1 quart wine	f 4/10

[remainder of the page is empty]

[8]
(325) --Credit-side--

Credit for Specie	f 10/-

[remainder of the page is empty]

[9]
(326) --Debit-side--

[the nine lines in this account, cr=satisfied]
1715 antony[36][,] hester's[37] son

on 1 stroud blanket	f 45/
on 1½ ells of cotton	" 10/
on hat and ribbon	" 14/
1719 July 19 on 1 ell of strouds	" 18/-

on 4 lb lead	" 4/-[38]
_____[thin line]_____	
on 1 duffels blanket	f 27/
on 1 knife	" 1/10
on money f8: on 1 coarse blanket ditto on	
1 coarse blanket	" 80/
	f108/10
Martie the savage woman	
on 4 kan rum	f 12/
on 5 ells of baize on 2 occasions	" 36/-

[the account below, cr=satisfied]

June 20

1719	naris the savage	
	from older times	" 4/
	on 2 ½ ells of baize	" 19/-[39]

[empty space]

[the account below, cr=satisfied]

1717	blandina[,] hend daughter[40]	
	on remainder on 1 stroud blanket	f 22/
	on 2½ ells of *fris*[41]	" 28/

[10]

(327) --Credit-side--

[the account below, cr]

Cred[it] for 1 deer and 2 turkeys	f 30/
for 1 deer f16	f 16/
for 2 deer quarters	" 6/
for 2 skins f 26 on 3 ½ lb beaver	" 46

	" 68/
for 1 doller[42] ditto	22/
	90/

[empty space]

[the entry below, cr]

Cred[it] for cuts of hare   f 18

[11]
(328) --Debit-side--

1717   august pamberoch quet[,] hans's wife[43]
       remains indebted at balancing the account   f 32/

[empty space]

1715   _____
       Kegkenond's[44] sister
       on remainder on strouds   f 26/
       on ½ lb gunpowder and shot   " 6/
                                                        f 32/

[empty space]

1712   _____
       ~~nane~~ nanemkis
       on 1 white coarse blanket   f 35/-

[Inserted leaf; recto]

Albany 25 April 1729

Received of Cap.t Albert Pawling.

40 Dr[essed] Deer w[eigh]ᵗ . . . 114 lb	£ 16/19/-
31 beavers w[eigh]ᵗ 54 lb . . . . . . @ 6/	16/ 4/-
10 bear hides . . . . @ 7/	3/10/-
5 D[itt]° smaller . . . . @ 5/	1/ 5/-
7 hairy Elks w[eigh]ᵗ 140 lb . . . @ 9/	5/ 5/-
6 foxes . . . . @ 3/3	-/19/3
6 Martins . . . . @ 4	1/ 4/-
1 wolf	-/ 3/-
2 fishers . . . . @ 5/6	-/11/-
8 Catts . . . . @ 2	-/16/-
2 otters . . . . @ 3/6	-/ 7/-
2 small Raccoowns . . . . @ 1/3	-/ 2/6
2 Minks . . . . @ 1/6	-/ 3/-
11 Musquashes[45] . . . . @ 3	-/ 2/9
	£ 50/11/6

p Ph: Livingston

[verso]
pawlings acct. f Livingston

[12]
(329) --Credit-side--

[empty page]

[13]
(330) --Debit-side--

[all accounts on this page, cr=satisfied]

<u>1717</u>   october 25 nawoghquarry[46]
          remains indebted at balancing the account   f 67/
          <u>on 1 string of beads   " 6/</u>

[empty space]

Krwamo[47]['s] daughter

1719	april 17 sar[,] hendreck hekan's wife[48]	
	on 7 lb lead	f 7/
	on 1 lb gunpowder	" 6/-
	on 2 ells of penneston	" 14/-
		" 27/
	on 1 stroud blanket	" 45/
		72/

1719	Kegkenond[49]	
	on 2 ells of cotton	f 12/
	on remainder on strouds	" 5/-
	on 2 ells of baize	f 12/-
	his daughter on 1 blanket	" 36/-
	on remainder from older times[,] this is	
	her father	" 9/-
	on 1 pt rum	" ~~2/~~
	she has again 1 duffels blanket	f 28/
	to the smith[50] for the axe	" 2/
	to her husband 1 ell of strouds	" 20/-

1719	hans or kwatten the savage	
	on remainder on duffels	f 12/
	on remainder on strouds and lead	
	and gunpowder	" 9/-
	on ½ lb gunpowder and lead	" 8/
	on remainder on 2 lb kettle	" 6/
	balance	f 35/-

[14]

(331) --Credit-side--

[empty space]

Cred[it] for 1 bear hide	f 16/
for 1 fisher	" 12/-
	" 28/
for remainder on a skin	" 6/-
	34/

72
34
38

1720 July 14 Cred[it] by y[our] H[onor's] daughter	f 6/-
Cr[edit] deerskins	" 40/
for 1 deer meat[51]	" 12/-

[the last two lines in the account above, cr]

[empty space]

Cred[it] for deer meat	f 8/-
for 1 *kno*[,] settling the account balance	" 27/-

72
28
44

[15]
(332) --Debit-side--

1719	Kawahym[,] Sander's[52] mother	
	on 14 kan rum	f 42/
	on ribbon and textiles by her son	" 10/-
	on 1 jackknife	" 3/-
	on 1 cap by her son	" 6/
	on 1 ell of strouds	" 18/-

remains indebted at Balancing the account

the sum of   f 52/-

---

sander's mother

on 1 pair of scissors f2 on 1 pair of

seyette[53] stockings   f 17/

on 10 kan rum   " 30/-

on 1 p^t rum f1:10 on 1 hat f9: on 1 girdle   " 14/-

on 2 lb shot   " 2

   63

on 1 gall molasses   " 2/10

on 1 ell of floret   " 1/10

1719   november 2 quakesas[54][,]karwamo[55]['s] son   f 6[7/-][56]

on 1 lb gunpowder on 1 lb lead   f 8/

on ½ ell of strouds   " 10/

on 1 hat   " 11/

on remainder on 1 dufels blanket   " 16/-

on molasses   " 2/-

   f 47/

His wife on 7 kan rum   f 21/

on remainder on blue textiles   " 4/

on beads   " 4/

   29/

1721/2 march 24 on 9 ½ kan rum   " 24/-

the savage woman who he escorted

has 4 kan   " 10/-

on 1 ell of strouds   " 20/-

   83/

[all accounts above, cr=satisfied]

Jan palin[57][,] nenison[58][']s son

On 1 girdle   f 4/10

1725   may 13 his brother on 1 knife   " 1/10

ditto on 2 ells of cotton sawis['s] son[59]   " 12/-

[16]
(333) --Credit-side--

Cred[it] for 1 dressed skin   f 24/-

[empty space]

___

Cred[it] by his wife for beavers   f 20/-
for 1 pig   " 60/-
                                                f 80

[remainder of the page is empty]

[17]
(334) --Debit-side--

[the account below, cr=satisfied]
1719   november 22
        Sander the savage[60]
        have coming to us at balancing the account   14/-
        January 1 on 1 cap f6 on 1 ½ ell of blue
                                        textiles   " 18/-
        on 19 quart rum   " 57/
        on ½ lb gunpowder   " 3/10
                                                    f 92/10
        on 3 ells of strouds   " 54/
        on 1 girdle   " 4/
        on 1 coarse blanket   " 35/-
        on 1 shirt   " 20
        _____   1 bucket of beer   " 3/
        remains indebted at balancing the account   f 81/
        on 1 small glass bottle f10 1 qt rum   f 13
                                                    f 97/

___

1719   M:ˣ Sawenakies[61]   D[ebit]

December 8 I have coming to me at balancing

                                                  the account   f 3/-   3

    on 1 hat f 14 on 1 cap   " 20/-   29

    on 1 stroud blanket   " 48/   41

    on remainder on strouds for stockings   " 08/   6

    on 18 lb lead and 2 knives   " 24/-   24

    on 4 ells of white baize   " 27/   27

                                           f130/   30

  X his son remainder on strouds   " 27/   16

    his wife on baize and 2 pairs of stockings   " 30/   f176

    also to this small savage woman f 16   " 16/-

  X on 1 dufels blanket on 1 ell of strouds

                                   his son   " 48

  X on 1 string of beads   " 6/-

[the account below, cr=satisfied]

1719/20 Sander the savage

    anew on goods   f100/

    on 1 bottle of rum   " 2/10

  X on rum and beer for 2 raccoons   "[empty]

    on 1 coat f 60 on 1 stroud blanket   "110/

    on 1 lb gunpowder f 6 on 6 lb lead   " 13/-

    on 6 ells of cotton   " 36/

    on 2 ells of red penneston   " 14/-

    on buttons   " 6/-

    on 2 gall rum   " 20/

                                         f301/10

1721

march 20 on 2 gall rum for his brother's

                                     daughter   f 20/-

    on 1 stroud blanket   " 50/-

    on 1 qt rum   " 3/

    on 1 qt rum and 1 *sch* Indian corn   " 7/

    on 1 stroud blanket   " 45/-

on 1 qt rum	" 3/
on ½ gall rum	" 6/
on 1 lb gunpowder and 1 bar of lead	" 8
	f443/10

[18]
(335) --Credit-side--

[the account below, cr]

1719 november 22	Cred[it]
for 2 dressed skins	f 26/
for 3 bear hides	" 60/-
for 5 martens	" 30/-
for 1 raccoon	" 3/
	"119/
by benyamen du pri[62]	" 5/

[the account below, cr]

for 1 bear hide	" 12/
for 1 fisher	" 9/
for 2 raccoons	" 6/
for 34 lb deerskins	" 55/
	f 82/

[empty space]

		27
		54
		81
		4
Cred[it] for his note[63] for moses du pri[64]	f 48	f85
for 2 deer meat	" 24/-	
for 20 dressed skins	" 40/	
for going to namesinck[65] with herij[66] $\sqrt{3}$	" 20/	

	f124/
1721 may 1 for 1 trip to manesenck[67] f	" 45
	169/
for 1 deer quarter	[empty]
for 1 kno	" 63/
	f232/
for 4½ deer	" 60/
	f292/

Transported to folio 1722[68]

[19]
(336) --Debit-side--

1719 november 8	
the son of Sar[,] Jurewen's[69] sister[70]	
at balancing the account up to today	
the sum of	f115/-
on 10 kan rum	" 30/-
on 8 kan rum	" 24/-
on 1 cap and 1 knife	" 8/-
on 1 duffel stroud blanket[71]	" 50/
	f227/
on 1 lb shot f 1	" 1
1721 July on 1 lb gunpowder and 2 bars of lead	" 6/
	f234/
on remainder on 1 coarse blanket	" 12
1723 sep* 6 coming to me at balancing	
the account	f 50/-
on 1 pair of shoes	" 15/-
he is indebted f 34:=	

[the account below, cr=satisfied]
1719   december 30

antonij frinses[72]

at balancing the account the sum of	f 18/
on 1 stroud	" 8/
on 1 stroud 1 ¼ ell	" 20/-
on 1 stroud blanket	" 50/
on silk ribbon	" 15/
on 1 lb gunpowder and [empty]	" 6/
to willam douty[73]	" 3/
	f120/
on 1 blanket and short pe[74]	" 55/
	f175/

1721	July 8 Young Abraham[,] Abraham's son[75]	
	on 1 dozen buttons	f 6/
	on ½ lb gunpowder	" 3/
	on 1 bar of lead	" 2/-
	on 1 kan rum	" 3/-
		f 14/

[the account below, cr=satisfied]

_____[thin line]_____

Sawanagki[']s son[76]

on 2 lb gunpowder and lead and bread	f 20/-

_____[thin line]

Matekie or hans Jacob[77]

at balancing the account	f 38/-

[20]
(337) --Credit-side--

Cred[it]

for 4 skins f 31: for raccoon	f 35/-
for 2 beavers	" 24/-
for 1 fat sow or pig	" 80/
	f139/

	For 4 sch cranberies	" 24/-
1721	July 8 for 2 deer quarters	" 4/
		f167/

1723	sep[t] 4 on 1 sow	" 50/
	1724 July for 4 days on the farm 4 days	
	for <u>his wife</u>	[empty]
	[I/we] owe his wife f 22:=	

[the account below, cr]

Cred[it] for 1 turkey	f 3/
for 1 skin	" 14/-
	f 19/[78]
for 8 raccoons	32/
	" 51/
for 8 ½ lb beaver	" 51/-

1722 april 15 for 1 elk skin	f 14/-

[21]
(338) --Debit-side--

[all accounts on this page, cr=satisfied]

1719	January	
	Lendert the savage[,] Sander's brother[79]	
	anew on various goods	f 44/-
	on 1 lb gunpowder	" 6/-
	for his mother's debt	" 52/
		f102/

---

anew on 1 pair of buckles	f 5/
on [1] string of beads and 1 girdle	" 10/-
on 1 gun for £ 6:-[80]	"240/

on 2 ells of white baize	" 14/-
on 1 shirt	" 20/
on 1 bottle of rum	" 3/
	f292/
on 1 dufels blanket	" 30/-
	f322/

1721	balanced accounts with Lendert he remains	f102/-
	on 1 qt rum	" 3/-
	on 3 pᵗ rum	" 5/-
	on 1 kan rum new Year	" 3/
	on 1 qt rum	" 4/10
		f117/10
	balanced accounts and he remains indebted	f 63/-
	on 6 kan rum	" 18/
	on 3 lb gunpowder and 1 bar of lead	" 6/10
	on 8 kan rum	" 24/-
		f111/10

_____[thin line]_____

1719	January 23 norman the savage[81]	
	on remainder on a coarse blanket by antony[82] f 6/	
	on his son's account the sum	" 33/
		49/
	Anew 1 ½ ell of strouds f 30 on 8 ells	
	of ribbon	" 38/
	on 4 ¼ ells of linen	" 17/
	on 1 kan rum	" 3/-
		f107/

Jores[,] hester's son[83]	
on remainder on strouds	f 18/-
on ½ ell of strouds for 1 savage	" 9/
on 3 kan rum	" 9/
on 1 stroud blanket	" 50/
on 1 sword	" 55/

1721	november on 1 dufels blanket	" 28/
	on 4 ells of garters linen	" 18/-
	on 1 qt rum	" 3/-
	on 1 bar of lead	<u>" 2/-</u>
		f192/
1721/22 march 2 on dufels		" 24/
	on 8 ells of *oosburgh*	<u>" 24/-</u>
		240

[22]
(339) --Credit-side--

[the account below, cr]

Cred[it] for 2 bear hides	f 38/
for 10 martens	" 60/
for 1 katlos[84]	<u>" 3/</u>
	"101/

Cred[it] for 2 deer	f 26/-
~~for 20 dressed deerskins~~	~~" 40~~
~~for going to nawesingh[85]~~	~~" 20/-~~
	f 86/
	f 26/
returned the gun[,] the stock brok[en]	<u>"200/</u>
	f226

X for dressing skins	f 45/-
X for 1 bear hide	<u>" 10/</u>
	f 55/
on 1 shirt	f 20/-
from the other side[86]	"111
on 1 gun for £ 6	<u>"240/[87]</u>
	f361/
on 1 shirt f 12 on gunpowder and lead	" 17/
on 1 ell of strouds	<u>" 20/-</u> 326

	f398/-
1727 on 1 ell of strouds — anew	" 16
	414/
Cred[it] for 5 day [*sic*] mowing	44 118
	55
	63

[the account below, cr]

1719 Cred[it] for 1 skin	f 24/
for 8 lb beaver	" 48/
	f 72/

107
72
f35:

Cred[it] for 3 deer quarters	f 6/-
for deer meat and 1 turkey	f 8/-
for 2 deerskins	36/
for 2 raccoons	" 6/-
	" 56/
1723 march 7 for 1 deerskin	" 24/
	f 80/
from the other side[88] his debt	f184/
of his wife[,] Jan van gelder's[89] sister	" 40/-
	f224/-

1723 november 24 then with Jors[,] hester's son
of f151:=:[90]
Cred[it] on 1 skin by pitt[91] van Cornels f24

[23]
(340) --Debit-side--

1722 april 9 Jacob the savage[92]	
on debt from older times in all	f 9/-
on 1 sword	" 60/-[93]
on 1 string of beads 1 girdle	" 10/

on remainder on strouds	" 9/[94]
on 1 shirt and 1 girdle	" 24/
on rum	<u>" 5/-</u>
	"057/[95]
on 1 lb gunpowder and 4 lb lead	" 10/
on 1 lb shot f 1	" 1
on 1 lb gunpowder on 1 bar of lead	<u>" 8/</u>
	f 76/

[empty space]

_____

1719 tatapagh[96]['s] wife	
on 11 kan rum	f 33/
on 12 kan rum	" 36/-
1725 on 4 kan rum that she carried with her	<u>" 10/-</u>
to trade for me[97]	<u>f 79/-</u>
at balancing the account I have coming	
to me	f 80/-

[empty space]

[24]
(341) --Credit-side--

Cred[it] by nicklas mayer[98]	f 33/
for ½ day mowing	<u>" 4/</u>
	f 37

[empty space]

Cred[it] for 4 days cutting twigs	<u>f 16/-</u>

[remainder of the page is empty]

[25]
(342) --Debit-side--

1715	my 2 Sawis[,] dorso['s] son[99]	
	on debt from older times	f 2/10
	on gunpowder and lead	" 27/
	on 2 quart rum f 6 on 1 ½ ell of *flinnen*[100]	" 15/
	on 1 lb shot f 1 [and] 1 quart wine	" 5/
	on 1 ell of strouds f 10 on 2 ells of baize	" 26/
	on 1 kan rum on 1 stroud blanket	" 53/
	on 2 kan rum on 22 kan rum	" 50/
	on beads	" 6/
		f184/10

[empty space]

1720	may 13 the small deaf savage[101] his gun is a security	
	on 9 kan rum f 27 for 3 ½ kan f 10:10	f[empty]
	on 1 small cask	f 5/

[empty space]

[26]
(343) --Credit-side--

Cred[it] by his mother	
for 3 bear hides	f 51/
for 6 raccoons	" 24/-
	f 75/
for 1 Elk skin by Jores meddagh[102]	" 20/-

[empty space]

Cred[it] for 2 skins at f 5 kan rum[103]	f 15/

[empty space]

[27]
(344) --Debit-side--

[the account below, cr=satisfied]

1720   marinham[104]['s] son barnnet[105]

on remainder on 1 coarse blanket	f 20/-
on 1 ½ ell of pinneston	" 9/-
on 2 ½ ells of pinneston	" 15/-
his wife on remainder on dufels	" 8/
on 2 sch Indian corn	" 10/
on 4 ells of ribbon	" 3/-
on remainder on 1 kettle	" 10/-

1721   on 1 small coat for his child   " 25/

June 17 on another small coat for the small[106]   " 15/

on 2 bars of lead	" 4/-
on 3 ¼ ells of strouds	" 58/10
on 2 juices	" 4/
on 1 pair of stockings	" 2/
	" 160/10[107]
on 8 kan rum	" 20/-
on 1 stroud blanket	" 45/-

-----

           f225/10[108]

1720   Kenoeghteck[']s wife

anew on ½ ell of strouds	f 10
on 13 kan rum	" 35/-
on 1 ½ ell of colored cotton	" 15/
on 6 lb lead	" 6
	" 66/
anew on 1 dufels blanket	" 28/
on 2 ells of cotton and 1 knife	" 15/
on 2 small axes	" 8/
on 1 lb gunpowder and lead	" 10/-

on 1 lb gunpowder and lead	10	" 1[0]/ [blotted][109]
on 5 kan rum	12	" 1[2]/10 [blotted]
on 3 ells of white baize		" 18/
on 2 ells of baize — her husband		" 12/
on 1 quart rum		" 2/
		f181/

Jamijn the savage woman	
on remainder on baize	f 6/-
on 7 kan rum	" 18/-
her niece[110] on 8 kan rum	" [empty]

----

nanset the deaf savage[111]	
on 2 ells of white baize	f 12/-
on 1 quart rum	" 3/
on 13 kan rum on 1 small cask	" 25/

[28]

(345) --Credit-side--

[the account below, cr]

Cred[it] for 1 bear hide	f 10/-
for 9½ deerskins for 120 in[112] lb gunpowder	"120/-
	f130/
on 1 bar of lead	" 2/
on 1 coarse blanket f 36 on ½ lb gunpowder	" 39/
on 2 bars of lead	" 4/
on 2 ½ ells of strouds	" 50/-
on 1 gall molasses f5 on 1 pair of scissors	" 7/-
on ¼ ell of strouds	" 5/-
on 1 bell	" 4/-
	f111/

[empty space]

Cred[it] for 2 ½ deer   f 34/

for 14 lb deerskins   " 21/

     f 53/

[remainder of page is empty]

[29]

(346) --Debit-side--

1721   march 28 tappose[113]['] son[,] Kattis[114]

on goods and rum   f 58

for which his trap is a security

1722 July 20 on 1 barrel   " 24/-

[the account below, cr=satisfied]

1721   august Jan van gelder[']s sister[115]

on goods f 31   f 31/

on 11 ½ kan rum   " 29/-

on 1 ½ ell of white baize   " 9/

1721   may 20 tamnat[116]

At balancing the account the sum   f 25/

on 2 coats for 14 lb beaver or [sic]   " 42/

on remainder on strouds   " 4/-

for repairing his locks   " 8/-

on 1 stroud blanket   " 45/

on 3/4 of on ell of strouds   " 13/-

on 10 bars of lead   " 20/

on 6 lb gunpowder   " 40/-

     f197/

on pipes   " 3/

on 9 knives   " 13/10

on 1 string of beads   " 5/

on 2 gall rum and 1 small cask   " 20

on 1 shirt   " 18/-

	f257/[117]
on 2 bars of lead by his boy	" 10/[118]
took with him 1 iron trap	f261/

[the account below, cr=satisfied]

1721 the 8th of June	
the savage women who have brought meat	
the one has a debt to the sum of	f 31/
~~the other is indebted~~	~~" 18/~~
X the 2 small savage women 1 string of beads	" 6/

---

the one savage woman is indebted from	
older times	f 13/
on 1 small frock for her child	" 16/
on molasses and 1 pt rum	" 3/
	f 32/
on 2 ells of white baize by their[119] mother	" 16/

[30]
(347) --Credit-side--

[empty space]

| Cred[it][120] by Coll gasbeek[121] | f 10/- |

[remainder of the page is empty]

[31]
(348) --Debit-side--

1721 June 4 norman[122]	
at balancing the account the sum of	f 35/-
on 2 bars of lead	" 4/-
on 4 ½ ells of Calamanco[123]	" 27/-
on ½ ell of *sallon*[124]	" 3/-

on 4 ells of strouds	" 80/-
on 2 kan rum	" 5/
	f154

1729	July 21 at balancing the account	
	then comes to me	f 61/-
	on 1 kan rum f3:= on 1 kan rum	" 6/-
	on 2 stroud blankets	" 68/-
	on 2 bars of lead	" 4/-

[empty space]

1721	may 30 meckeck who [at/with] Norman[']s[125]	
	Remainder on Cotton f 5 on lead	f 7/-

[32]
(349) --Credit-side--

1722	may 25	
	for 2 bear hides and 1 raccoon	f 27/-
	for 5 lb beaver	" 35/
		" 62/
1729	July 20 by derck westbroek[126]	" 26/
		f 88/-

[remainder of the page is empty]

[33]
(350) --Debit-side--

1721	June 12 Jott[,] tamnat['s] brother[127]	
	on 1 ell of duf[128] strouds	f 18/
	on 1 stroud blanket	" 45/

[empty space]

1721 June 12 pitgas   tamnat['s] brother
      on 1 stroud blanket   f 45/
      on 1 string of beads   " 5/

[empty space]

1721 July 1 kakepan
      paid f 3::- on 1 kan rum
[not crossed out, but also no debt entered in monetary unit(s)]

[empty space]

[34]
(351) --Credit-side--

[empty page]

[35]
(352) --Debit-side--

<u>1721</u> august 9 Keghkenond[129]['s] daughter
      on 1 dufels   blanket f 28/
      on 1 axe from the smith[130]   " 2/
      by her father remainder on textiles " 9/
      to her husband 1 ell of strouds   " 20/
      on 14 kan rum   " 35/
      on 4 ells of fine colored textiles " 32/
      on 1½ ell of white baize   <u>" 9/-</u>
                                  f135/

      a savage woman who she escorted on 8 kan
                      rum 1 small caske f 25/-
      her husband for repairing his lock <u>" 11/-</u>
                                  171

[empty space]

1721	Juren[131] and hanna	
	on 3 ½ ells of baize	f 21/
	on 1 bar of lead	" 2/
	on 6 ells of penneston	" 36/
	on ½ ell of strouds	" 11/
	on gunpowder	" 1/10
	on 11 ½ kan rum	" 29/-
	on 1 bottle of rum	" 3/
	on 4 ½ ells of Cotton for their daught[er]	" 36/-
	on 1 dufels blanket	" 30/-
		169/10/

[empty space]

[36]
(353) --Credit-side--

[empty space]

Cred[it][132] for spinning	f 36/-
For 5 days spinning	" 10/
	46/

[remainder of the page is empty]

[37]
(354) --Debit-side--

1721	september 17	
	watpotgau or pitter[,] tamnat['s] brother[133]	
	on 1 stroud blanket	f 50/
	on 2 lb gunpowder	" 12/
	on 3 bars of lead	" 6/
	on 2 awls	" /15/
		68/15/

1732 June 28 on 1 stroud blanket f 36 on 12[134]

	1 piece of *gemp*	f 48/-
		f117/-

[account above, cr=satisfied]

[empty space]

1721 september 17 barnanschetnat

on 2 lb gunpowder and 3 bars of lead	f 18/
on 3 knives and awls and on gunpowder	" 10/-
on 1 ell of strouds	" 18/
on 3 pᵗ rum	" 4/10
on 3 pᵗ rum	" 4/10
	f 55/ 0/

[empty space]

1721 septemeb [*sic*] 17 Kesenat

on 1 lb gunpowder — paid	f̶ 6̶/̶[135]

---

[38]
(355) --Credit-side--

[empty page]

[39]
(356) --Debit-side--

1721 september nemham[136][']s sister

on remainder on [a] stroud blanket	f 20/
on stroud stockings	" 16/-
on remainder on a shirt	" 9/
on ½ lb gunpowder and 1 bar of lead	

	2 flintstones	" 6/-
on 2 lb lead		" 2/-
		f 53/
His mother on 9 kan rum		" 23/-
november on 1 ell of strouds		" 20/
on 1 coarse blanket		" 36
on 1 shirt		" 20/
on gunpowder and lead		" 5/-
on 1 coarse blanket		" 36/-
on rum and beer		" 3/-
		f196/
remains indebted the sum of f		" 94/-
anew on 1 stroud blanket		" 45/
on 1 pair of black stockings		" 20/-
on 1 lb gunpowder and 2 bars of lead		" 9/
on 1 small box with paint		" 3/
on 1 kan rum		" 3/-
		f174/-
on remainder on 1 coarse blanket		" 12/
		"186/

tabarhekan[137]['s] wife[']s sister

1722	november balanced account and remains	f 64/-
on 2 ells of cotton and ¼ of an ell		
	of strouds	" 19/-
on ½ gall molasses on 2 lb lead		" 4/-
		f 87/-
July 26 on 1 knife and 1 bar of lead		" 4/-
		f 91/
on 1 comb f 3 on 1 ell of strouds f 18		" 21/-
		112/
now remains indebted at balancing		
	the account	f 88/-

[40]
(357) --Credit-side--

1721   november 14:-

Cred[it] for 2 deer	f 24/-
for 1 deer	" 15/
for 27 lb skins	" 54/-
for 9 lb grease	" 9/-
	f102/
for 1 deer	f 20/
	f122/-

---

the boy who she escorts[138]	
X on remainder on dufels[139] ½ deer	9/-[140]
on ½ lb gunpowder	" 3/-
for repairing 1 gun and lead	" 4/-
Cred[it] for 1 gourd with beargrease[141]	f 4/-

[empty space]

Cred[it] for 1 deerskin	f 12/-
1723 august 6 for her part of deer meat	" 12/-
	f 24/-

[remainder of page is empty]

[41]
(358) --Debit-side--

[the account below, cr=satisfied]

1720 Sander the savage[142] from folio 1719[143]	f151
on 1 lb gunpowder and 1 bar of lead	" 8/-
his youngest brother on 2 blankets dufels	" 60/-
his mother's account is 67 guil[ders]	" 00[144]
sander and his younger brother fall short	47/-
	f266/-
decem[ber] 18 1 ~~dufel~~ stroud blanket	" 50/

on 1 pᵗ rum	" 1/10
on 1 kan rum	" 3/-
	320/10

1721 January 25 balanced the account and	
he remains	f171/-
on 4 kan rum	" 12/-
on 3/4 lb gunpowder on 1 bar of lead	" 6/10
on 1 lb pepper	" 8/-
on 5 ells of linen	" 20/-
	f218/

on 1 ell of linen [and] 1 pair of	
stockings f 22	" 27/
on 7 kan rum f 21:= on 1 bar of lead	" 23/-
on 1 dufels blanket	" 28/-
on 6 kan rum	" 18/-
	f314/-

1727 at balancing the account I have	
coming to me	f214/-

[account above, cr=satisfied]

[empty space]

Sander[']s brother[,] willam[145]	
at balancing the account	f 10/-
on 4 lb sugar	" 5/-
on 5 kan rum f 15 on 1 axe and	
1 *beversteker*[146]	27/-
	" 42/-
on 1 ell of strouds	" 20/
on 1 ½ ell of ribbon	" 6/
	f 68
1728 June 24 on 1 dufels blanket	" 24/-
on 2 lb gunpowder f 14 on 2 lb lead	
[and] flintstones f 3	" 17
on 2 ells of band and awls f 1-	" 4/-

	f113/-
on 3 ells of stocking garter	f 3/-
	f116/
on 1 shirt on the farm on 1 p^t rum	" 14/-
on 1 colored shirt f 24 on 2 bottles of	
rum f 6	f 30/-

[42]
(359) --Credit-side--

[the account below, cr]

His brother is Cred[itor] for 2¼ deer meat	f 39/-	
for 4 deerskins	" 54/-	
	f 93/-	
for preparing skins	f 57/-	
	f150/-	
for 1 trip to menisenck[147]	f 20/-	
for 4 days working at [the] southfield	" 24/-	
	f 44/-	
for 1 know	" 56/-	
	100/	314
		100
		214

[empty space]

1727 his wife on 1 p^t rum and 2 ells of band	f 3/-

[empty space]

_____ [thin line] _____

Cred[it] for 1 beaver	f 12/
1729 July for 10 days mowing on the farm	" 90/
	102/-

for cutting the meadow	" 20/-
	122

_____ [thin line] _____

1729 July 1 on another colored shirt	f 24/-
on 1 kan rum f 4:10	" 4/10

_____

1729 July 20 at balancing the account I have	
coming to me	f 86/
on 1 ell of strouds f 12	" 12/
	f 98/-
	20/[148]
	78/-

[43]

(360) --Debit-side--

[the account below, up to "299/, cr=satisfied]

marenghan['s] son[,] ~~tan~~ barnat[149]	
anew on 2 ells of dufels	f 22/-
on 1 coarse blanket	" 36/-
on 2 ells of swan stock[ings]	" 16/-
on rum	" 3/-
from the other side[150]	"207/-
on 2 small shirts	" 15/-
	"299/
on 1 qt rum	f3:=
his account stands at f431:-	f431/
1721 december 28 they anew coarse blanket	
by t: tapes[151]	" 2:10
1721 december 28 anew	
on 1 pair of black stockings	f 20/-
on 1 fine shirt	" 20/
on 2 ditto shirts	" 32/
on 1 coarse shirt	" 12/-
on 2 ells of white baize — has not	

received these[152]	" 00/
on 1 stroud blanket	" 50/
on 2 ells of ditto strouds	" 40/
on 1 ell ditto	" 20/-
on 3 ells of colored cotton	" 24/-
on 4 ells of *eysersterck*	" 24/
on 2 lb gunpowder	" 12/
on 4 bars of lead	" 8/-
on 1 *bleckyie*[153]	" 11/
on 2 small ells [for?] shirts	" 15/
	f278/-
1722 april 25 on 1 striped shirt f20:-	" 20/
on 6½ <u>kan</u> rum	" 19/10
~~on 2 small shirts for his children~~[154]	
on flintstones f1:10 on his gun f9:10	" 11/
on 1 kan rum and 1 small cask	" 30/
	f358/10
on 1 shirt	" 12/
Jacob the big[155] savage	f370:10
the big savage woman on 1 coarse blanket f 36:-	f 36/
on old debt	" 10/-
on 1 quart rum	" 3/-
	49
on 1 stroud blanket	f 45/
	94
his wife remains indebted in total	f 15/
on 2 qt rum on 2 bars of lead	" 9/
his wife on on [*sic*] 6 kan beer 1 qt rum	" 6/
	f 30/

[44]
(361) --Credit-side--

[all accounts on this page, cr]

Cred[it] for 7 deer	f 90/

for 1 otter		" 5/
for 19 lb grease		" 19/
for 97 lb deerskins	f 160:-	"160/
		274/-
for 1 bear hide		" 12/-
for 12 lb deerskins		" ~~18/-~~
		f286/-
for 1 beaver		" 8/-
his goods come to 431 guilders that is		f431/
from the other side[156]		f370/
on 3 ells of strouds		" 60
on 2 small shirts		" 15/-
		f445/-
for repairing 1 sight		" 7/-
on 10 kan rum fetched by his daughter		" 25/-
on 1 gall ~~rum~~ molasses		" 5/-
		f482/
on 1 lb gunpowder on 2 lb lead		" 8/
on ½ sch Indian corn [and] 3 qt molasses		" 6/
		f496/-
1722 december 7 on 1 stroud blanket		f 45/
on 1 dufels blanket and 1 kan		" 30/
		572/-[157]
1722 december 7 he then remains indebted		f343/
£ 8:11:6		
for 70 lb raw skins		f122/
1722 november 1 for 1½ lean deer		f 22/
for [a] plain meal[158]		" 8/
for 4½ deer		" 67/-
for 10 lb fat		" 10/-
		f229/-
1722 december 8 remains £ 8:11:6		f[empty]
indebted		
for 34 lb deerskins		f 68/

for 10 lb grease | " 10/-
 | 78/-

[45]
(362) --Debit-side--

1721 January 1
 tatepagh[159]
 on 2 kan rum his brother 1 comb | f 9/
 on 1 shirt | " 12/-
 on rutsen['s] old debt 1 skin | " 12/-
 on 1 fine shirt | " 24/-
 on 1 small cask of rum | 5
 | 62/-

[empty space]

1721 January 1 the savage from across the river
 on 2½ kan rum | f 7:10

[empty space]

1721 January 1 sawangh['s] son[160]
 on 1 shirt of rutsen | f 18/
 on 1 small box with paint | " 3/10
 on 2½ ells of dufels | " 23/-
 on 2 lb gunpowder on lead and 1 bread | " 22/-
 on ½ of an ell of strouds | " 14/
 | f 80/-[161]
1722/3 feb[ruary] 5 for 1 stroud blanket | f 50/-
1723 sept 28 on 1 fine shirt | " 36/-
 | f166/-
 balanced accounts and he remains indebted | f 32/-

on 2 qt rum and 1 qt rum	" 7/10
on 1 small axe by nicklas hofman[162]	" 6/-
	f 45/10

[46]
(363) --Credit-side--

for 1 kettle f 24[163]

[empty space]

1722 Cred[it][164] for 40 lb raw skins	f 70/-
feb[ruary] 4	
1723 october 29 for 2 deer	" 24/-
	94/
1723/4 march 21 for 32 lb raw skins	" 48/
	f142/-

[47]
(364) --Debit-side--

[all accounts on this page, cr=satisfied]

Willam Krom[165][,] tatepagh[166]['s] son[167]	
1721 on 1¼ ell of strouds	f 25/-
on 1 bottle of rum	" 2/10
	f 27/10

1725 april 24 anew 1 piece [of fabric]	f 9/-
on 1 shirt f12 on 2 ells of white baize f12	" 24/-
on 2 pint rum f3:=	" 3/-
on 1 p^t rum f1:10	" 1/10
on 1 knife f1:10	" 1/10
on 1 p^t rum f1:10 on 1 lb gunpowder	" 4/10
	f 42/10

may 17 on 1 shirt	<u>" 12/-</u>
	f 51/-
1726 sept 30 on 1 dufels blanket	" 26/
on 1 lb gunpowder and lead by y[our]	
H[onor's] mother	<u>" 8/</u>
	f 85/-
november 22 on 1 coarse blanket	" 33/-
on lead	<u>" 2/-</u>
	120/
1727 on remainder on 1 coarse blanket	
and strouds	" 9/
on 1 coarse blanket f33 on 1 Duffels	
blanket	" 58/-
on 2 kan rum and 4 kan rum	" 16/-
on gunpowder and lead and flintstones	
and remainder on rum	" 14/
on 5 kan rum	<u>" 15/-</u>
	f232/
on ½ lb gunpowder and 1 knife and 4 awls	" 8/-
1728 his wife on 10½ kan rum	<u>" 31/10</u>
	f271/10/-

[entire account above, cr=satisfied]

1721/2 march 23 abramhans[168]['s] daughter[,] menckesonghua	
on [ ] old debt	f 20/
on 12 kan rum for which the gun is	
a security	" 30/
on 1 ell of strouds for which [a] belt of	" 18/
wampum is a security 5 kan rum	" 12/10
on 1 pᵗ rum	" 1/10
on 2 kan rum	" 6/-
on 1 pᵗ rum	" 1/10
on [[169]] kan on the gun[170]	<u>" 25/-</u>
	f114/10
on ½¼[171] ell of strouds	" 2/10

on 3 kan beer and 1 kan rum " 6/-
on ½ strouds[172] " 3/-

[account above, cr=satisfied]

[48]
(365) --Credit-side--

[the account below, cr]
1725 for skins[,] settling the account f 27/10

1726 october 10 for 1 elk skin weighs £[173] 11 lb f 14/-

1728 february 1 for 4½ lb beaver f 46/
for 1 sch grits and ½ sch small beans " 9/-
for 11 skins, not dressed " 53/-

for 1½ lb beaver f 12/-
f 75/-[174]
85
14
71

120
14
106
271
59
£ 212[175]

[remainder of the page is empty]

[49]
(366) --Debit-side--

1722 april 1 on ½ ell of strouds f 10/-
Ragel

1722 may 1 the lame savage his gun is a security
    for 31 kan rum and 1 small cask   " 82/-

[empty space]

    tabarhekan[176][,] marinham[177][']s son
1722 december balanced accounts with him for all
    and he remains indebted £ 8:11:6   f343/-
1723 July 26 on 1 bar of lead on 1 knife   " 3/-
    for repairing 1 axe   " 4/-
    3¼ ells of cotton and 1 piece of duffels   " 29/
                                  379/-

    Now remains indebted at balancing
                         the account   f319/
1723 sept 2 on 1 stroud blanket   " 45/
    on 1 dufels blanket   " 30/-
                                    f394/

[remainder of the page is empty]

[50]
(367) --Credit-side--

[beginning of the page is empty]

1723 july 26[178] for deer meat   f 10/-
august 6 on his part of meat   f 60/-

1723 sept 2 for 4 lb deerskins   f 27/-[179]
    for 2 deer quarters   " 5/-
november 15 for 6 deer   " 61/-
                              f 93/-

[51]

(368) --Debit-side--

<u>1722</u> april 1 tamror[,] ~~nimhan~~[']s wapsto's son

on 1 stroud blanket	f 50/-
on ½ ell of strouds	" 9/
on 1 ell of strouds	" 18/-
on Ribbon	" 17/-
on 3 kan and 1 p[t] rum	" 11/-
on money for his gun[180]	<u>" 6/</u>
	f111/
on 1 p[t] rum f1:10 on 1 shirt	" 21/10
on 2 lb gunpowder	" 12/-
on 1 bar of lead	" 2/-
his wife stockings and ribbon and 1 q[t] peas	" 17/10
hi[s] w:[181] 1 shirt	" 10/-
on 2 pairs of stockings black	" 40/
on 1 q[tt] [sic] rum	" 3/-
on 1 ell of strouds	" 20/
on 12 flintstones	<u>" 2/-</u>
	f239/0

[empty space]

[the account below, up to the 1722 entry, cr=satisfied]

peghtarend[182]	
on 3½ quart rum	f 11/10
on money f1 on ½ ell of strouds	" 9/
on 1 p[t] rum	" 1/10
his wife on stroud stockings	" 15/
on remainder on 2 stroud blankets	" 10/-
on 1 bar of lead and some paint	" 5/-
on 3 qt molasses	" 5/-
on 1 ell of strouds on 1 bot[tle] of rum	" 21/

on remainder on strouds		" 6/-
on ¼ ell of strouds on 1 barrel		
	by his wife	" 28/10
		f112/10

1722 november 27

his wife again 2 ells of dufels	f 22/-
she on strouds	" 23/
he on 1½ ell of strouds	" 30/
on 1 barrel	" 24/-
to mary stenbergen[183]	" 12/
on 1 bread	" 2/-
	f113/-

[52]
(369) --Credit-side--

for remainder on his skins	f 30/-
he was indebted from older times 40 which has been paid	
1722 july 20 on deer meat	f 8/-

[empty space]

for 2 horses[,][184] settling the account[185] _____

from the other side[186]	f113/-
on 1 saddle	f120/
	f233/

[53]
(370) --Debit-side--

1722 april piswijn's[187] wife

on 1 box with paint	f 4/-

1722 feb[ruary] 1 Symon the savage[188]
    on 2 kan rum   f 6/-

_____   _____

    Joghem[,] Sawanagh['s] son[189]
1723 on remainder on 1 dufels blanket that not   f 6/ on the farm[190]
    on [s]trouds   " 5/-
sept 26 on 4 ell of fine colored cotton — yarn   " 33/
                                        f 44/-
    on 1 axe by _of_[191] hofman   " 6/[192]
                                        f 51/
                                        37/
                                        14/

[empty space]

_____

symon the savage has borrowed my gun
1723   on 1 knife for 5 kan beer   f 4/-
        on 2 ells of cotton   " 16/-
                                        20

[54]
(371) --Credit-side--

[beginning of the page is empty]

_____

1723 october 29[193]
      for 5 raccoons   f 15/-
      for 3 raccoons   f 9/-
      for 2 beavers   f 13/-
                                      f 37/-

_____

[remainder of the page is empty]

[55]
(372) --Debit-side--

1723 december 10
    Jors[,] hester[']s son[194]
    Remains indebted at balancing the account   f151/

[empty space]

    agpettos
    on 2 ells of baize for stockings   f 14/-
    on 1 piece of strouds   " 10/-
    on rum and beer   <u>" 5/-</u>
        f 29/-

[empty space]

    [the account below, cr=satisfied]

1724 sept 1 hendreck hekan[195]
    on 2½ gall beer   f 2/-
    ~~on remainder on 1 kettle 1 goat skin~~
november on 4 lb gunpowder on 4 lb lead   " 28/-
    on 3 half gall beer   " 3/-
may 11 on rum f3:= on 4 lb gunpowder and lead   <u>" 33/-</u>[196]
        f 66/-

1725 on ½ ell of strouds   f 9/-
    on 1 p^t rum his ~~son remainder on 1 piece~~
                ~~of strouds~~   " 1/10
    ~~his son on 1 lb gunpowder and 1 bar~~
                ~~of lead~~   " 8/=
    her[197] on 4 bottles of rum   " 12/-
    on remainder on his kettle 1 goat skin[198]

on 1 bar of lead and flintstones　　　　　" 2/10

~~his son on 1 ell of strouds f18~~

　　　　~~on 1 fine shirt f 20~~　　　　　　~~" 38/-~~

~~ditto son on 2½ lb gunpowder~~　　　　~~" 13/-~~

he on 4 lb gunpowder　　　　　　　" 24/-

on 3 quarts rum　　　　　　　　　" 9/-

on 1 bar of lead　　　　　　　　　" 3/-

on 1 bottle of rum and 1 bread　　　" 5/

on lead 4 on remainder on cotton f3　" 7/-

on his wife on 1 knife　　　　　　　" 3/-

his younger son　　　　　　　　　" 2/10

on 1 coarse blanket　　　　　　　<u>" 26/-</u>

　　　　　　　　　　　　　　f150 10

on 1 quart rum f3:-　　　　　　　" 3/

febwary [sic] 20 on 1 pint rum f1:10 on 2 pᵗ rum　　" 6/-

on 5 lb gunpowder f30 on 3 bars of

　　　　　　　　　　lead f6　　" 36/-

on 8 kan rum in his small cask　　　" 24/

on 2 kan rum f6　　　　　　　　　" 6/-

[　] lb gunpowder　　　　　　　　<u>" 3/</u>

　　　　　　　　　　　　　　228/10

[56] --Credit-side--

(373)

<u>1723</u>[199]

december 20 for 1 deerskin by pitt:v:C[200]　　f 26/-

1726 may 25 for 14 lb skins from a: stenberge[201]　　<u>" 98/-</u>

　　　　　　　　　　　　　　f124/-

　　　　　　　　　　　　　　　　70

　　　　　　　　　　　　　　　　<u>20</u>

　　　　　　　　　　　　　　　　90

[empty space]

28
14
42
11
53

Cred[it][202]

1725 for 42 lb Elk skins	f 53/-	
february 18 for 3 martens	" 21/-	42
for 1 otter	" 6/	21
	f 80/-	11

his wife anew on Linen for		
a shirt	f 12/-	
		169/10
		53
		116

[the account below, cr=satisfied]

his wife is indebted from older times	f 38/	
1726 july 13 on 2 kan rum still owes me	" 6/-	228
on 1 bar of lead by his wife	" 3/-	10
he on 1 bottle of rum	" 2/10	218
on 2 *musis* rum f1	" 1/	74
on 2 lb gunpowder	" 12/	144
from the other side[203]	" 148/-	
	f171/10	228
on ½ ell of strouds	" 9/	80
	f180[204]	148
on 1 bottle of rum	3/	

[57]
(374) --Debit-side--

[all accounts on this page, cr=satisfied]

1724 Sep[t] 1 abraham[205]['s] Youngest daughter

    on 4 kan rum   f 16/-

1726 may 30 on 8 kan rum   " 20/-

    on 1/8 ell of strouds   " 2/-

                                             f 38/-

    on 1 duffels blanket by her father   " 24/-

                                                62/-

    on remainder on a dufels blanket   " 17/

                                               f 79/-

                                                 39

                                                 40

1724 sep[t] 1 pensogh's wife[206]

    X on 12 kan rum and 1 small cask   f 30/-

Pooni[,] ~~marija~~ Catrin['s] husband[207]

ponij

1724 septemb[er] on 7 kan rum   f 17/10

    on 5 kan rum his wife   " ~~14/~~

    on 1 bar of lead f2 on flintstones   " 3/-

    on ½ lb gunpowder f3   " 3/-

                                              f 24/10

January 10 on 1½ ell of white baize   " 9/

    on 1 lb gunpowder f6 on flintstones f1:10   " 7/10

    on 1 coarse blanket   " 26/-

    on 1 p[t] rum on 8 kan rum   " 17:10

                                              f 85/10[208]

1724 sept 29 andris the savage[209]

    on 1 lb gunpowder on 3 lb lead   f 9/-

    on 3 ells of white baize on 1 knife   " 23/-

    on ½ ell of strouds f10 on 2 ells

                            of baize f15   " 25/-

    on 1 coarse blanket   " 36/

    on 1 lb gunpowder on 2 lb lead   " 8/

	f101/
his wife's brother[210] on gunpowder and lead	f" 6/10
ditto on ½ ell of strouds	" 9/-
on 1 white shirt by his wife	" 12/
on 1 lb gunpowder by his wife and	
1 *mutsie* rum	" 6/10
1725 sept 20 then balanced accounts with andris	
and he remains indebted	f 22/-
on 1 knife and 1 bar of lead	" 4/10
on remainder on Cotton 3 ells of cotton	" 18/-
~~his wife on 1 coarse blanket~~	~~" 34/-~~
	~~f 78/10~~
anew on pipes	f 44/10
	" 1/10
	f 46/00

[58]
(375) --Credit-side--

[the account below, cr]

Cred[it] for 1 small bear hide	f 8/-	
for 1 fox skin	" 5/-	
for 1 skin	" 7/-	
	f 20/-	
X ~~for 1 piece of silver~~	~~12/-~~	
	f 32/	
for 1 piece of copper	" 6/	38
	26/-	22
1729 july 8 for remainder on skins	" 13/	16
	39/-	79
		26
		53:-
paid by Kattener[211]	f 30/-	

[the account below, up to the 1724 entry, cr]

1724 january 10 for dressed skins	f 20/-
march 8 for 1 bear hide	f 10/-
for 1 beaver f12: for 1 raccoon	" 15/-
	f 45/-
1725 march 8 then balanced accounts with him and	
he remains indebted	f 39/
on 1 lb gunpowder f3:- on 1 lb gunpowder f6	
on 3 lb lead	" 12/
at balancing the account remains	f 50/-
anew on 1 kan rum f3:-	" 3/
on ½ lb gunpowder and 2½ lb lead f5:10	
for repairing 1 lock[212]	" 13/10
july 13 balanced accounts with him	
and his days on the farm	" 36/10
on 1 colored shirt	" 24/
	60/10[213]
1724 november 14 for 1 otter and 1 fox	f 10/-
for 1 pig	" 92/-
	f102/-

[the account below, cr=satisfied]

1726 may 22 for skins by her brother	f 34/-
1726 august 4 from the other side[214]	f 46/-
on 3½ ells of cotton	" 24/-
on 1 kettle from Catharina	" 16/-
	" 86/
on 1 knife and flintstones f3:10	" 3/10
	f 89/10
on 2 ells of cotton on 3 lb lead	" 17/-
on pipes	" 1/-
	f108/-

[59]
(376) --Debit-side--

1724 november 14 runup[215][,] the husband of queck[216]['s] daughter

on 20 kan rum	f 45/-
his wife on 1½ ell of cotton	" 9/-
~~on 1 box of [paint] f3 on strouds~~	~~" 27/-~~
his wife on remainder on strouds	" 8/-
his wife on 12 kan rum	" 36/-
on remainder on one coarse blanket	
for hops[217]	" 20/-
	f118/-

[the account below, cr=satisfied]

1717 wieijiekas[218][,] former husband of kisay[219]['s] daughter

on remainder on a gun and gunpowder and lead	
also 14 martens	f[empty]
again balanced everything	f 8/-
on 1 pint rum	" 2/-
on 1½ ell of baize f9 on 3 pint rum	" 13/10
1724	
january 30 on 1 shirt f12:-	" 12/
	f 35/10

1727 moskono[,] or wiyiekas['s] daughter margriet

on 1 shirt colored on remainder on	
stockings	" 28/10
on 10 kan and p^t rum	" 31/10
	f 60/00:-
1728 november 10 on 4 kan rum	" 12/-
	72

[the account below, cr=satisfied]

1724 november 5 wieijiekas's daughter

on remainder on rum	f 4/-

novemb[er] 7 on 7 qt rum and 1 small pint rum	" 19/-
may 10 on 7 kan rum	" 15/-
on 1½ ell of blue eysersterck	" 10/-
1726 december 2 on remainder on stockings	" 4/10
on 1 colored shirt	" 24/

[60]
(377) --Credit-side--

1725 august 13
    for 1½ lb dressed skins   f 12/-

[empty space]

  [the account below, cr]

1724 october 1 for 1 small deer	f 0/-[220]
for 1 wolf head	f 18/-

1728 by teunus meddagh[221] — Cr[edit]   f 33/-

[empty space]

  [the account below, cr]

1724 november 7 for 1 marten	f 6/-
for [a] note[222] from klas roosa[223]	f 12/-
for [empty]	

[61]
(378) --Debit-side--

1724 october 24 ~~andris the s~~

1724 november 1 gasrit the savage[224]

       ~~tam nat~~[225] weghtagkarin

    On 1 coarse blanket   f 30/-

november 6 on 1 coarse blanket f33 on 1½ ell of

                                  cotton f9   " 42/

    on strouds 7 on 1 colored shirt f24-   " 31/

                                         f103/

[from here on, all accounts on the page, cr=satisfied]

1725 october 26 then balanced accounts with him   f 35/-

    on 1 lb gunpowder f6 on lead and

                              flintstones   " 9/

    on 1 knife   " 2/10

    his wife on 1 knife f3 on 1½ ell of cotton   " 12/-

    on 1 piece of strouds   f 7/10

    paid his debt apart from his wife's

                              account   f 66/-

1726 april 11 anew remainder on a stroud blanket f 26/-

    on 1 lb gunpowder and 1 bar of lead and

                            flintstones   " 9/-

                                         f 35/

    for 5 days working on the farm   " 35/

1724   mocka[']s ~~gasris~~ brother

        ~~tam nat~~

november 1 on 2 kan beer and 1 pint rum   f 3/10

    on remainder on goods — 4 martens   " 24/-

    on 1 gun for 20 martens hendreck hekan[226]

    is his guarantor for the gun   ~~f120/-~~

novemb[er] 7 on ½ lb gunpowder and 4 lb lead   " 7/

    on 1½ ell of white baize f10   " 10/

    on ¼ ell of baize f2 on 3 kan cider   " 5/-

                                     ~~f189/10~~[227]

1724 on 1 coarse blanket f 26 on 2 lb

                        gunpowder f12   " 38/-

    on lead and 1 knife   " 4/

1725 december 27 then balanced accounts with him

	and he remains	52/-
	besides the fact that the gun is *slanner*[228]	
	on beer f2:- on 1 p^t rum f1:10 on 1	
	kan beer	" 4/10
	on 8 kan rum	" 24/-
	on 1 lb gunpowder f6- on 1 bar of lead	" 9/-
1726 october 12 on 1½ lb lead f[229]		89/10

1724 november 10 the sawonossie[230]

	on remainder on goods — 4 martens	f 24	
	on 1 pint rum	" 1/10	
1725 april 27 on 1 lb gunpowder and 5 lb lead		f 11/-	
	on 2 lb gunpowder strouds flintstones	f 19/10	
		f 30/10	
	anew on ½ gall rum	" 6/-	
1725 november 4 remainder on cotton		f 10/-	56
	on 1 coarse blanket	" 26/-	42
	on 2 lb gunpowder and 2 bars of lead	" 16/=	14
	for borrowing 1 skin weighs 1¼ lb[231]	f 52/-	
	for *omlegen*[232] of his axe	" 4/-	
1726 april 10 his wife's son on strouds and lead		" 18/	
	anew remainder on strouds	f 20/	
	on 1½ lb gunpowder and 2 bars of lead	" 3/	
	on ½ ell of cotton and 1 lb sugar and		
	flintstones	" 5/-	
		f 38/	
	on 1 juice on ½ sch wheat	f 11	

[62]

(379) --Credit-side--

1724 november 6 for 6 martens	" 36/-
	for 1 elk skin	" 19/-
	for 1 small mink	" 1/10[233]

	f 56/10	
by Klas Roosa	" 8/-	
by Jacob the savage[234]	" 14/-	
	f 78/10	

[from here on, all accounts, cr]

1726 april 10 for 1 elk skin	f 12/	
for 7 martens	" 49/	
for 2 bear hides	" 20/	
he has 27 guilders coming to him paid settled		

1725 for remainder on martens	f 46/-	
his wife blandin[235] from older times	f 26/	
1725 november on 1 copper pot with legs	" 36/-	
his wife on 3½ kan rum	" 10/10	
	72/10	187
she Cred[it] for 30 lb raw skins	f 60/	46
for 1 raccoon	" 3/	141
balanced accounts with her and she remains indeb[ted]	7/-	90
for 4 skins f30 for 1 skin and 1 beaver f27	f 57/	57
		f 33

1725 april 24 for 1 wolf pelt and head	f 25/10	
for 1 skin 25	f 25/-	28
february 18 for 6 martens by hend hekan[236]	" [ ][237]	13
1726 april 16 towis[238] who was escorted here by the sawanos[239]		15
on gunpowder and lead flintstones and		46
strouds	f 9/10	
on [sic] wife's daughter[,] gasris['s] wife		
on 1½ ell of cotton 1 knife	" 12/-	36
have paid him 1 lb gunpowder and 1 kan rum		3

for preparing the skins   49
1726 july 29 of   f 46/-
  anew on kettle and 1 knife f3   " ~~43/-~~
           89/-

  Cred[it] 1726 october 25 for 48 lb elk skins   ~~52/-~~
           f 37/-

[63]
(380) --Debit-side--

1724 pansogh's wife and son[240]
december 27 on 1 ell of white cotton   f 6/-
  his son remainder on stockings[241]   " ~~10/10~~
  he on 1 pint rum still   " 2/-
his father on 1 lb gunpowder and 4 lb lead   " 10/-
april 19 by his son remainder on a shirt[242]   " ~~6/-~~
1725 april 26 on 4 ells of baize white   " 24/-
  his son on 1 knife f1:10 his wife on
          1 knife   " 3/10
  his wife on 3½ ells of blue baize   " 21/-
  ~~his son on remainder on a colored shirt f3~~   ~~" 3/-~~
  ~~on ditto on 1 knife f4- his son~~
       ~~on cotton f4~~   " ~~8/-~~
  ~~to his son f3 ell of blue baize[243]~~   " ~~12/-~~
  on 2 ells of white baize   " 12/-
  ~~his son on 6 kan rum~~   " ~~15/-~~
           f 78/10
1727 he remains indebted for everything   f 36/-
  her sister at kesegton[244] on remainder on
     duffels and colored textiles   " 20/-

1724 january 1 Eijsack[,] Abraham[245][']s son
  on 1 coarse blanket by his mother   f 28/-
  on 1 lb gunpowder and lead   " 10/-
  on 2 kan rum f6:- on 4 kan rum   " 18/-

		f 22/-
his wife[,] sawegonck hendreck['s] daughter[246]		
	on 12 kan rum	f 23/-
his wife anew on 11½ kan rum		f 37/10
to barent niew kerck[247] f35:10 for		
	2 goat skins	" 35/10
on 1 bar of lead f 1:10		" 1/10
		f 69/10

1724 january 5 Jan Roos[,] domeni[']s[248] son		
on 1 knife and flintstones and 1 awl		f 3/10
on 2 ells of baize by Catrijn[,]		
	nanado['s] daughter[249]	" 12/-
anew on 1 lb gunpowder		" 6/-
1725 june 14 on 2 lb gunpowder and ½ ell		
	of strouds	" 21/-
on 1 dufels blanket		" 28/-
		f 55/-[250]
on 1 lb gunpowder and 1 bar of lead		" 9/-
on 1½ lb gunpowder		" 9/-
		73/-
1727 a piece of strouds f7:-		" 7/-
		80/

[64]
(381) --Credit-side--

1725 april 12 for 1 beaver by his son	~~f 10/-~~
for 1 bear hide f 13 for 1 marten	" 18/-
for 1 leg and 1 piece of rump meat	" 3/-
for harvesting flax	" 9/-
his *som* still has coming to him on	f 30/-
his bill f 21:-[,] paid with 1 colored shirt	
1727 for harvesting 1 sch flax[251]	f 12/-

f 42/

		78
		42
		36

for 1 bear hide and grease for the coarse
blanket   f 28/-

his wife Cred[it] for skins ———————————— f 21/10

for 1 bear hide	f 12/-	
for 1 wolf pelt	" 3/10	
for remainder on his skins	f 11/-	
1726 july 4 for 1 skin	" 10/-	73
	f 21/	21
		f52:

[65]
(382) --Debit-side--

[all accounts on the page, cr=satisfied]
Keman the savage[,] or watschap[252]

on 1 stroud blanket	f 45/
on blue textiles 17 on beer f3:-	" 20/-
on 2 ells of flinnen f10 and lead and	
1 knife f5	" 15/
on 2½ ells of baize f20 on 1 colored[253] f12	
on wine f2	" 34/-
at settling the account I have coming	
to me	f 60/-
1724 june 7 on ½ ell of strouds	" 9/-

1724 his wife[,] kisay['s] daughter[254]
december [ ][255] on remainder on rum   f [8/, cr]

on 1 coarse blanket	" 26/-
on 1 bread	" [2/-, cr]
the son[256] of her brother wappenack[257]	
on 1 colored shirt　　　paid	f[24/-, cr]
her brother remainder on strouds	" 2/
remainder on 1 shirt for which he has	
paid 1 marten	" [6/-, cr]
~~ditto on 2 lb gunpowder and 3 lb lead~~	
~~and 1 kan molasses~~	" ~~17/-~~
june 30 his remainder on a colored shirt for	
his wife	"[10/-, cr]
1725	
july 18 his gun is a security for 12 kan rum	
and 1 small cask	" 24/-
~~his wife remains indebted on rum 8 kan~~	" ~~16/-~~
on 1 bottle of rum f3:-	" 3/
his wife on 1 shirt f24	

Kobes[258][,] sawagonck hendreck['s][259] son who has kisa[']s daughter[260]	
1725 june 7 on remainder on white baize	f 4/10
his wife on remainder on a colored shirt	" [8/-, cr]
remainder on a white shirt by her brother	" 6/-
~~his wife on 10 kan rum~~	"[20/-, cr]
he on 1 qt rum f3:-	" 3/
~~his wife on 6 kan rum~~	"[12/-, cr]
his brother	
on 1 lb gunpowder	f 4/-
he anew on 1 coat	f 60/-
his wife on 1 stroud blanket	"[44/-, cr]
he on 1 coarse blanket	" 34,-
	94/
paid thereon 4 lb beavers	" 40/
remains indebted at balancing the account	54/-
on 1 knife f3 on [empty]	" 3/-

on rum by westbrock[261]	" 3/-
on 1 pᵗ rum f1:10	" 1/10
on 1 kan beer and 1 bread	" 3/-
on ½ gall cider	" 1/-
balanced accounts	" 65/10
anew 2 kan cider	" 2/
on 1 qt rum	" 2/

[66]
(383) --Credit-side--

[all accounts on this page, cr]

Cred[it] for 1 kno	f 60/-
for 1 deerskin	f [9/-, cr]
~~for remainder on a bear hide f 9~~	
~~wappenak[262]['s] son for 1 skin~~	~~f 9/-~~
paid his wife's account with skins	
for remainder[263] on 1 skin[264]	f [2/-, cr]
1725	

1725	~~she remains indebted the sum of~~	~~f 24/-~~
	she remains indebted on 1 stroud blanket	f 12/-
	on 1 quart rum	" 3/-
	on 1 kan rum	" 3/-
	on 4 kan rum	" 12/-
		f 30/-
	on 1 kan cider	" 1/-

[67]
(384) --Debit-side--

[all accounts on this page, cr=satisfied]

1725 march 14 manonck[265] and his wife and son
    then balanced accounts with her and she
    remains indebted   f 300/10
    ~~to hendreck hekan's boy[,] kryn~~[266]
    ~~on gunpowder and lead~~   " 7/-
    ~~his son's wife remains indeb~~ted on 1 shirt   "[18/-, cr]
april 19 on 6 gall rum   " 60/-
    on 2 p[t] rum f 3:- another pint rum   " 4/10
    ~~on 1 stroud blanket~~   "[45/-, cr]
    on 2 colored shirts   " 48/-
    on 5 kan rum   " 12/10
    on 1 dufels blanket by the sawanosse[267]   " 25/-
may 15 on ½ ell of strouds for Cattener[268]   " 9/-
    on ½ gall rum   " 5/-
    for repairing his lock   " 12/-
    his son Jacob[269] on 1 colored shirt   " 24/-
    ditto on 1½ ell of cotton   " 9/-
    he on 6 kan rum f15:- his wife on
                      1 colored shirt   " 39/-
    on 2 kan rum f6:-   " 6/-
    his wife on 2 ells of cotton for
                 kwakesas[270]['s] son   f 12/-
    on 4 kan rum   " 19/-
    his son Jacob on 1 kan rum   <u>" 3/-</u>
                             f586/10[271]

1725 july 20 then balanced accounts with manonck
    and he remains indebted   f100/-
    his son jacob f[empty] on 1 colored shirt
               and 1½ ell of cotton   " 33/-
    on 1 kan rum — his son   " 3/-
    anew on 1 quart rum f2:- paid a guilder
                  thereon   " 1/10
    his wife on 2 lb tobacco   " 3/-
    on 1 sheath knife f4:-   " 4/-

august 21 on 4 kan rum f12 on his wife

on 1 p^t rum   " 13/10

on his son mattiso[272] on ½ gall rum   <u>" 6/-</u>

1725 august 26 I have coming to me

up to this date   f 72/-

     X anew on 1 lb gunpowder and ½ gall cider   " 7/-

     X on 6½ kan rum — him and his wife   " 19/10

sep^t X on 1 stroud blanket   " 48/-

     X on 1 dufels   blanket   " 28/-

     X on remainder on a kettle   " 50/-

     X on 1 fine shirt   " 18/-

     X on 5½ gall rum   <u>" 55/-</u>

f294/10

     X on 1 coarse blanket f8 his wife on 1

coarse blanket f   " 68/-

     X he on 1 coarse blanket   " 30/

     X on ½ lb gunpowder — and drink   <u>" 6</u>

f 398/10

     X on 7 kan rum at abram[']s burial[273]   " 21/-

1726 may 25 his wife on 10 kan rum   " 30-

July X 25 on ½ gall rum on 1 p^t rum   " 7/10

     X his wife on 1 gall rum   <u>" 12/-</u>

f469/-

october 20 on 8 kan rum by mannonck   " 20/-

his wife remainder on a ketel f4:-

she on 1 p^t rum f1:10   " 5/10

[68]

(385) --Credit-side--

[the account below, cr]

     1725 april 19 for 1 skin   f 20/-

     ~~for 8½ lb beaver @ 10 each lb~~   " 85/-

     for 1 beaver weighs 2 lb   <u>" 20/-</u>

July 20 for 7 pigs   "360/-

		to
his son has paid for the cotton by going	f 9/-	Kingston
by his son Jacob by Cornelis in addition	" 22/-	
for 1 kno f [empty]		

[the account below, cr]	
1726 april 25 for skins for the kettle	50/-
he for skins	" 10/-
october 20 for 6 lb skins by manonck	f 42/-

Catryn[274] on 1 quart rum f3:-

[69]
(386) --Debit-side--

[the account below, cr=satisfied]
1725 march 14 kattias[,] manonck['s] son[275]

on 2 ells of cotton by his mother	f 12/-
may 15 on remainder on a fine shirt	" 14/-
ditto on 8 kan rum by his wife	" 16/-

[account above, cr=satisfied]

[the account below, cr=satisfied]

then balanced accounts with him and he remains indebted	
apart from his wife's debt	f 24/-
~~his wife remainder on~~ on [sic] 1 pair of dutch shoes	" 16/-
X on 1 pair of stockings for 1 skin[,] paid	
X on remainder on 1 skin for 1 coarse blanket fetched by his wife	"[16/-, cr]
he on 1 gall rum	" 12/-
	f 68/-

on remainder on strouds	" 28/-
1726 july 21 on ½ pint rum	" 1/-
on 1 pᵗ rum at the burial	" 1/10
	f 98/10
on remainder on cotton by mattiso[276]	" 4/-
on 2 lb lead	" 2/10
	f105/-
1727 march 5 on ½ gunpowder and 2 lb lead	" 5/-
	f110/-
july 20 at balancing the account I have coming to me	f 34/-
[account up to here, cr=satisfied]	
july 27 on remainder on gunpowder	" 12/-
on 1½ ell of cotton	" 9/-
on 3/4 ell of strouds by his wife	" 16/-
on 10 kan rum and 1 pᵗ	" 31/10

---

abraham or kwakasagh[277]	
1725 on gunpowder and lead	f 7/-
april 28 on 4 kan rum	" 10/-
on 1 shirt f12:-	" 12/-
he must still work 13 days[,] then he will have paid[278]	
on rum f 2: on ~~16 kan rum f40~~	" 36/-[279]
on 1 coarse blanket and remainder on 1 dufels blanket	" 56/-
on 1 otter for 1 marten f6:-	" 7
on 1 bar of lead	f 2/-
on 1 knife and rum	" 3/-
	68/

[70]

(387) --Credit-side--

[the account below, cr=satisfied]

his wife[,] tatapagh['s] daughter[,] pitternel[280]

on remainder on a colored shirt	f 18/-	
on 8 kan rum	" 18/-	
on remainder on 1 coarse blanket	" 16/-	
	f 52/-	
Cred[it] for 1 day of harvesting flax	" 12	
she remains inbebted	40 guild[ers]	" 40/-	
from her mother	f80	" 80/-	24
			16
			12
			28
			1
			5
			86

[the account below, cr]

1727 march 5 for 2 bear hides	f 20/-	
for 8 lb dressed skins	" 56/-	
	76/-	
for 4½ [days] mowing	" 36/-	110
		76
		f34

for remainder on his skins for the rum[281]	f 7/-	
by his daughter[,] Jan Ros['s] wife[282]	" 24/-	

[71]
(388) --Debit-side--

[all accounts on this page, cr=satisfied]

Winhas[,] sawagonck hendr[ick's][283] son

1725 may 12 ½ ell of strouds	f 9/-	
on 1 lb gunpowder f6:- on 1 knife	" 9/-	

comes to me	" 4
	f 22/
1726 march 7 on ½ ell of strouds	" 9/-
	31/
on 1 dufels blanket	" 24/-
on 1 lb gunpowder and lead	" 8/-
wenagsen[,] sawangonck hend[rick's] son	
paid	63/-
1727 march 2 anew on goods	f 40/-
on ½ gall rum	" 6/-
on 1 skin borrowed f6:-	" 6/-
april 20 on 3 gallon rum f36 on 5 pint	
ditto f7:10[284]	" 43/10
on 1 gun of mother £6:10	" 280/-[285]
	f375/10
on 1 white shirt f12:- on 1 lb gunpowder	
and lead	24/-

1725 june 18 Jacob the savage[,] gerti's husband[286] at paponeck[287]	
on 1 lb gunpowder f6 on ½ ell of strouds	f[15/-, cr]
anew on gunpowder f4.- on 2 guilder cider	" [6/-, cr]
his wife on remainder on strouds on 4 kan	
cider	" [5/-, cr]
she on 4 kan cider f4 on rum f2	" 6/-
he on 1 ell of strouds and 1 kan cider	" 18/-
his wife on 2 kan cider	" 2/-
on 1 bread	" 2/-
he is indebted in all	f 28/-
his wife gertie in all	" 15/-

---

gertie remains indebted - paid 4 guilders	f [4/-, cr]
he remains indebted on gunpowder and lead	" 7/-
on 1 lb sugar — he	" 1/10
1726 his [wife] on 14 kan rum	"[42/-, cr]

	her husband on 4 kan rum by sar[,]	
	kisay['s] daughter[288]	" 12/-

1725	kisay the savage woman[289]	f 18/10[290]
	on remainder on 7 kan rum for which she	
	gave a skin	" 6/-
	~~her husband arent fynhout[291] on 1 knife~~	
	~~by her daughter~~	~~" [4/]~~
	for 3 martens in the year 1715[292] for which	
14	he had rum	" 12/-
14	~~her small daughter remainder on 2 ells~~	
	~~of dufels~~	~~" 3/~~
28	~~her youngest son on 1 dufels blanket~~	~~" 24/-~~
<u>7</u>	~~on remainder on 1 stroud blanket~~	~~" 16/-~~
35	~~anew remainder on a coarse blanket~~	~~" 29/-~~
<u>26</u>	anew on 3 kan rum by her husband	" 9/
<u>10</u>	on 2 kan rum by her daughter the youngest	<u>" 6/-</u>
20	on 1 bread f2: she is indebted in all	f 22/-
	her youngest daughter on strouds	" 14
	her husband on 2 pint rum f3:- on [ ]	" 5/-
	he [remains] indebted from older times[,]	
	her husband	" 12/-
	her youngest daughter on 6 kan rum	" 15/-
	Ditto on 7 ells of *gemt* or ribbon	"[14/-, cr]

[72]
(389) --Credit-side--

[the account below, cr]

1726	march 2 for 1 bear hide	f 12/-
	for 1 elk skin by blandine[293]	<u>" 18/-</u>
	375	f 30/-
	<u>134</u>	
	241:-	
1727	march 1 for 10 martens — paid	<u>f 70/-</u>

april 18 for 3 bear hides   f 36/-
for 14 martens   " 98/-
                                                   f134/-

[the entry below, cr]
for 1 skin[294] f13:[295] [and] remember on good lock for him
                                                              247

[the account below, cr]
her husband[296] 3 martens and 1 raccoon   f 25/-
she for 1 marten   " 7/-
~~1726 july 30 she remains indebted~~   ~~f 10/-~~

~~for remainder on 1 skin~~   f 4/-

her youngest daughter for 1 bear hide   f 9/-
1726 for 3 martens her daughter f[empty]   " 21/-
                                                   f 30/-
_____   14
[the account below, cr]   15
            kisay   14
her daughter[,] winasenck['s] wife   43
remains indebted f13 anew on 1 shirt f12   " 25/-   30
kisay from older times f20 anew on 2 ells
                                 of cotton   " 32/-   13
for 1 bear hide   " 12/-   15
balancing the account comes   paid   f 20/-[297] 14
                                                             34
                                                             21
                                                             15

[73]
(390) --Debit-side--

[all accounts on this page, cr=satisfied]

1725 august 2 debora[298][,] maggel[']s wife or wido[w]

on remainder on a shirt	f 6/-
on remainder on white baize	" 6/-
on remainder on a stroud blanket	" 20/-
on 12 kan rum	" 30
	62/

---

mattiso[,] mannock[']s son[299]

1725 august 28 on remainder on a colored shirt	f 5/-
on 1½ gunpowder and 3½ lb lead	" 13/-
Sep[t] 28 ~~on remainder on 1 stroud blanket~~	
~~by y[our] H[onor's] mother~~	~~" 28/-~~
on his lock	" 2/-
	48/
on 1 *dobelstin* shirt	" 24/-
on 4 kan rum at abram[']s burial[300]	" 12/-
1726 july at balancing the account I have	
coming to me	f 24/-
ditto 18 on 1 lb gunpowder and 1 bar of lead	" 8/-
on 1 p[t] rum by y[our] H[onor's] brother	
at the burial of kattener[301]	" 1/10
on 2 p[t] rum f3:- on 1 p[t] rum	" 4/10
	37/0
on 1 lb gunpowder and 3 lb lead by	
his father	" 9/-
	f 46/-
on gunpowder 2 lb f12 on 4 lb lead f4	" 16/-
on 5 kan rum	" 15/-
decemb: 3 on 1½ ell of strouds for his father	" 27/-

1725 Sep[t] 6 arrons[302] with the lame arms	f104/-[303]
on 1 p[t] rum f1:10 on ½ gall rum f6	f 7/10
on ½ gall rum ditto also ½ gall	" 12/-

on 1 lb gunpowder and 1 bar of lead f2	" 8/10
	f 27/10
on remainder on stroud stockings	" 7/-
on 1 qᵗ rum f3:-³⁰⁴	
1726 july 22 anew on remainder on a kettle	f 10/-
on 1 bucket or that he and hend have lost	" 3/-
on 1 pt rum	" 1/10
on lead f1:10 on 2 ells of cotton	" 13/10
	f 25/⁰⁰
on remainder on 1 coarse blanket	" 3/-
on 1 lb gunpowder and 2 lb lead	" 8/-
1727 may 14 on account remains	f 36/-
	f 1/-

[74]
(391) --Credit-side--

[empty space]

1725/6³⁰⁵

january 30 for 2 dressed skins 2 lb	f 14/-
1726 july 15 for 3 days on the farm	f 18/-
for 1 deer by his mother	" 12/-

[from here on, all accounts, cr]

1726 january 4 on [empty]³⁰⁶

1726/7 march 3 for 2 skins weighs [sic] 6½ lb	f 45/10
1726/7 march 4 then balanced accounts with him	
and he remains indebt[ed]	" 59/
on remainder on a shirt	" 1/-
on strouds — and lead	" 8/-

C[redit] for 3½ lb skins	f 24/10 35
1727 may 14 for 28 lb elk skins	f 35/-

[75]
(392) --Debit-side--

[the account below, cr=satisfied]
1725 Sept wiijekaswedie[,] kessa[307]['s] daughter

on 6 kan rum f12:- on 1 bottle f3-	f 15/-
on 1 pint rum	" 1/10
on 3 p^t rum by her brother	" 4/10
	f 21/-
~~1726 may 20 on 2 kan rum~~	~~f 5/-~~
on 1 bottle anew	" 1/10
on 5 kan rum	" 12/10
on 2 ells of ribbon	" 6/-
	f 20/-
1726 july 26 on 3 p^t rum	" 4/10
on 2 pt rum f3:-	" 3/-
on 1 pair of stroud stockings	" 14/-
on 1 kan rum	" 3/-
	f 44/10
on 2 kan rum	" 6/-
on pipes	" 1/-
on 1 kan rum f3:- on remainder on a	
shirt f3	" 6/-
1727 on 1 ¼ gall rum	" 15/-
	f 72/10

[the account below, cr=satisfied]
Tatteu[,][308] andris['s] wife's brother

1724 on ½ ell of strouds by his sister	f 9/-
on gunpowder and lead	" 6/-
1726 may 22 on remainder on rum	f 14/-
on 1 bottle of rum	" 3/-

on Beer f6:- on ½ lb gunpowder and

	1 knife f3	" 12/-
		31
on ½ lb gunpowder		" 3/-
		f 34/-
on strouds		" 12/-
on 1 pᵗ rum f1:10		" 1/10
on 1½ ell of cotton		" 9/-
		f 56/10
1727 on 1 coarse blanket		" 33/-
		f 89/10
on 3 ells of white baize		" 18/-
on ½ lb gunpowder and lead and 1 bottle		
	of rum	" 7/-

---

abraham's old[309] wife	114/10[310]
on 1 dufels blanket	f 28/-

[76]
(393) --Credit-side--

[the account below, cr]

1725 november for skins	f 7/-
for 2 martens	" 14/-

[the account below, up to the March 9 entry, cr]

1727[311] for 1 deerskin with hair 4 lb	f 8/-
for 1 marten	" 7/-
for 5 lb dressed skins	" 35/-
	f 50/-

march 9[312] tateu[313] has had 5½ kan on the promise	f 16/10	80
1727/8 to show a mine in the Spring[314]		52
on 1 stroud blanket at the mine	" 45/-	f28
to nackarend[315] 2½ ells of baize at the mine	" 15/-	9

ANNOTATED TRANSLATION, DUTCH-ENGLISH | 155

for martens	f̶ ̶1̶5̶/̶-̶	6
		18
for bear meat	" 8/-	33
for 1 bear hide and 2 raccoons 2 skins	" 33/-	89
	f 41/-	41
		48
Tatweu		114

1727 remains indebted at balancing the account		
I have coming to me	f 73/-	41
on 1 dufels blanket and 1 lb gunpowder	" 32/-	73
on ½ lb gunpowder and 1 pipe	" 3/15	
on 2 kan rum	" 6/-	
on 1 shirt from Catharina	" 6/-	
on 1 small coat for his child	" 12/-	
on 1 kan rum	" 3/-	
on 3 kan rum f9 on ½ ell of strouds f9	" 18/-	
on 1 stroud blanket at the mine	" [45/-, cr]	
on 1 quart rum and 1 bread	" 5/-	
on 1 qt rum f3 also 1 kan f[empty]	" 6/-	
on 1 shirt f12:- on 1 knife f3:-	" 15/-	
	f180/-[316]	
on 1 kan rum f3 on 1 colored shirt f24	" 27/-	
on 1½ ell of cotton f9 on ½ lb gunpowder		
and lead	" 6/-	
on 8 kan rum to drink at his sister's grave	"24/-	
on 4½ kan rum	" 13/10	
on 8 kan rum f24 on 1 colored shirt f24	" 48	
on 2 kan rum f[empty]	" 6/-	
on 3 ells of gemt [and] on flintstones	" 4/-	
	f308/10	
his wife's account	" 62/-	
on 1 shirt and 1 ell of strouds	" 30/-	
on 3/4 ell of strouds for his wife's		
stockings	" 14/-	
on goods received at the mine from above[317]	" 76/10	

f491/~~10~~

[77]
(394) --Debit-side--

[the account below, cr=satisfied]
1724 pony[318] at balancing the account

remains indebted	f 60/-
octob[er] 10 on 4 kan rum fetched for sundagh[319]	" 12/-

1729	porrick[, a] kasegton savage[320]	
	at balancing the account	f 78/-
	on 1 silver gorget[321] and ribbon	"160/-
	on 1 coarse blanket f28 on 1½ ell of dobelstin	" 37/-
	on 1 coarse blanket f28 on 3/4 ell of strouds f12	" 40
	on 1 dufels blanket f22:-	" 24/-[322]
	on 1½ lb lead[323]	f339/-
	on 1 axe - - lesys[324] comes to £ 8:10:	
	on on [sic] 5 lb gunpowder £ 9:10	" 12/-
	"00:15	
	6	
	£10:1:-	

his[325] sister on 1 stroud blanket 1 kan rum	f 32/10
on 1 dobelstin shirt	" 14/-

[the account below, cr=satisfied]
hendreck hekan['s] oldest son[326]

1725 on remainder on a piece of strouds	f 1/-
on 1 lb gunpowder and lead	" 8/-
on 1 ell of strouds f18 on 1 fine shirt f20	" 38/-
on 2½ lb gunpowder	" 15/-

on 2 lb gunpowder f12 on lead and

      flintstones   " 16/-

on 1 knife f3:-   <u>" 3/-</u>

         f 81/-

febewary [*sic*] 20 on 1 ell of strouds   " 20/-

on remainder for 1 doller[327] for 1 fisher   " 2/-

on 2 bars of lead   <u>" 5/-</u>

         f108/-

1726 on 1 bread   " 2/-

his brother on 2 lb gunpowder and 2 bars

       of lead   " 16/-

his brother on 1 shirt f12 on 1½ ell of

        cotton   " 27/-

on remainder on rum and flintstones   <u>" 24/-</u>

1726 may 26 then balanced accounts with him

       remains   f 58/-

on 5 kan rum   <u>" 15/-</u>

         f 73/-

on 1 lb gunpowder f6 on lead f3 on

       strouds f6   <u>" 15/-</u>

         f 88/-

october 25 on 1 lb gunpowder f6:- on 3 lb lead   <u>" 9/-</u>

         f 97/-

october 26 balancing the account   f 70/-

on flintstones 6 by sawannes[328]   " 1/-

on 2 lb gunpowder and 3 lb lead   <u>" 15/-</u>

         f 86/-

on remainder on a coarse blanket   <u>" 3/-</u>

on ½ bread   f 90   f 89/-

[78]

(395) --Credit-side--

Cre[dit] for remainder on deer meat   f 8/-

[entry above, cr]

1729 his wife remains at balancing the account	f 58/	
on 10 kan rum	" 25/-	
on 1 coarse blanket f28 on 6 ells of		
gemp f12	" 40	
on strouds f12:- on strouds	" 17/	
	f140/-	
on 1 colored shirt	" 22/-	
	f162/-	

[from here on, the accounts below, cr]

1725 november 4		
for 1 skin	f 22/-	97
febewar [*sic*] 18 for 6 martens	" 42/-	27
	f 64/	70
for 1 bear hide and 1 fisher	" 22/-	
	86/-	22
1726 october 25 for 1 elk skin 22 lb	f 27/5	5
		27
		106
		84
		f22
his brother for 2 martens and remainder		
on 1 marten	f 18/-	
1726 july 18 then balanced accounts with him		
and remains	f 19/-	37
hend youngest son on 1 lb gunpowder and lead	" 9/-	18
	f 28/-	19
november 13 on 1 duffels blanket	" 24/-	17
	f 52/-	97
January 8 on remainder on cotton by y[our]		
H[onor's] brother	" 3/-	28

he has 1 skin weighs 4 lb and 1 marten f32[329]   <u>f 55/-</u>   9
1726/7
feberary [sic] 27 for 16 lb elk skin   <u>f 16/-</u>
                   Still remaining   f 39/-

Wadde[330] is indebted   f 90
Cre[dit] for 1 beaver   <u>f 12</u>
Still remaining   78

[79]
(396) --Debit-side--

[all accounts on this page, cr=satisfied]
1725 november 8
    ~~the savage from kisechton~~[331]~~[,] perraris['s] brother~~[332]
    ~~for goods~~   <u>~~f 30/-~~</u>
    perraris
1726 ~~june 1 on rum and goods in total~~   <u>~~f 40/-~~</u>
    ~~his brother~~ on 1 kan rum and lead   " 4/10
    also he on 1 knife   " 3/-
Sep^t 28 parraris on remainder on the silver cup   " 80/
    ~~and 10 guilders on meat~~ — his wife
                     on 1 kettle   " 12/-
    his wife on remainder on strouds f13 -   " 13/-
    on 1 coarse blanket by his wife   <u>" 33/-</u>
    he on 5 kan rum   " 12/10
    on 2 coarse blankets   " 66/-
    on 3 ells of baize white f18 on 6 lb
                   lead f6-   " 24/-
    on 3 lb gunpowder   <u>" 18/-</u>
    that savage woman on 2 kan rum f5:-   <u>" 5/⁰⁰</u>
                               f271/-

---

    mack[,] pansogh['s] son[333]
1725 on remainder on a colored shirt   f 3/

on 1 knife f4 on remainder on cotton f4	" 8/
on 2 ells of baize for stockings	" 12/
on six kan rum	" 15/
on remainder on a coarse blanket	<u>" 21/-</u>
	f 59/-
1726 on 1 lb gunpowder	" 6/-
july 4 on 1 shirt	<u>" 12/-</u>
1726 july 18 at balancing the account	
I have coming to me	f 29/-
on 1 qᵗ rum f3:-	" 3/-
novemb[er] 8 on 1 coarse blanket	<u>" 33/-</u>
	65/-
on 1 lb gunpowder f3 on 2 lb lead	" 5/-
on 2 ells of cotton	" 17/-
feb[r]u[ary]:26 on 1 ell of strouds	<u>" 18/-</u>
	f100/-
on 2 kan rum f6:- on ½ lb gunpowder f3	" 9/-
on 1 kan rum f[empty]	" 3/-

	<u>f112/-</u>[334]
1727 then balanced accounts with him and I have	
coming to me	f 24/
on 1 ell of strouds and 3½ ells of	
colored textile	" 20/-
on 1 lb gunpowder and 2 lb lead	" 9
on remainder on a coarse blanket	" 10
on 1 knife f[empty]	<u>" 3/</u>
	f 77/-
on 1 quart rum f3 on 1 dufels blanket f25	<u>" 28/-</u>
	<u>f105/-</u>
1727 he remains indebted 71 and on the coarse	
blanket of his father 4	f 75/-
on pipes f1:- on 2 kan rum	<u>" 7/</u>
	f 82/-

[80]
(397) --Credit-side--

1726 ~~may 29 for skins~~   ~~f 30/-~~

    ~~perraris has paid f16:~~ his brother paid   ~~f 16/-~~

[empty space]

  [the account below, cr]
1726[335] july 16 8 days on the farm   f 48/-
                                                                    65
january 4 for 1 deerskin   f 24/-   24
on 1 beaver   " 11/-   41
                                                           " 35/-   112
for 7 days on the farm   " 42/-   77
balancing the account   f 77/-   35
                                                                    77
───   30
for 10 raccoons   f 30/-   47
                                                                     4
                                                                    43
                                                                   105
                                                                    30
                                                                    75
[the account below, cr=satisfied]
1728 october 20 from the other side[336]   f 82/-
  on 1 lb gunpowder by sar the savage woman[337]   " 7/-   84
  on 1 guilder on beer f1:-   " 2/-[338] 12
                                                           f 91/-   72

1729 for 1 bear hide f12
  at balancing the account I have coming to me   f 72/

[81]

(398) --Debit-side--

1725 abraham[,] son of abraham
　　on remainder on a 1 [sic] coarse blankets　　f 16/-

[half a page of empty space]

　　[the account below, cr=satisfied]

---

wappaneck[339][,] kisay's son[340]
1725 on remainder f2 on gunpowder and lead
　　　　　　　　　　　　　　and molasses　　" 19/
november 29 on 1 coarse blanket　　　　　　" 33/
　　on cider f3 on rum f2　　　　　　　　　" 5/-
　　on 1 lb gunpowder f6 on lead f2　　　　" 8/-
　　remainder on a shirt from older times　　" 6/-
　　anew on remainder on gunpowder　　　f 4/-
　　on lead and flintstones　　　　　　　　" 5/-
　　on ½ sch flour f3 on ½ ell of strouds f 9　" 12/-
　　on 1 marten for 1 stack of cards　　　　" 7/-
　　on 1 sheath knife[341]　　　　　　　　　" 4/-
　　　　　　　　　　　　　　　　　　f[34/-, cr]
　　on goods and rum in total　　　　　　　f 14/-
　　on 1 sch Indian corn by y[our] H[onor's]
　　　　　　　　　　　　　　　mother　　" 5/-
　　on 1 kan rum by arent[342]　　　　　　　" 3/-
febru[ary] 4 on 2 ells of baize white　　　　" 14/-
　　on 1 bottle　　　　　　　　　　　　　" 3/-
　　　　　　　　　　　　　　　　　　　39
　　on 2 bottles of rum　　　　　　　　　　" 6/-
　　on 3 pint rum　　　　　　　　　　　　" 4/10
　　on 3 pt rum by his father　　　　　　　" 4/10
　　on 1 shirt　　　　　　　　　　　　　　" 22/-
1725/6 march 10 then balanced accounts with him

and he remains indebt[ed]	"[ ]343	
	f 68/-	
april on 1 lb gunpowder	" 6/-	
1726 august 6 on 1 shirt and 1 piece of strouds	" 20/-	
on 3 lb gunpowder	" 18/-	
	112/-	

[82]
(399) --Credit-side--

[half a page of empty space]

[the account below, cr]

1725344 for 1 skin	f 9/-
for skins[,] settling the account	
1726 Cred[it] anew for on [sic] 2 bear hides	f 20/-

1726 august 18 then balan[ced] accounts		
with him	f 92/-	
on 1 kan rum f3;-	" 3/	
~~october 27 paid 1 lb gunpowder and~~		
~~4 lb lead~~	~~" 10/-~~	
on 2 lb gunpowder	" 12/-	112
on 1 kan rum	" 3/	20
	f110/-	f92

his wife[,] sawagoneck hend[rick's] daughter345		
on 12 kan rum f30 on 11½ kan rum f34:10	" 64/10346	74
paid on this with skins	" 21/10	20
still remaining	f 43/00	54

[83]
(400) --Debit-side--

[all accounts on this page, cr=satisfied]

1725 Keman[347] remains indebted at balancing the

   account   f 69/-

      on 12 kan rum his gun is a security[348]   " 24/-

      on 1 kan rum   " 3/-

                                                 96

    X his wife[349] on 8 kan rum   "[16/-, cr]

      his wife on 1 coarse blanket   " 25/-

      ~~on remainder on lead f1 on 1 shirt by~~

                          ~~his wife~~ f24   [24/, cr]

    X his wife on 1 coarse blanket by

                       her mother[350]   "[30/-, cr]

      his wife remains indebted   anew   " 1/-

      on 3/4 ell of strouds his wife   " 14/-

      his wife on 4 p[t] rum by her father[351]   " 6/-

      his wife on 1 pair of stroud stockings   " 14/-

      his wife   " 3/-

      his wife remains indebted   f 20/-

      his wife on 1 shirt   " 13/-

      keman's wife remainder on a coarse blanket f 10/-

      his wife on strouds   " 14/-

1726 at balancing the account he remains

                      indebted in all   f 76/-

november 20 on 2 ells of cotton f12 on gunpowder

                      and lead   " 20/-

      on 1 lb gunpowder and 1 knife f3   " 9/-

                                     f105/-

      he on 1 kan rum f3:- and cider   " 5/-

1727 on 1 p[t] rum f1:10   " 1/10

                                       f111/10

      on 1 coarse blanket f33 on rum and

                      cider f5   " 38/

    pogrons[352]

1726 june kampo['s] son he lives at mamme kattin[353]

on 1½ ell of strouds	f 24/-
on 1 lb gunpowder and 2 lb lead	" 8/-
~~on 4 kan Beer f4:-~~	[empty]
on 1 stroud blanket	" 50/-
on remainder on ribbon	" 1/15
	f 83/15

novemb 10 on 1 coarse blanket f33 on 2 ells of dufels f20	" 53/-
on 1 pᵗ rum	" 1/10
	f138/ 5
on 1½ ell of dufels	" 15/[354]
	f153/ 5
on 1½ gall cider	" 1/-
on 1 lb gunpowder on lead [and] 3 lb lead f3	" 9/-
on 4 kan rum by matisso[355]	" 12/-
on 1 jackknife	" 3/-
	f178/ 5

january 3 for manonck[356]['s] burial	
on ½ of 3 ells of strouds	" 27/-
on 1½ ell of strouds	" 27/-
on 1 fine shirt	" 20/-
on 2¼ gall rum at the burial of manonck[357]	27/-
on ½ lb gunpowder	" 3/-
	282/ 5

1727 Sepᵗ 8 on balancing the account I have coming to me	f190/-

[84]
(401) --Credit-side--

[all accounts on this page, cr]

1725 he has coming to him on his skins	[f30/-, cr]	96
		25
his wife for 2 martens	f 14/-	121

his wife for 1 skin	f 4/-	45
	f 18/	76
1726 november 13 for 1 pig	f 45/-	
1727 november 14 on 1 deer	f 15/-	
for 1 deerskin that has not been dressed	[empty]	
~~his wife~~ on 1 shirt	f 13/-	
on remainder on 1 coarse blanket f10		
on strouds f14	"24/-	
1726/7 march 18 on remainder on rum by arrons[358]	" 10/10	
	f 41/10	
1727 august 15 maycke his wife on goods anew	" 47/-	
november 30 on 10 kan rum	" 30/-	
on remainder on 1 colored shirt	" 12/-	
	89/	
maycke Cred[it] by her brother[359] on		
1 marten	" 7/-	
for 12 lb skins	" 87/	44
f 9 comes	78/	25
12	9	8
21		78
21		
42		

~~1726 remains for him on 1 skin~~	~~f 3/10~~	
1727 sep[t] for 12 lb dressed skins	f 84/-	282
		84
		f198
His wife on 1 stroud blanket	f 40/-	

[85]
(402) --Debit-side--

[all accounts on this page, cr=satisfied]

1725 december 30 kosoes or kobes[360][,] hendreck sawagonck['s] son[361]

at balancing the account I have coming

	to me	f 65/10
anew 1 kan cider and 1 bread		" 6/
on 1 gall rum		" 12/-
on ½ ell of strouds f9:-		" 9/-
		f 92/10
on 1 jackknife		" 2/10
on 1 bread and *eysen*[362] flintstones		
	stroud[s]	" 5/-
on tobyas hornbeck[363]		" 6/
		f106/[00]
on rum		" 1/10
on 2 bars of lead		" 4/-
on 1 shirt		" 24/-
the savage boy who they escorted		
~~remainder on dufels f7 on ½ lb gunpowder~~		~~" 10/~~
on the debt of wiijakas[364]		" 18/-
		f149/-
1726 november 15 at balancing the account		f 69/-
on 1 kan rum f3:- on flintstones f1		
	on stroud[s] f12	f 16/-
on 1 lb gunpowder		" 6/-
		f 91/-
on 1 p[t] rum f[empty]		" 1/10
on cotton f12 on 1 knife f3		" 15/10
		f108/[00]
on cider		" 3/
		f111/-
on 1 lb gunpowder		" 6/
		f117/-

1725 his wife[,] kesay['s] daughter Cattrijn[365]

on remainder on strouds	f 12/
on 2 quart rum	" 6/-
on 1 gall rum f12 on ½ gall cider	" 13/-

on 8 kan rum   " 24/-

             f 55/

on 1 kan rum   " 3/-

             f 58/-

on ½ lb gunpowder by gertie[366] " 3/-

       balance f 61/-

1726 november 21 on 1 coarse blanket f 33/-

 on 7 kan rum   " 18/-

             f 51/-

 on pipes   " 1/-

 on cider   " 1/-

             f 53/-

 on 2 ells of cotton   f 12/-

 on 1 kettle f69 and ½ deer[367] " 60/

             f125/-

1727 at balancing the account I have coming

         to me f 36/

 and ½ deer on borrowing 1 skin 1 lb " 15/-

 on 10½ kan rum   " 31/10

             f 82/10

[86]

(403) --Credit-side--

[all accounts on this page, cr]

1726 for remainder on martens f 6/-

 for 2 bear hides   " 24/-

             f 30/-

 november for 7 lb skins f 50/-

             f 80/-

 for 3 raccoons   f 9/-

 ~~for skins~~   ~~24/-~~

transported from the other side[368]	f108/-
on ½ lb gunpowder and flintstones and	
2 lb lead	" 7/-
1727 on ½ ell of strouds	" 9/-
at balancing the account I have coming	
to me	f115/-[369]
on 2 lb gunpowder	" 12/-
	f127/-
on 1 knife f[empty]	" 3/-
Kobes[370] remains indebted at balancing	
the account	f120/-[371]
on 1 lb gunpowder and 1 lb lead	" 8/10
on 1 kan cider f1	f128/10
for 12 lb dressed skins	" 84/-
	f 44/10
for 62 lb elk skins	" 88/-
Cred[it] for 1 skin	" 18/-
for 1 raccoon	" 2/10
	f 20/10
for 1 elk skin and 4 martens	" 41/-
balance	f 61/~~10~~
1726/7[372] febewary [sic] 26 for 6 martens	f 42/-
for 2 minks f4 for 1 bear hide f8	" 12/-
	f 54/-
for deerskins	" 34/-
	f 89/-[373]
on 2½ gall cider f2:-	
for 10½ lb skins	f 73/10
she remains indebted f3 and ½ deer	f 3/
1728 anew on 4 ells of cotton	f 24/-
	f 27/
for 1 bear hide	f 12/-
for 1 elk skin f15	f 15/-

[87]
(404) --Debit-side--

[the account below, cr=satisfied]
          blandien the savage woman[374]
1726 on remainder on rum f4:- on 1 colored
shirt f24   f 28/-
          on 1 pᵗ rum f1:10   " 1/10
                                                       f 29/10

1726 july 19 remainder on a dufels blanket   f 24/-

1726 october 14 on remainder on a coarse blanket   f 11/-
          on 1½ ell of cotton f[empty]   " 9/-
          on flintstones f1:- on 1 kan cider f1   " 2/-
          on ½ ell of strouds   " 10/-
          janu[ary] 14 on 4 ells of oosburgh f12-   " 12/-
                                                       f 44/-

[the account below, up to the entry "at balancing the account — anew,"
cr=satisfied]

1725 july 13 pony[375] at balancing the account
                              remains indebted   f 60/10
          for sett for rum   " 4/-
          his wife Catrin remains indebted   f 78/-
1726   his[376] 1½ ell of cotton for kettene[377][']s
                              dead child   " 9/-
     X he anew on ½ ell of strouds   " 9/-
          on ½ lb gunpowder and 1 bar of lead   " 5/-
          he anew on 2½ ells of strouds   " 44/-
          also 1 ell of strouds for which he has
                         given 3 grease[378]   " 15/-
                                                       f 59/-
1726 may 25 on 10 kan rum   " 30/-

	f 89/-	
july 18 on 1 lb gunpowder and 1 bar of lead	" 8/-	
	f 97/-	
on 1 knife	" 3/-	
	f100/-	
1727 march 2 on ½ lb gunpowder and 1 knife	" 6/-	
	f106/-	
on 1 p^t rum	" 1/10	
on 1 stroud blanket	" 45/-	
	f152/10	
on borrowing 1 skin 1½ lb[379]		
on 9 p^t rum f13:10	" 13/10	
	f176/^{00}	
at balancing the account remains indebted	f108/-	
at balancing the account — anew	f 65/-	
on 2 ells of baize and 2 lb lead	" 14/-	
on 2 kan rum	" 6/-	
on 1 knife f3 on 1 dufels blanket f25	" 28/-	
	f113/-	
on 1 dufels blanket	" 24/-	
	f137/-	
1729 january 16 at balancing the account I have coming to me	f104/-	
on 1 kan rum f3:-		

[88]
(405) --Credit-side--

[the account below, cr]

1726 april for 1 beaver	f 12/-	33
for 1 bear hide	" 10/-	22
f 22/-		11
for 1 skin	" 7/10	
[the account below, cr]		
		29

1726[380] october 14 for 4 lb skins	f 28/-	22
for 2 lb beavers	" 16/-	7
	f 44/-	46
		24
		f22

[the account below, cr]

1725/6 march 10 for 3 raccoons	f 9/-
1726 april 15 for 1 bear hide	" 8/-
for 12 martens paid	" 84/
	f 92/-[381]

1727 march 1 for 7 martens	f 49/-	
for 1 bear hide f12 for 1 marten f7	" 19/-	
balancing the account	f 68/-	
		108
[the two entries below, cr]	43	
1727 july for 1 skin	f 7/-	65
for 5 days on the farm	30/-	113
	f 37/	37
		76
28 november for 1 pig	f 33/-	

[89]
(406) --Debit-side--

[all accounts on this page, cr=satisfied]

1726 july 13 small fellow[,] or sansis Rennos	
on strouds	f 0/[382]
on 1 knife	" 3/-
on strouds f12	" 12/-
on 1 shirt f12:-	" 13/-[383]
	f 28/-

on 1 kan rum f3 on 1 lb lead	" 1/-
	f̶ ̶2̶9̶/̶-̶
1728 on 1 shirt from older times	" 17/-
on stockings f11	" 11/-
	f 28/-
on 1 kan rum on 1 lb gunpowder and	
2½ lb lead	" 13/-
on remainder on 1 knife	" 1/10

---

arent fynhout[384]	f 42/10[385]
1726 july 19 anew on remainder on strouds	f 21/-
on 1 kan rum f3:-	" 3/-
anew on 1¼ ell of cotton	f 7/10
on 3 pᵗ rum	" 4/10
	f 12/-
on 1 kan rum f3:-	" 3/-
on 2 shirts for his children	" 24/-
	f 39/-
1727 april 24 he has coming to him on	
his goods f45:-	" 45
he has paid 3½ lb beavers f28: remains	" 16 on the beavers
for his daughter f12 f̶6̶3̶:̶-̶[386]	61
deter[387] on 1 pᵗ rum f1:10 on 1 kan f3:-	f 4/10

1726 august jacob or nockkehan[388]	f 56/10[389]
on gunpowder and lead from older times	" 7/10
on 1 lb sugar on pipes	" 1/10
on 4 kan rum by kisa['s][390] daughter	" 10/-
his wife gertie[391] on 1 small kettle	" 12/⁰⁰
on pipes f1 on 1½ ell of cotton	" 10/-
her husband on rum — pipes	" -1-/10
he on 1 kan rum by sawanosse[392]	3/-
on 1 kettle f36	" 36/-
he is indebted in all	f 59/-
his wife in all	" 22/-

his wife for 1 knife by arent[393]	" 4/-
	26/
1727 april 22 at balancing the account I have	
coming to me	f 10/-
on 1 pᵗ rum f1:10 on 1 pᵗ rum f1:10	" 3/-
on 1 pᵗ rum another pᵗ rum	" 3/-
	f 16/-
on 1 pᵗ rum f1:10	" 1/10
	f 17/10
X his wife gertie on rum and 1 small cup	~~" 28/-~~
X he on 1 lb gunpowder f 7 on 3 pᵗ rum f4:10	" 11/10
X on ½ sch bran	~~" 3/-~~
on 1 gall rum 12:-	" 10/-[394]
X she on 2/3 ell of strouds	~~" 12/-~~
gertie remains indebted	f 18/-
she on 2 kan beer	" 2/-
gertie is indebted	f 8/-

[90]

(407) --Credit-side--

~~1727 april 22 for 1 marten f 0/-~~[395]	
~~1728 for 1 elk skin~~	~~f 25/-~~

[all accounts on the remainder of this page, cr]

1728 april 29 at balancing the account	f 42/10
on 1 small looking glass his belt of	
wampum is a security	" 7/-
on 2 lb gunpowder and 2½ lb lead	" 18/-
	f 67/10
Cred[it] for 1 skin	f 21/-
Remains indebted at balancing the account	f 46/10
Cred[it] for 6½ lb skins	" 45/10
	f 1/00

1727[396] april 23 for 1 wolf head	f 24/-	
for 1 bear hide	" 12/-	
for 1 wolf pelt	" 6/-	

[empty space]

		59
		42
1727 april 21 for 1 elk skin and		17
1 bear hide and beaver	f 42	
for 1 marten	" 7/	19:-
	" 49	
for 1 marten f7 for 1 fisher f11	" 18/	26
gertie has coming to her f11.- on beer		18
and rum f2:10"	3/-	-6
she on 1 knife	" 3/	
he has brought 1 skin for the lock		9
of his gun	f[20/ ,cr]	2
he for 1 skin f7:-	" 7/-	12
		3
		52
1727 for 1 marten	f 7/-	34
for skins	" 27/-	18
	f 34/-	
she for harvesting flax	f 12/-	

[91]
(408) --Debit-side--

1726[397] august 20 hend hekan[398]

I have coming to me at balancing	
the account	f183/-
on 1 dressed skin on a kettle	"[empty]
on lead by his son	" 3/-
on 1 lb gunpowder on 2 lb lead	

by sawannos[399]	" 8/-
on 3 lb gunpowder on 3 lb lead	" 21/-
	"215/-
1727 on bread f1:10 on remainder on gunpowder f11:10	13/-
	"228/-
on 1 knife and flintstones	" 4/-
on 1 bottle of rum f3:- on 1 kan rum	" 6/-
	"238/-
on 1 coarse blanket by his son waddie[400]	" 33/-
on remainder on duffels for his son	" 4/-
on flintstones	" 1/-
on 1 piece of strouds	" 9/-
on 4½ lb lead by sawanos	" 6/15
	f291/15
on 1 kan rum	" 3/-
	294/15
1728 on 1 kan rum f3 on 2 lb gunpowder f14.- april 28	" 17/-
on 3 lb lead and flintstones	" 5/-
	f316/15
sep[t] 12 on 5 lb gunpowder — by mary pawling[401]	f 35/-
on 7 flintstones f1: on 2½ lb lead on 1 p[t] rum" 5/10	
on 1 coarse blanket f27	" 27/-
	f384/5
on 2 p[t] rum f3:- on ½ lb gunpowder f3:	" 6/-
on 4 p[t] rum f6:- on rum f2 for 1 marten	" 8/-
on 1 lb gunpowder and 1 bar of lead	" 9/-
on 1 bottle of rum f3 on 1 bucket of cider	" 8/-
on 2 lb gunpowder f14:- on 2 kan rum f6	" 20/-
	f435/5
on 1 lb gunpowder and 1 bar of lead f9:-	
on ½ lb gunpowder f3	" 12/10
	f447/15

[the account below, cr=satisfied]

Sar[,] hendreck hekan[']s wife[402]

on her old account in kingston	f 38/-
on 1 shirt of linen therefor	" 12/-
on kwakesas[403]['s] account her part	" 33/-
	f 83/-

1728 ~~I have coming to me at balancing~~

~~the account~~ f 55/-

1728 october 15 they remain indented balancing [*sic*]

the account	f 30/-
~~on 1 dufels blanket for her son~~	~~" 24/-~~
on ¼ lb gunpowder	" 1/15
~~her son the boy on 1½ ell of cotton~~	~~" 9/-~~
~~her son on ½ lb gunpowder f3:10~~	[empty]
his wife on 10½ kan rum	" 31/-
	61
on 1 kan rum at bur[ial] f 3:- of	
andries['s] child	" 3/-
on remainder on strouds [and] on the pig	" 12/-
on 3/4 ell of strouds	" 12/-
	f 88/-

[92]
(409) --Credit-side--

1726 november 20 for 1 pig	f 70/-
january 10 for 1 skin — 1 lb	" 7/-
	f 77/-
1727 for ½ lb dressed skins on the coarse	
blanket	" 10/10
for 1 elk skin	" 15/-
	f102/10
1728 sep[t] for 1 elk skin weighs 13 lb	f 16/-
for 2 skins 2 lb	" 14/-

	f132/0
for 1 marten f8:-	" 8/-
	f140/10

1729 from the opposite side[404]	f447/15
on borrowing 1 skin of 1 lb on 1 bar	
of lead[405]	" 9/-
on 1 kan rum f3:- on 3 lb gunpowder f18	
on 4 lb lead 5	" 26/-
	f483/15

wissandiys's son	
at balancing the account f12:10 on 1	
coarse blanket f26	f 38/10

[the account below, cr]	
1728 april 24 for 4 lb skins	f 28/-

~~by his son 3 martens~~	~~f 24/-~~

[93]
(410) --Debit-side--

1726 october 12 hend sawangock['s] wife[406]	
on 1 coarse blanket	f 33/-

[the account below, cr=satisfied]

sawannos[407] ~~from balancing~~	~~f 37-~~	
his daughter[,] gasris['s wife][408]	f 12/-	
his wife['s] son on strouds f 18 and 2 knives	" 24/-	" 24/-
the sawannos ~~on~~ at balancing the account	f 37/-[409]	
1726 october 25 on 2½ ells of cotton	" 15/-	

on ½ lb gunpowder and 3½ lb lead	" 7/-
on 3½ ells of cotton	" 21/-
	f 80/-
on strouds	" 3/-
on trading of 1 gun	" 80/-
on 1 lb gunpowder	" 6/-
	f169/-
november 10 at balancing the account I have	
coming to me	f113/-
on 1 dufels blanket	" 24/-
on gunpowder and lead	" 11/-
on flintstones on 1 knife	" 4/-
	f152/-
on ½ lb gunpowder f3:- on 1 kan rum f3	" 6/-
	f158/-
on 2 lb gunpowder f14 on 3 lb lead f3	" 17/-
on 1 lb gunpowder f7	" 7/-
	182/-
on having borrowed 1 skin 1¼ lb	" 8/10
	f190/10
on ½ lb gunpowder and 2 lb lead	" 5/-
	f195/10

1727 at balancing the account I have	
coming to me	f 83/

~~touwas[410] who was escorted by the sawonnos~~
~~on gunpowder and lead and flintstones~~
~~strou[ds]~~ ~~f 9/10~~

[94]
(411) --Credit-side--

1726 november 14 by her son 6 lb skins	f 33/

1726 october 29 for 1 deer	f 16/-
for 6 lb dressed skins	" 40/-
	f 56/-

[the entries below, cr]
    1727 april 22 for 1 bear hide f10

for 2 martens	f 24/-
for 4/3 [sic] lb beaver	" 6/-
	f 30/-
for 4½ lb skins	" 31/10
	f 61/10
for 8½ day [sic] on the farm	" 51/-
	f112/10

190
112
f78
5
f83

[95]
(412) --Debit-side--

[the entire account below, cr=satisfied]
1726 mattasson[,]411 wappeneck412['s] son

at balancing the account	f 93/
on 1 kan rum	" 3/
on 2 small cups of rum	" 2/-
on 2 lb gunpowder on flintstones	" 12/10
	f110/10
1726 november 28 at balancing the account	f 40/-
on 1 lb gunpowder f6 on 4 lb lead	" 10/-
on 2 kan rum	" 6/-
on 1 stack of *rarten*413 [and] on cider	" 6/-

	f 62/-
1726 december 28 at balancing the account	
I have coming to me	f 58/-
january 3 on 1 shirt f13:-	" 13/-
	67/-[414]
1727 april 22 remains	f 11
on 1 lb gunpowder and 2 lb lead	" 1/-
on strouds	" 6/-
	f 18/
on 1 p^t rum on another p^t rum	" 3/-
on 1 ell of strouds	" 18/-
	f 39/-
on 1 shirt	" 12/-
	f 51
on remainder on 10 kan rum	" 21/-
	f 72/-
on 2 lb gunpowder f14 on 2 lb lead	" 16/-
on 2 kan rum	" 6/-
on 1 3/4 ell of cotton	" 10/-
on 1 bottle of rum f3:-	" 3/-
	f107/-
on 1 bottle of rum f3:- on 1 bottle of rum f3:-	" 6/-
on remainder on strouds	" 6/10
at balancing the account	f119/10
on rum	" 0/10
	f120/-
at balancing the account I have coming to me the sum of f110	f110/-
on 4 p^t rum and 2 kan beer	" 8/-
on pipes f1:- on 2 ells of colored textile on 1 p^t rum	" 4/-
on 2 kan rum	" 6/-
on 1 coarse blanket	" 33/-
	f161

on 2½ lb lead	" 3/-
febru[ary] 8 on 1 gun of pitter tappen[415]	f240/-
on 1 colored shirt f24 on 2¼ ells	
of strouds	" 38/-
	f442/-
on 1 p^t rum	" 1/10
1728 april 24 at balancing the account I have	
coming to me	f285/-
~~on 1 q^t rum f1:10~~	[empty]
on 1 bottle of rum	" 3/-
on 1 shirt and ½ gall cider	" 14/10
on 1 kan rum f3:-	" 3/-
	f305/10

[96]

(413) --Credit-side--

[the account on this page, cr]		110
1726[416] october for 1 beaver *lap*	f 7/-	67
for 1 pig	f 60/-	f40
~~for meat~~	~~f 61/~~	

his wife remains	f 43/-
Cred[it] 1726 october 30 for 1 beaver	" 12/-
Remains	f 31/-

balancing the account remains	f 31/-
anew on 1 dufels blanket	" 24/-
~~on molasses~~	" 1/10
	f 55/-
for 4½ lb skins	" 31/-
	f 24/-
his wife anew on cider	" 1/-

on 1 shirt	" 12/-
on cider f2:- on 1 bread f1:10	" 3/10
this is hendr[ic]k sawangonck['s]	
daughter['s][417] debt	f 40/10

1727 april for beavers f40 on 1 beaver f 16	f 56/-	67
for 1 bear hide credited f10:-	f 10/-	40
		27
for remainder on deer meat	f 12/-	161
for 15½ lb dressed skins	"108/10	12
for 6 lb fat or grease	" 6/-	149
	f126/10	

1727
april 23 for 1 bear hide

	f 12/-
	f138/10

for 1 elk skin	f 25/-
for 1 elk skin	" 30/-
for 9 lb beaver	" 72/-
	f127/-

[97]
(414) --Debit-side--

[the account below, cr=satisfied]
1726 november 10 kewesie[, a] keseton[418] savage

on goods as at balancing the account	f 40/-
on remainder on lead	" 2/-
on 2 coarse blankets	" 66/-
on 2 blankets dufels	" 40/-
on 3½ ells of cotton white	" 25/-
on remainder for salomon[419]	" 1/-
on flintstones	" -/10
	f183/10

1729 october 5 on 1 coarse blanket	f 28/-
on 2 kan rum f6:-	" 6/-
	f217/-
on 2 axes	" 18/-
	f235/-[420]
1729 october 7 on remainder on 1 colored shirt	f 6/-
on 2 pairs of stockings	" 20/-
on 2 blankets dufels	f46
on 1 coarse blanket f30	" 76/-
on 6 knives f14:- on 3 ells of gemp	" 18/-
	f120/-
on 1 dobelstin shirt	" 14/-
on 1 small shirt f7 on 1½ ell of	
dufels f21	" 28/-
	f162/-
on 2 kan rum 1 jackknife f2	" 8/-
£ 4:5-	f 170

parraris from kasegton[421] anew	
the savage woman who he escorted on 2	
kan rum	f 5/-
[the remainder of the account below, cr=satisfied]	
1727 april 24 for 3 stroud blankets	f120/-
on 2 small shirts f10 on gunpowder	
and lead f6:-	" 16/-
	f141/-
the old [debt] has been paid has been paid [sic]	
~~anew~~	
~~on strouds~~	f 8/10
his wife on 1 coarse blanket f33 on 1	
duffels blanket f24	" 57/-
on 1 stroud blanket f40 on 5 ells of band	" 40/15
on 3 coarse blankets and 7 lb lead	"106/-
on flintstones f1:- on 1 knife	" 2/10
on 1 piece of strouds	" 7/-

1728 october 25 on 1 coarse blanket anew	f 30/-
on 1 coarse blanket f30 on 2 blankets	
dufels f48	" 78
on 1 lb gunpowder f7 on flintstones f1	" 8/-
	f116/-
on 1 stack of cards	" 4/-
	f120/-
on gunpowder and lead and flintstones	" 9/-
on strouds for his daughter	" 11/-
1729 may 28 on 1 kan rum f2:10	" 2/10
	f142/10
on 10 kan rum f28:10 on 3 ells of	
strouds f42	" 70/10
on 1 stroud blanket f40	" 40/-
on 4 bars of lead f8 on 1 lb gunpowder	" 6/-[422]
1729 may 29 at balancing the account I have	
coming to me £5:4	"208/-
Cred[it] for 8½ lb dressed skins	"130/-
	f 78/10
1729 may 28 for 2 elk skins	f 60/-

[98]
(415) --Credit-side--

[all accounts on this page, cr]

1729 october 6 for 12 lb dressed elk skins	f 60/
for 1 bear hide	" 20/10
for 1 parchment[423] elk skin	" 36/-
for 8 lb beaver	" 90/-
for 40 lb dressed skins @ 7 each lb	"280/-
for 1 *vos kruys*[424]	" 10/-
for 25 lb fat — by pit lou[425] f13	" 38/-
for 1 otter f6: for 14 *wateratten*[426] f7	" 13/-
for 1 raccoon f1:- for 4 lb feathers	" 13/-
	f550/-[427]

he has coming to him on his skins[,] paid

with shot	~~14~~/-	
1727 for 11 lb dressed skins	f 77/- f7/lb	134
for 1 bear hide	" 8/-	77
f 85/-		57
for 5 lb skins	" 35/-	77
this has been paid	f120/-	134
1727 sept 10 for 5 lb deerskins paid		85
with gunpowder	f 35/-	f49
his old account has been paid		35
his wife's accounts [she] is still indebted[428]		14
his wife Cred[it] for 15½ lb dressed		
ski[ns]	~~f108/10~~	

~~his wife still has coming to her f9:-~~

his wife

on on [sic] 2 stroud blankets	f 80
on 3¼ ells of cotton f19	
on on [sic] strouds f18	" 37
on remainder on 1 shirt	" 11
	128/-

1729 for 10 lb skins — his wife	f 70/-

she has 1 lb gunpowder and lead	f 8/-
the savage woman Cred[it] for 5½ lb skins	
for which she must have a kettle	f 38/10
also 2 lb dressed skins	" 14/-

[99]
(416) --Debit-side--

1726 november 15 manonck[429] remains at balancing

the account	f 72/-
on 1 lb gunpowder and ½ gall cider	" 7/-
on 3 pᵗ rum f4:10 on 1 fine shirt f18	" 22/10
on 5½ gall rum	" 55/-
on 1 coarse blanket f34:- on gunpowder	
and rum	" 6/-
on rum at abraham's burial[430]	" 21/-
on 3 kan rum f9:-	<u>" 9/-</u>
	f192/10/

---

mack[,] pansogh['s] son[431]

1729 march 8 at balancing the account I have

coming to me	f 72/
on 2 kan beer f2:- on 1 bucket of beer f5	" 7/-
on ½ lb gunpowder f3:10 on 1 lb shot	" 5/
on ½ sch bran f3 on ½ ell of cotton	
by y[our] H[onor's] sister	" 12/-
on beer f½ on 1 sch bran f4:10	" 5/-
on 1 stroud blanket f40 on 1 ell	
for stockings f16	" 56/
on ½ ell of strou[ds] f9:- on 3 ells	
of gemp f3	<u>" 12/</u>
	f169/
on 1 lb gunpowder and lead f9 on ½ bread	" 9/10[432]
on 1 small skin for the smith[433] f3	" 3/-
on flintstones f1:- on 1 kan rum f3:-	" 4/-
on 1 colored shirt f24:- on 1 kan rum f3	" 27/-
on 1 bottle of rum	<u>" 3/</u>
	f216/

1729 july 20 at balancing the account I have

coming to me	f 82/-
on 1 raccoon[434] f3:- on 1 pᵗ rum f1:10	
on 1 kan [rum] f3	" 7/10
<u>on 1 pair of stockings</u>	<u>" 13/</u>

102/10

his wife[,] Catryn[435]
on 1 gall rum f12 on 1 stroud blanket f45   " 67/
on 1 dufels blanket f26 on 2 coarse
                    blankets f68   " 94/-
1726 on 10 kan rum f30 on 1 gall rum f12   " 42/-
october on 8 kan rum f[empty]   " 20/-
november 15 on remainder on a kettle f4:-
                  on 1 p^t rum f1:10   " 5/10
on 1 kan rum f3:-   " 3/-
on 4½ ells of cotton f27 on 1 knife f3   " 30/-
                            f261/10/-
on 1 knife f3:- on ½ lb gunpowder f3   " 6/-
1728 october 1 on 1½ ell of cotton and 1 kan rum   " 12/-
                            f279/10

[100]
(417) --Credit-side--

Cred[it] for remainder on skins   f 10/

for[436] 8 martens   f 64/-
1729 for 10 days on the farm   f 70/-
                            f134/-   216
for 1 skin   f 9/10   134
                                   82
1729 august 1 at balancing the account
                I have coming to me   f 93/-   102
for 1 kan rum by kobes[437] f3:- on 1 lb   9
                gunpowder and lead   f 13/-   93

1726[438] october for 6 lb skins   f 42/-

[the account below, cr]

1728 sept[em]ber 30 for 9 lb skins	f 63/	264
for 10 lb fat	" 10/-	_42_
for 2 lb skins[,] paid these skins		222
with strouds	" 14/-	
		299
		_42_
		257

[remainder of page is empty]

[101]
(418) --Debit-side--

1726 november 20 makwas

on 1 colored shirt f24	f 24/-
on 1 lb gunpowder f6 on 3 lb lead f3	" 9/-
on ½ ell of strouds	" 9/-
on 1 knife	" 3/-
	f 45/-
on 3 p^t rum	" 4/10
on 1 kettle	" 30/-
	f 79/10/
on 1 p^t rum	" 1/10/-
january 4 on 1 gall rum at the burial[439]	" 12/-
on 1 lb gunpowder f6 on lead f4	
on 2 knives f6	" 16/-
	f109/00/-
on 1 knife f3:-	" 3/-
1728 july 28 on 1 colored shirt	" 21/-
on rum f4:- on 2 ells of cotton f12:-	" 16
on beer f1 on 1 bucket of beer f3-	" 4

andris the savage[440]

1726   at balancing the account he remains

                                         indebted   f108/-

on ½ gall rum at manonck[441]['s] burial[442]   " 6/-

                                                    f114/

february 2 I have coming to me at

                        balancing the account   f 58/-

anew ½ lb gunpowder   " 3/-

on 1 stroud blanket f40 on 1 small piece

                           [of fabric] f3   " 43/-

                                                   f104/-

on 1 lb gunpowder by sawagonck[443]

                                      1 pipe -   " 6/5

on 1½ ell of cotton and 1 bottle of rum

                               by tateu[444]   " 12/

 122/-

on ½ ell of cotton on 1 bottle of rum f6   " 6/

on 1 lb gunpowder and 3 lb lead   " 10/

on ½ ell of strouds   " 9/-

                                                   147/-

1729 july 27 on 2 ells of cotton f12 on 1 bar

                               of lead f2   14/-

on 1 shirt for his child f8 on ½ ell of

                               strou[ds] f7   " 15/-

on 3 gall rum f36 on 2 ells of colored

                               textile f12   " 48/

on 1 kan rum f3:-   " 3/

                                                   227/

[102]

(419) --Credit-side--

[half of a page, empty]

1726[445] febewary 2 for 8 lb skins 3 skins	f 56/-	

1729 july 27 for 2 bear hides	f 24/-	114
on 1 fisher f11 on 2½ lb dressed skins f17	" 28/-	56
	f 52/-	"58

[remainder of page, empty]

[103]
(420) --Debit-side--

1727 april 20 Ragel[,] the savage woman from manisenck[446]

on 2 gall rum	f 24/-
X saij the savage woman who she escorted	
1 p^t [rum]	" 1/10
on 1½ gall cider	" 1/-
X on 2 ells of white baize	" 12/
on 1 coarse blanket	" 33/
on 1 dufels blanket	" 24/-
on 9 ells of floret band	" 6/15
	f101/15
her son 1 p^t rum f1:10 on 1 bucket	
of cider f5	" 6/10
also 1 bucket of cider and 1 bucket	
of cider	" 10/-
on 1 bucket of cider f5:- on 1 p^t	
rum f1:10	" 6/10
	" 24/-
on 1 lb gunpowder f7 for which wampum is	
a security	" 7/
	f 31/-

[the account below, cr=satisfied]

   arent fynhout the savage[447]

1726 on remainder on goods and rum	f 18/-
on 1 colored shirt	" 24/-
~~his wife on 2 kan rum by sar[448]~~	~~" 6/-~~
he anew on 1 stroud blanket	" 12/-
~~on 2 kan rum f6:-~~	
on 1 dufels blanket f24 on 3 kan rum f9	" 33/
on 1 kan rum f3:- on 1 pᵗ rum f1:10	
on [a] bottle f3	" 7/10
on 1 coarse blanket f33 on 1 duffels	
blanket f24	<u>" 67/-</u>
	f116/10[449]
on cotton	<u>" 8/10</u>
	f124/00
on 6 kan rum f18 on ½ ell of strouds	<u>" 26/-</u>
1727 then balanced accounts with him	f115/
on 4 galls cider	" 4/
on 1 qᵗ rum by mattison[450]	" 3/
~~on 1 kan cider f1 on 2 gall cider f2~~	~~" 3/~~
1728 on 2 kan rum f6:- on 2 kan cider f	f 8/-
on 1 pᵗ rum f1:10:-	<u>" 1/10</u>
	f131/10
april 28 at balancing the account I have	
coming to me	f 85/-
on ½ sch Indian corn	" 2/-
on cider by mattison	" 6/-
on remainder on strouds	<u>" 34/-</u>
	f127/-
~~on 1 pᵗ rum f1:10 on 1 lb gunpowder~~	
~~and 3 lb lead~~	~~" 12/-~~
on 1 blanket f24:-	<u>" 24</u>
151	f151/-
<u>107</u>	
44	

[104]
(421) --Credit-side--

1727 sept 10 for 1 skin weighs 1½ lb   f 10/10

[empty space]

[all accounts on this page, cr]
    1727[451] ~~july for 1 wolf head and pelt~~   ~~f 30/-~~
by johanes vernoy[452]   f 38/10
~~for 2 days on the farm~~   " 12/-
for 4½ lb dressed skins   " 31/10
for remainder on 1 marten   " 4/-
for 1 fisher   " 11/-

for 8½ lb skins   f 59/10
for 4½ lb beaver f45   " 45/-
     104/10/
     3/-
     107/10

1729 march 8 then balanced the account and
                 I have coming to me   44/-
on beer f10 on beer f1:-
                 1 bucket of beer f5   " 16/-
[text cr, illegible] on 6 kan beer f3   " 3/-
on 1 colored shirt f18:-   " 18/-
     f 81/-
on gemp f4 on 4 kan rum f12
                on 3 bucket of cider 15   " 31
on cider f1   " 1/-
     f113/-

~~his son on 1 colored shirt f18~~ *nan*[453] 1 p^t

1 kan rum f4	f 23/10	
on 1 kan rum f3:- on 1 dobelstin shirt f20	" 23/-	113
1729 july 16 on 1 stroud blanket f40		22
on 1 pᵗ rum f2:-	" 42	23
on 1 kan rum f3:- on 1 kan rum f3:-		42
on 1 kan rum f3:-	" 9/-	9
on 1 kan rum f3:- on 1 kan on 1 kan	" 9/-	9
1729 ~~for skins f20:-~~ on 1 kan rum f3:-		6
on 1 kan rum f3:-	" 6/	3
on 1 kan f3 on 2 kan rum f6 on		227
coarse blanket f24-	f 33	28
Cred[it] for 1 marten	f 8	199
for skins f20:-	" 20	
	28/-	

[105]
(422) --Debit-side--

[all accounts on this page, cr=satisfied]
1727 may 15 arronshagkie or ankerop['s] son[454]

on 1 ell of strouds and flintstones	f 20/-
on 2 lb gunpowder f14 on lead f3-	" 17/-
on ½ ell of strouds	" 9/-
on ½ gall rum	" 6/-
on 1 pᵗ rum 1:10 on 3 pᵗ rum	" 6/-
august 15 on 1 3/4 ell of baize f11	
on 3 ells of floret garters f2:5	" 13/10[455]
	f 71/10
on 2 lb gunpowder and 3¼ lb lead	" 18/-
	f 89/10
1728 may 26 I have coming to me at balancing the account	f 33/10
on flintstones f1:-	" 1/-
on ½ ell of strouds	" 7/-
	f 42/~~10~~

I have coming to me at balancing	
the account	f 3/-
on 1 colored shirt f24 on 1 ell	
of strouds f16	" 40/-
on 1 stroud blanket f40 on band	" 43/-
on 3 lb gunpowder f21 on 4 lb lead f6	
on flintstones 2	" 29/-
	f115/-
on 1 knife	" 6/-

	f121/10[456]
kisay[457] on 2 kan beer	2
on 2 kan rum by sar[458]	f 6/-
~~her youngest daughter on strouds~~	~~" 10/-~~
on 1 shirt colored	" 24/-
on 1 shirt f12:-	" 12/-
~~her daughter on 1 q' rum f3-~~	~~" 3/-~~
she on 7½ ells of floret	" 6/-
	f 50/-
~~on 1½ gall cider f1:10 on 4½ gall cider 6~~	~~" 6/10[459]~~
~~on 1 shirt and ½ gall cider~~	~~" 14/10~~

she is by at balancing the account	f 27/-
~~her young daughter~~	~~" 41/-~~
1729 may 29 on 15 kan rum by jawis['s][460] son	" 45/-
~~her daughter on 12 kan rum~~	~~f 36/-~~
~~on 1 dufels blanket f25 on 1½ ell~~	
~~of cotton 9~~	~~" 34/-~~
	~~f183/~~
1728 kisay remains at balancing the account	f 27/-
on 1 ell of cotton	"
on beer f2:- on 1 lb sugar	" 3/-
on 1 frying pan on 1 bleaching kettle f9	" 17/-
remains indebted	f 48/-
on 10 kan 1 pint rum by matteson[461]	" 31/10

1729 march 8 I have coming to me at balancing

the account	f 21/-
on 3 lb sugar f3:10:- on 1 skin f2	" 6/-[462]
	27/-
on 1 sch bran f6:- on bcer f4:-	" 10/-
on penneston f11:- on 1 coarse blanket	
for the girl	f 35/-
on 1 sch wheat f6	" 6/-
	f 78/-

[106]
(423) --Credit-side--

[all accounts on this page, cr]
1728 may 25 for 2 elk skins 56:

arons haghkie	f 56/-
1728 july 21 I have coming to me at	
balancing the account	f122/10
on 5 kan rum f15-	" 15/
	f137/10
for skins and otters	" 78/-
	f 59/10

for skins	f 12/-
for 4 days on the farm	" 27/
	f 39/-

her daughter[463] on remainder on 1 shirt	" 5/-	41-10
her daughter on 1½ gall cider	" 1/10	12:
1727 for elkskin her daughter	f 8/-	29:10
her daughter[,] wynne[']s wife[464] on		
remainder on strouds	" 10/-	
on 1 qᵗ rum f3 on stroud stockings f13	" 16/-	
	26/-	

her daughter for 1 marten by her brother   " 7/-
for 11¼ lb dressed skins   " 78/10
for 1 marten

~~kisaij Cred[it] for 2 martens~~
                    ~~and 9 on skins   f 23/-~~

~~her younger son is indebted on [a] strou[d]~~
                          ~~blanket   f 12/-~~
~~her daughter Cred[it] for 1 skin   f 12/-~~
for 2 fishers and 1 marten   " 32/-
for beavers   " 30/

~~she still has coming to her on her pig   f 8/-~~

kisay['s] daughter annatie[']s ~~part~~   f 00/-[465]
~~she remains~~ from older times at balancing
                          the account   " 9/-
1729 march 8 on beer f3:-   " 3/-
on 1 ell of strouds f16:-   " 16/
                                                 f 28/-
on 4 ells of gemt f4:- on 1 bread f2:   " 6/-
on 1 ell of strouds f8:   " 8/-
on remainder on 1 dobelstin shirt   " 18/-
on 3/4 ell of strouds f10:-   " 10/
                          1 kan rum   " 3
                                                 73/-

~~kisay Cred[it] for harvesting flax   f 18/-~~

[107]
(424) --Debit-side--

[the account below, up the 1728 April entry, cr=satisfied]
         matisso[,] manonck['s] son[466]

1727 I have coming to me at balancing

        the account f 59/-

  on remainder on 1 shirt f1 on strouds

       [and] lead f8 " 9/-

  on 6 kan rum by ponij and 1 colored shirt " 42/-

  ~~on 1 lb gunpowder and lead and flintstones~~ " 11/-

  on[467]   f110/-

1728 april remains indebted at balancing

        the account f 74/-

  on 2 ells of cotton f[empty] on 1 lb

       gunpowder " 19/-

  on 1 knife f3 on lead f4 on 1 colored

       shirt f24 " 31/-

            f124/-

[the account below, cr=satisfied]

  at balancing the account remains indebted f 60/-

1728 sep^t 30 on 1 ell of strouds by y[our]

      H[onor's] mother " 16/-

           f 76/-

  on 1 kan rum f3:- on 2 ells of cotton f12 " 15/-

  on remainder on strouds f16 on 1 bucket

      of cider f6 " 22/-

           113/-

  on ½ lb gunpowder f3:10 on ½ gall rum f6 " 9/10

  on 1 gun £ 6 "240/-

           f362/10

  anew on 1 lb gunpowder and 2 bars of lead f 10/-

  on 1 dobelstin shirt f20 on 1 ell of

      strouds f6 " 36/-

  on *manetvel*[468] " 3/-

1729 june 8 I have coming to me at balancing

      the account "110/-

  on 1 kan rum f3:- on 1 kan rum f3:-

      on 1 kan [rum] f3 " 9/-

1727 Catrijn[,] nanondo['s][469] daughter

-at balancing the account f78 on [empty]		f 78/-
on 1½ ell of cotton for ketternar[']s		
	child	" 9/-
on 2 kan rum		" 6/-
on 10 kan rum and 1 pᵗ		" 26/-
on 1 shirt f12:-		<u>" 12/-</u>
		f131.

[108]
(425) --Credit-side--

[the account below, cr]

     his wife[,] pitternel[470] at balancing the account

	remains indebted	f 40/-
on her mother[']s account		f 80/-
1728 on 4 lb beavers	36	f 36
1729 october for 4½ lb skins		" 31/10
for 7½ lb skins		" 52/10
for 1 beaver		<u>" 12/-</u>
		f 64/10

[the account below, up to "for 1 day" entry, cr]

1729 january 16 for 16 lb skins	f160/-
for 2 lb skins	" 14/-
for 1 fox and 2 cats	<u>" 14/-</u>
	f188/-
for skins and beavers	<u>f113/-</u>
	f301/-
for 1 day shooting fire[471]	" 9/-
for 4½ lb dressed skins	" 31/-

[empty space]

1727 for 2 skins paid with rum   f 25/

[109]
(426) --Debit-side--

[the account below, up to the 1728 April entry, cr=satisfied]
    Waddie[,] hendreck hekan[']s son[472]
1727 remains on the account   f 78/-
    on remainder on 1 lb gunpowder on lead   " 2/-
    on remainder on lead f2:10 on flintstones   " 3/10
    on 1 ell of strouds   " 17/-
                                                f100/10
    on 1 knife   " 3
    on 1 piece [of fabric] by his father[473]   " 6/
                                                f109/10
    on cider   " 2/-
                                                f111/10
    on ½ turkey   on 1 kan rum   " 6/-
    on 1 shirt f12:- on 2 lb gunpowder   f 14   " 26/-
    on 4 lb lead f5 on 1 knife f3 on
               strouds f5   " 13/-
    on flintstones   " 1
                                                f157/10
1728 april 30 I have coming to me at balancing
             the account   f 37/-
    on 3½ lb lead   " 4/10
    on rum f1:- on 3 lb swan shot f4:10   " 5/10
    on remainder on strouds   " 4/
    on 3 ells of band   " 3
                                                f 54/00
    on 1 lb gunpowder   " 4/
    on remainder on 2 stroud blankets   " 10/-
    on 1 lb gunpowder and 2 lb swan shot   " 10/-
    on 2 ells of cotton f12 on remainder on

	1 blanket f4	<u>" 16/-</u>
		f 94/-
1729 january 15 on 1 gun for £ 8		<u>f320</u>
Transported to the other side[474]		f414/-

[the account below, cr=satisfied]

    magh[,] hend hekan[']s son[475]

1727 on the account		f 39/-
on 1 stroud blanket		" 45/
on 1½ ell of ~~strouds~~ cotton		<u>" 9/-</u>
at balancing the account		f 13
on 2 lb gunpowder		" 12
on remainder on 1 duffels blanket		
and flintstones and lead		<u>" 5</u>
		30/-
on strouds f7 on 1 lb ~~gunpowder~~ lead		" 8/-
on strouds		<u>" 8/-</u>
		f 46/-
on 2 ells of gemp f2 on ½ sch Indian		
corn f2		" 4/-
on strouds f15- on 1 kan rum f4		" 19/-
on rum for 1 marten on 1 lb gunpowder and		
1 bar of lead 9		<u>" 18/</u>
		87/-
on ½ bread and flintstones		<u>" 1/10</u>
		f 88/10
on 1 shirt f13:- on 1 kan rum f3-		" 16/-
on 6 ells of gemp f6:- on 1 stroud		
blanket f38		" 44/
on 7½ ells of gemp f7:10 on 2 pᵗ rum f3:-		<u>" 10/10</u>
		f158/00
on 1 pᵗ rum f1:10		f 1/10
1729 august 8 I have coming to me at balancing		
the account		f 46/-

[110]
(427) --Credit-side--

[the account below, cr]
1728 for 2 martens
      for 1 elkskin   [upper right-hand corner
      for elkskins   ___ torn off]
                                   f120

1728 october 12 for 1 deer meat	f 12/-
for 14½ lb skins	" 101/10
	f113/10
for 2 elkskins	" 51/10

1729 january 18 from the other side[476]	f301/-
on 1 piece of strouds	" 8/-
on 1 lb gunpowder and 2 lb lead	" 9/-
on 2¼ [lb] lead f3:10 on 1 lb gunpowder	
by kisay[477]	" 10/10
on gunpowder f3 on 1 sch Indian corn f4	" 7/-
on 1 ell of strouds	" 16/-
	f351/10
on 1 bucket of cider	" 5/-
on 1 pᵗ rum f1-10 on 1 kan rum f3	" 4/10
on 1 kan cider f1:- on 1 bottle of rum	" 4/-
on 2 lb gunpowder and 1 bar of lead	" 10/-
on 1 kan rum f3:- f383	f383/-[478]
~~Cred[it] for 42 lb elkskins~~	~~f 51/10~~
1729 july 5 for 1 bear hide	f 12/-

[the account below, cr]
      for[479] 8½ days binding[480]   f 51/-
      for 2 small skins   " 7/-

      for 1 bear hide and 1 marten   " 20/-

for 10 days binding on the farm	" 66/-	
for cutting in the meadow	" 27/-	88
	f100/-[481]	20
for cutting in the meadow	" 7/-	68

~~his younger brother on 1½ ell of cotton~~ ~~f 9/-~~

[111]

(428) --Debit-side--

[the account below, cr=satisfied]

[upper left-hand	rokehan[,] gertie[482][']s man	
corner torn	remains at balancing the account	f 31/10
off]	remains indebted	" 8/
	strouds	" 11/-
his wife on 1 lb gunpowder on 1 knife		" 8/
she on 1½ ell of baize and 1 bottle of rum		" 12/
he on 1 bottles [sic] of rum		" 3/-
she on 2 kan rum on 2 mussen rum		" 7/-
she on 1 kan rum f3:-		" 3
he is indebted at balancing the account		f 22/
~~gertie at balancing the account~~		~~" 39/~~
he on 1 lb gunpowder f1:- on 2 ells		
	of cotton	" 19/
		f 80/-
~~he is indebted~~		~~f 41/~~
gertie on ½ ell of cotton		" 3/-
~~on 2 p' rum -- and pipes~~		~~" 3/10~~
gertie on 1 kan rum remainder on cotton		" 4-
on 2 jackknives		" 6/-
on 1 shirt for her		" 11/-
she on ½ gall cider		" 1/[10]
on 2 kan cider		" 2/- 43
on 1 kan cider f1:- on 1 kan cider		" 2/- 14

on 1 kan rum f3   " 3/-   29
                                                            f 29/

on 1 kan cider f1:10 on ½ lb gunpowder and
                        5 lb lead   " 6/
                                                            " 35/-

on remainder on flour f2   " 2/-
on remainder on rum f6:-   " 6/-

Lendart the savage[483]
indebted from older times[484]   f398/-
on 1 ell of strouds on 1 lb gunpowder   " 22/-
                                                            410/

1728 june 24 on 1 colored shirt f24 on 3 awls f1
                        on 1 knife f3   " 28/
on 7 ells of colored woolen f5:5 on 1 dufels
                        blanket f24   " 29/-
on 4 lb lead   " 6/-
                                                            473/-
on rum f1:-   " 1/-
                                                            f474/-

---

        waddie from the other side[485]   f374/
1729 on 2 ells of cotton f12 on 1 kan rum f3:-   " 15/
on 2 bars of lead f4:- on 1 dufels
                        blanket   f24   " 28/
on strouds f6:-   " 6/
                                                            f423/

on 2 lb gunpowder f12:- on 3 lb gunpowder
                        f18   " 30
                                                            f453/

[END OF TRANSLATION]

====================

Notes to the Annotated Translation

1. For this native man, see also the appendix: Esopus, "Mannonck." "[M]anonck," his wife, and two unnamed sons reappear together on pages [2] and [67]; these page numbers have been allocated in editing the account book. The activities on those accounts span the period between an undetermined month in 1717 and October 1726. In addition, "manonck" himself appears on [99], with an account dating from November 1726. His burial in January 1727 is mentioned on [83] and referred to on [101]. An unnamed son is active on the account of the Indian man "Kattener" on [5], in September 1724. Several of his sons are mentioned in the account book with their names: "Jacob" on [2] and [67]–[68]; "kattias" on [69]; and "mattiso" (also "matisso") on [67] through [69], [73], [83], and [107]–[108]. The latter's wife, "pitternel," appears with her own account on [108].

"[M]anonck" and his kin developed the highest recorded debt in this account book; the third largest in this account, of 566 guilders; and the largest, amounting to 586 guilders and 10 stivers (half a guilder). See the account on [67].

2. The Spanish "peso," consisting of eight "reales."

3. This total is incorrect; it should have been 232 guilders.

4. A *tromp*, in this context, can be a part of a horn, a gun barrel, or a Jew's harp. Considering the low price of the item, the latter is the most likely possibility.

5. The remainder of this line is empty.

6. Sentence ends abruptly; *hat* (had) would be expected here.

7. This debt is among the highest in the account book.

8. All accounts on this page relate to the account of "manonck" and his relatives on [1].

9. The tax assessment of Ulster County in January 1716–17 listed Jan van Kampen Sr. as living in Marbletown and Jr. as residing in Rochester. It is unclear which of the two is recorded in the account book; see UCTAL.

10. It is possible she reappears in an account of almost six years later on [73], as "debora[,] maggel[']s wife or wido[w]."

11. For a note on this individual and his relatives, see [1].

12. A son of "manonck." He reappears in the account of "manonck" and his relatives on [67]–[68]. It is uncertain if he is the same individual as "Jacob the savage" on [23],

"Jacob the big savage" on [43], or "Jacob the savage[,] gerti's husband at paponeck" who is described elsewhere as "jacob or nockkehan"; see [71] and [89].

13. *Opleggen*, of which *gelyt* may be derived, in commercial exchanges is "to raise" or "to lay onto/on top" (of a price for instance).

14. In this manuscript, the pages are not numbered, and the page number used in this reference cannot be checked. It is the only internal reference of this kind in the account book. But "manonck," his wife, and two sons reappear frequently in the pages of this account book.

15. This individual and many of his relatives occur frequently in the pages of this account book. For a profile of this Esopus leader, see the appendix: Esopus, "Hendrick Hekan." He has his own accounts on [55] and [91], and is active on other Indians' accounts on [61], [62], and [109]. Together, these activities cover the period between September 1724 and September 1728. His relatives who are listed with an account of their own are: his wife "sar," "Krwamo['s] daughter," on [13] and [91]; his son "wadde" (also "waddie") on [78] and [109] through [111]; his other son "magh," on [109]; and his "oldest son," on [77]–[78]. Other relatives are active on the account of several Indian customers. They include: his son "kryn" on [67]; an unnamed daughter on [77]; and, besides the unnamed son on this page, one or various additional unnamed son(s) on [55], [77], [78], [91], and [110] (twice). His relatives' accounts and appearances in accounts of others cover the period between April 1719 and August 1729.

Robert S. Grumet lists this prominent native man's occurrences in colonial records that span the period 1699–1758 in "The Minisink Settlements: Native American Identity and Society in the Munsee Heartland, 1650-1778," in *The People of the Minisink: Papers from the 1989 Delaware Water Gap Symposium*, ed. David G. Orr and Douglas V. Campana (Philadelphia, PA: National Park Service, 1991), 205. In one of these instances, in 1730, he was involved in a dispute about land boundaries around Mamakating. For an appearance of that locality in this account book, as "mamme kattin," see [83] and the note there.

It seems entirely likely that Hendrick Hekan was related to the Esopus Indian "Harman heakan" (and variations thereof), who was involved in land sales on the west side of the Hudson River in the 1670s–90s; see for 1674, TDRK, book 2:347–48 (two occurrences); for 1677, *NYCD*, 13:507; for 1679, TDRK, book 2:253–54; for 1682, TDRK, book 2:629–30 and 632–33; for 1683, TDRK, book 3:41–42, 43–44, 52–53; for 1684, TDRK, book 3:17 and NYBP, 5:82–84; for 1696, UCDB, CC:145. For the latter, see also UCDB, DD:89–91. We have a profile of this individual on file.

16. This name reappears on [7] as "Samtie," where it is used to identify his daughter, wife of "warangau." That account is dated one day after the one on this page.

17. His name also appears on [63] and [107], as "nanado" and "nanondo," in all cases to identify the same daughter. Together, the accounts cover the period between August 1717 and an unspecified month in 1727.

18. For other appearances of this woman, see the previous note. On [63], she is active on the account of "Jan Roos[,] domeni[']s son," who is also mentioned on the following page [4]. She is not the same person as two other women listed in the account book with this Dutch

given name; see their appearances on [57], [87], and [99]. The occurrence of a "Catrin" on [68] is more ambiguous.

19. Probably the Spanish "peso" or "piece of eight." Such coins consisted of eight "reales."

20. The nature of this transaction remains obscure, and no credit was recorded for the Indian woman. She did not pay a mink fur with a value of a *doller*, since a small mink would fetch only 1½ guilders and a larger mink 2 guilders; see [62] and [86]. A doller is taken to mean a Spanish piece of eight, which was usually valued at or around 12 guilders. This account book contains a transaction where 1 doller was worth 22 guilders, see [10].

21. He reappears as "Jan Roos[,] domeni[']s son" on [63] and "Jan Ros" on [70]. Entries on accounts on [69] and [70] describe his wife as the daughter of "abraham or kwakasagh." On [63], the Indian woman "Catrijn[,] nanado['s] daughter," who is also mentioned on the preceding page [3], is active on his account.

Other Indians who are listed with a full European name (usually in Dutch) in this account book are "Jan Palin," [16]; "Jan van gelder," on [22] and [29]; "Willam Krom," on [47]; "arent fynhout" on [71], [81], [89], and [103]–[104]; and possibly "antonij frinses" and "hans Jacob," both on [19].

22. He reappears in a later account from the same year on [13], as "nawoghquarry." See the appendix: Esopus, "Nawoghquarry."

23. For this native man, see the appendix: Esopus, "Kattener." He reappears in an undated account (later than September 1724) on [58], where he paid the debt of "pensogh's wife," and on [67], where "manonck" or one of his relatives bought strouds for him in April 1725. His burial is recorded on [73], where it was dated July 1726. In the present account, however, he appears to be trading in September of that year, and possibly also in April 1727. His "dead child" is mentioned in an account of an unnamed month in 1726; see [87].

24. A 4 was changed into 0.

25. For a note on "manonck" and his relatives, see [1].

26. The charges for this rum were not crossed out.

27. The date has been wiped away.

28. See the remark on [73].

29. See the remark on [73].

30. These credit transactions pertain to the account of "nanoghquarij" on the opposite page.

31. These credit transactions pertain to the account of "Kattener" on the opposite page.

32. See the appendix: Esopus, "Walengaghkin."

33. For an earlier appearance of this name, see [3]. It occurs in an account that is dated one day earlier than this one.

34. 1716 has been overwritten by 1717, or vice versa.

35. An Esopus leader, he does not reappear in the account book and neither does his wife. But their son (named "arronshagkie or ankerop's son") has an account on [105]–[106],

covering the period between May 1727 and July 1728. See the appendix: Esopus, "Ankerop II/Tackawahkin."

36. An Indian named "antony" also appears on [21] but it is not certain that he is the same individual, although this seems likely. It is unclear if this "antony" is identical to "antonij frinses" on [19].

37. Hester has no accounts of her own, but another son of hers appears as "Jores" and "Jors" on [21]–[22] and [55].

38. A 2 was changed into a 4.

39. A 5 was changed into a 9.

40. She also appears on [62], [72], and [87], and has an account on the latter as "blandien the savage woman." Together, the appearances cover the period between an unknown month in 1717 and October 1726. On [62], she is listed as the wife of "mocka[']s brother." She was connected to both "hendreck hekan" and "hendreck sawagonck."

41. This refers to *fries*, a coarse woolen fabric.

42. Probably the Spanish "peso" or "piece of eight." Such coins consisted of eight "reales."

43. The man named "hans" may be the same individual as "hans or kwatten" on [13] or "hans jacob" on [19]. But note that this entry can also be read as "pamberoch[,] quet hans's wife."

44. For this native man, see the appendix: Wappinger, "Kechkenond." For his own account, on which "his daughter" and "her husband" also traded, see [13]–[14]; "Keghkenond['s] daughter" with "her father" and "her husband" are also listed with a sizeable account on [35]. Together, the activities on these accounts cover the period between an unknown date in 1715 and August 1721.

45. Muskrat.

46. For an account of the same individual, listed as "nawoghquarry," see [5] and note 22 there.

47. "quakesas[,] karwamo['s] son" (noted elsewhere as "Kwakesas" and as "Abraham or Kwakasagh") and "his wife" are active on an account on [15]–[16]. See the appendix: Esopus, "Crawamogh."

48. She has an additional account on [91]. For a note on her, her husband, and their relatives, see [2]. Possibly she is also listed as "sar[,] the savage woman" on [80] and [103]. She is not the same woman as the "sar" who was described as "kisay['s] daughter" on [71] and [105].

49. For a note on "Keg(h)kenond," his daughter, and her husband (who are active on this account and the one on [35]), see [11].

50. A person identified as "the smith" also appears on [35] and [99]; see also note 324 on [77].

51. In cases where he lists specific quantities of "deer meat," such as "1" in this case, the trader does not usually describe the measuring unit of this type of product.

52. See the appendix: Esopus, "Sander/Nachnawachena." An Esopus sachem, this individual and his relatives appear frequently in the account book. "Sander," his brother "Lendert," and another unnamed "brother" are recorded as traveling to earn credit against their debts; see [18] (twice), [22], and [42].

"Sander" has accounts of his own on [17] and [41]; together, they span the period between November 1719 and an unspecified month in 1727. Besides her own account on this page, his mother is active on her son's account on [41]. His brother "Lendert" has accounts on [21]–[22] and [111]; together, they span the period between January 1719 and June 1728. "Willam," another brother, has an account on [41]. Other relatives of his are active on accounts of various native customers: "his brother's daughter" on [17], his "youngest brother" on [41], his "brother" and his wife on [42].

53. *Sayette* or *sajet*, a type of uncombed woolen.

54. See the appendix: Esopus, "Kwakasagh/Old Abraham." "quakesas" reappears on [67] and [91] as "kwakesas," and as "abraham or kwakasagh" on [69]. Together, the accounts on these pages cover the period between November 1719 and around September 1728. His wife is active on this account and pays off part of their debt on [16].

This individual is not the same as the other Indians with the name "Abraham" who appear in the account book. See note 75 on [19].

55. See note 47 with "Krwamo" on [13].

56. The amount of the total debt (67 guilders) disappears into the binding of the manuscript; it pertains to the preceding account.

57. For Indians with Dutch given and last names, see note 21 on [4]. For this individual, see the appendix: Esopus, "John Pauling."

58. See the appendix: Esopus, "Nanisinos."

59. See the appendix: Esopus, "Achpalawamin/(Old) Suwies" and "Tanksetackin/Young Suwies." "sawis[,] dorso['s] son" appears with an account on [25].

60. For the appearances of "Sander" and his relatives in this account book, see note 52 on [15].

61. See the appendix: Esopus, "Schawenackie." The meaning of the annotation "M:ˣ" that precedes his name remains unclear. His wife is active on this account, his unnamed son has a sizeable account on [19] and [45]–[46], and a son named "Joghem" has an account on [53]. Taken together, the activities on the accounts of "Sawenakies"/"sawanagki"/"sawangh"/ "sawanagh" and his relatives cover the period between December 1719 and March 1724.

62. This surname was also written as "Du Puis" or "De Pue." "Benjamin De Pue" married Elisabeth Schoonmaker on September 1719; both were living in Rochester; *BMK*, 536.

63. The exact nature of this transaction remains obscure, but it involved some type of written bill from the Indian to "moses du pri" that earned the customer a credit of 48 guilders. For a similar instance, see [60].

64. This surname was also written as "Du Puis" or "De Pue." In the tax assessment of Ulster County in January 1716-17, Moses Du Puis Sr. was recorded as living in Rochester.

He had the one-but-largest estate in town and acted as one of the fourteen assessors. The 1716–17 tax assessment and a list of freeholders in Ulster County in 1728 also list Moses Jr. as a resident of Rochester; it is unclear which of the two was recorded in the account book; see UCTAL and *DHNY*, 3:971.

65. Nawesinck at the Neversink River; it also appears on [22]; see also map 1.

66. An Indian called "Heerij" traded in Albany with Evert Wendell in July 1707. Wendell described him as a "Mahican who stays with Awanwaghquat's people." Information from Blair Rudes shows that, while Algonquian, the name "Heerij" cannot have been Mahican. Mahican names do not have an *r* or an *l* in them; *WAB*, 98, 112.

67. A reference to Minisink, a multiethnic native community at the Delaware River; see map 1. It also appears on [42] and [103].

68. A reference to [41], although none of the entries there shows transactions in 1722. The balance of 151 guilders, listed on [41], is arrived at by subtracting his payments from the debt on [17]. An amount of 10 stivers (0.50 guilder) was not transported to [41].

69. See the appendix: Esopus, "Lewahlauqua."

70. The son's wife appears in the credit account on the opposite page. It is unclear whether the "Sar" on this page is the same as Hendrick Hekan's wife; see note 10 on [2]. It is very likely that "Jurewen" himself appears as "Juren" in an account that he shared with his wife "hanna" on [35].

71. The bookkeeper made an error in describing the type of blanket; the price is consistent with that of a stroud blanket.

72. It is unclear whether this Indian man has a Dutch surname; for Indians with Dutch given and last names, see note 21 on [4].

73. "Wiljem Douwty" married Marya Doritea Beem in Kingston on December 10, 1715. At that time he was registered as having been born in England. No place of residence was stated; *BMK*, 530. In 1728 "William Doughty" was listed as a freeholder in Kingston; *DHNY*, 3:969.

74. Probably short for penneston. It has been counted as such in table 3 in the introduction.

75. An almost identical combination of names appears in an account on [81]. Together, the entries span the period between July 1721 and an unspecified month in 1725. The burial of an "Abraham" was recorded in November 1726; see [99]. "abraham['s] Youngest daughter" has an account on [57]; "her father" was still active on the account in May 1726. "Eijsack, abraham's son" is listed in January 1724 with an account on [63], on which "his mother" and "his wife[,] sawegonck hendreck['s] daughter" were also active. See also the appendix: Esopus, "Kwakasagh/Old Abraham" and "Metmahes/Young Abraham." For a note on another individual with the name "Abraham," see [15].

76. For a note on his father and other relatives, see [17].

77. For Indians with Dutch given and last names, see note 21 on [4].

78. This subtotal is either incorrect or the writer has taken into consideration a transaction that was recorded elsewhere in the account book.

79. For the appearances of "Sander" and his relatives in this account book, see note 52 on [15].

80. This is one of the few cases where pound sterling was used. For the other cases, see [22] (the same amount as here), [44], [48], [49] (the same amount as on [44]), [71], [77], [97] (twice), [107] (the same amount as here), and [109].

81. See the appendix: Esopus, "Norman." He also appears with an account on [31]–[32]. Together, these activities occurred between January 23, 1719, and July 21, 1729.

82. For another appearance of an Indian man named "antonij," see [9] and note 36 there.

83. The activities of "Jores," listed as "Jors" on [22] and in his account on [55]–[56], cover the period between November 1721 and December 1723. For a note on another son of "hester," see [9].

84. *Katlos* (elsewhere *catloes/katloes/katlos*): lynx and other closely related catlike predators, such as bobcat. Both the bobcat and the lynx ranged throughout colonial New York; see for instance Adriaen van der Donck, *A Description of New Netherland*, ed. Charles T. Gehring and William A. Starna, trans. Diederik Willam Goedhuys, foreword by Russell Shorto (Lincoln: Univ. of Nebraska Press, 2008), 160n78.

85. Nawesinck at the Neversink River; it also appears on [18]; see also map 1.

86. Although the total debt on the facing page is 111 guilders and 10 stivers (0.50 guilder), this is a reference to Lendert's account on [21].

87. The same transaction is listed on [21].

88. Such (sub)total is not on the previous page, nor can it be located anywhere else in the account book.

89. For this Wappinger Indian, see the appendix: Wappinger, "John van Gelder." His sister reappears with an account of her own on [29]–[30]. For Indians with Dutch given and last names, see note 21 on [4].

90. Although the sentence is not intelligible, it is a reference to [55], where the book-keeper transported "Jors's" balance.

91. "Pitt" and "pitter" are variations of the Dutch first names Piet and Pieter.

92. He also appears on [62]. Together, his appearances occur in the period between April 1722 and November 1724. It is uncertain if he is the same individual as "Jacob," a son of "manonck" on [2] and [67]–[68], "Jacob the big savage" on [43], or "Jacob the savage[,] gerti's husband at paponeck" on [71] who is described elsewhere as "jacob or nockkehan"; see [89].

93. A number has been changed into 60.

94. A number has been changed into 9.

95. The origins of this subtotal are unclear.

96. He reappears with his own account as "tatepagh" on [45]; his brother is active on that account as well. On [47], his son "Willam Krom" is listed. See the appendix: Esopus, "Tautapagh." "tatapagh" also appears in the description of his daughter "pitternel," wife of "kattias[,] manonck['s] son," on [70]. Her mother, presumably the same woman as in this instance, is active on that account.

Robert Grumet describes him as an "up-and-coming sachem named Tatapagh (fl. 1683–1715)," related to land acquisitions by New York Governor Dongan in 1685. Grumet adds that "Tatapagh" disappeared from the records after 1715; Robert S. Grumet, *The Munsee Indians: A History* (Norman: Univ. of Oklahoma Press, 2009). The account on [45] shows him trading actively in January 1721.

97. The Indian woman was supposed to trade the rum elsewhere, but the keeper of the account book applied the regular price for rum.

98. In the tax assessment of Ulster County in January 1716–17, "Nicolas De Meyer" was recorded as living in Kingston; see UCTAL. In 1728 he was listed as freeholder there; *DHNY*, 3:969.

99. See the appendix: Esopus, "Achpalawamin/(Old) Suwies," "Tanksetackin/Young Suwies," and "Doesto." An account of "sawis['s] son" appears on [15].

100. The meaning of this term remains obscure.

101. It is uncertain if he is the same individual as the Indian man listed on [27] as "nanset the deaf savage."

102. In the tax assessment of Ulster County in January 1716–17, "Joris Middagh" was recorded as living in Marbletown; see UCTAL. In 1728 "George Middagh" was listed as a freeholder there; *DHNY*, 3:970.

103. The author made a small error here; by removing the *f*, the sentence is clear and logical.

104. He also appears with the same name on the account of his other son, "tabarhekan," on [49], and on [43] as "marenghan." It is plausible that he is the same individual as "Marringgamahhan," and variations (fl. 1671–1739), connected to land sales along the southern and middle sections of the Hudson River and to disputes over land in and around the Minisink area. He and his wife were described as "frequent visitors to White settler's homes." See Grumet, "Minisink Settlements," 210.

105. He reappears as "barnat" on [43], where his father is listed as "marenghan." Combined, the accounts are dated between an undetermined month in 1720 and April 1722. The account on this page shows activities by his wife and "child"; "his daughter" is active on the account on [43]–[44].

106. Presumably *kent* (child) should have been written after "small."

107. This subtotal is incorrect.

108. Total from the previous account.

109. In this and the following entry, the blotted figures were repeated to the left of the tally.

110. Or cousin; the Dutch *nicht* makes no distinction between the two.

111. It is uncertain if he is the same individual as the Indian man listed on [25] as "the small deaf savage."

112. In seventeenth- and eighteenth-century Dutch, *in* (in) and *en* (and) were often used interchangeably; in this instance, *in* was intended.

113. Robert S. Grumet lists occurrences of (an) Indian(s) named "Taphow"—and many variations, some of which are similar to the one used in this account—in colonial records that span the period 1667–1720. On some occasions he was described as a sachem and "Commander in Chief of all Indians inhabiting northern New Jersey" or "the north part of the Jerseys"; "Minisink Settlements," 221–22. For a discussion of the roles of this individual, see Grumet, "Taphow: The Forgotten 'Sakemau and Commander in Chief of All Those Indians Inhabiting Northern New Jersey,'" *Bulletin of the Archaeological Society of New Jersey* 43 (1988): 23–28.

114. This appears to be a different individual than "Kattias" on [69], described as "manonck['s] son." He does not reappear in this account book; see appendix: Esopus, "Kattkies."

115. She appears with the same description in the account of her husband, "Jor[e]s[,] hester's son," on [22].

116. While this is the only account of this native customer, three of his brothers also developed an account of their own: "Jott," on [33]; "pitgas," also on [33]; and "watpotgau or pitter," on [37]. Only the latter extended his trading contacts beyond June 1721; he remained active until June 1732. The name "Tamnat" appears twice on [61] but it is crossed out in both instances.

117. This subtotal is incorrect, it ought to have been f246/10. Perhaps the difference can be explained by assuming that the transaction recorded in the last line of the account was incorporated in this tally.

118. Although the bookkeeper made an error (two bars of lead did not cost 10, but 4 guilders), he correctly calculated the following total.

119. Although the bookkeeper described the mother as *syn* (his), there are other cases in the account book where *syn* is clearly used in the sense of "them" or "their." See, for instance, the entry of October 15, 1728, in the account on [91] that was shared by "hendrik hekan," and his wife and son.

120. This credit line pertains to the account of "Jan van gelder[']s sister" on the opposite page.

121. Abraham Gaasbeek Chambers (1679–1759), as Thomas Chambers's stepson, inherited the lordship and manor of Foxhall; Cuyler Reynolds, ed., *Hudson-Mohawk Genealogical and Family Memoirs*, 4 vols. (New York: Lewis Historical Publishing Co., 1911), 1:207–10.

122. For a note on this individual, see [21].

123. A woolen cloth of a fine gloss.

124. It is unclear what type of fabric is listed here.

125. The entry is left incomplete. "Norman" may have escorted "meckeck," or the latter may have stayed or lived with "Norman."

126. In the tax assessment of Ulster County in January 1716–17, "Dirck Westbroek" was recorded as living in Rochester; see UCTAL. In 1728 "Dirik Westbrook" was listed as a freeholder there; *DHNY*, 3:971.

127. Note the other brother in the next account. For a note on the activities of "tamnat" and his relatives, see [29].

128. The author began writing *duffel*, apparently made an error and crossed it out.

129. For a note on "Keg(h)kenond," his daughter, and her husband (who are active on this account and the one on [13]–[14]), see [11].

130. For other appearances of "the smith," see [13] and [99]; see also note 324 on [77].

131. The name also appears in an account on [19], where it is used to identify his sister's son.

132. These credit transactions pertain to the account of "Juren and hanna" on the facing page. It may be assumed that either "hanna" or "her daughter" did the spinning.

133. For a note on the activities of "tamnat" and his relatives, see [29].

134. The 12 (guilders) was inserted just above the word *gemp*, to indicate the value of the one piece of gemp.

135. The 6 was changed into a 0, and was crossed out.

136. For this native leader, see the appendix: Wappinger, "Old Nimham/Sackoenemack."

137. An account in his own name appears on [49].

138. The remaining transactions on this page pertain to the debit account of "tabarhekan['s] wife['s] sister" on the opposite page.

139. A word is missing here. It could be *voor* (for), meaning that the remainder of the debt equals half a deer.

140. The 9 has been crossed out.

141. Already in the 1640s the Dutch Rev. Johannes Megapolensis reported that Mohawk Indians carried grease with them in this fashion, "Kort ontwerp van de Mahakuase Indianen in Nieuw-Nederlandt," in J. Hartgers, *Beschryvinge van Virginia, Nieuw-Nederlandt, Nieuw Engelandt en d'Eylanden Bermudes, Berbados en S. Christoffel* (Amsterdam: N.p., 1651), 46. His account is also published in Kees-Jan Waterman, Jaap Jacobs, and Charles Gehring, eds., *Indianenverhalen: De eerste beschrijvingen van Indianen langs de Hudsonrivier, 1609–1680* (Zutphen, the Netherlands: Walburg Pers, 2009), 101–11, see 107.

142. For the appearances of "Sander" and his relatives in this account book, see note 52 on [15].

143. The reference is to [18], where the balance of Sander's account came to 151 guilders and 10 stivers (0.50 guilder). The stivers were not transported here.

144. The original amount of 67 guilders has been changed into 00.

145. See the appendix: Esopus, "Willemachecane." For a note on the appearances of "Sander" and his relatives in this account book, see note 52 on [15].

146. The exact nature of this tool, probably used to hunt or prepare beaver, remains unknown.

147. Minisink; see note 67 on [18].

148. Apparently this was deducted from the debt.

149. For a virtually identical combination of these names, see [27] and notes 104 and 105 there.

150. Such (sub)total does not appear on the facing page, nor can it be located anywhere else in the account book.

151. Possibly Teunis Tappen of Kingston; see UCTAL. The appearance in the account book of Pitter (Pieter) Tappen from the same town on [95] supports this possibility. Teunis married there on October 10, 1695. He was registered as being born in Albany, his spouse was born in Kingston, and both were living in Kingston at the time of their marriage; BMK, 511.

152. Apparently the customer did not take the baize with him or her. The charge at the right side originally showed a figure, but this was changed into oo.

153. Presumably a piece of bleached fabric.

154. No amount was entered to the right.

155. For a note on an Indian man with the same given name and several others with similar names, see note 92 on [23].

156. Although the total differs by 10 stivers (0.50 guilder), this is a reference to the account on [43].

157. This is a slightly incorrect total; it should be 571 guilders. This is the second largest debt in the account book, the highest being 586 guilders and 10 stivers, on [67].

158. The entry reads *maltyt sleght*, where *maltyt* is "meal." For the translation of *sleght* as "plain," we are indebted to Charles Gehring and Jaap Jacobs.

159. For other appearances of this name, see [23] and note 96 there.

160. For a note on his father and other relatives, see [17]. An individual named "hofman" is also active on this Indian's account on [53].

161. The author erred in computing the total: he left out 10 stivers (half a guilder).

162. In the tax assessment of Ulster County in January 1716–17, "Nicolas Hofman" was recorded as living in Kingston; see UCTAL. In 1728 he was listed as a freeholder there; DHNY, 3:969. It is likely he also appears in the account on an Indian man on [53]; the trade there also involved an axe.

163. Although this entry occurs on a page with credit accounts, it seems unlikely that this was a payment by the Indian. Also, other credit pages show purchases by customers, and the explicit insertion of the word "Cre[dit]" in the next entry suggest a shift from debit to credit accounts.

164. This pertains to the last account on the debit side.

165. See also the appendix: Esopus, "Allamaaseeit"; compare Robert S. Grumet, "Minisink Settlements," 200, that lists occurrences of "Allamanseet" in colonial records that span the period 1745–61.

For Indians with Dutch given and last names, see note 21 on [4].

A settler with the same name, "Willem Crom," married Wyntje Roosa in Kingston on November 12, 1699. He was recorded as being from Marbletown, his spouse as being from Hurley; *BMK*, 515. He does not appear on the list of freeholders in Ulster County in 1728; *DHNY*, 3:969–71.

166. For other appearances of this name, see [23] and the note there.

167. On two occasions in the account book, the author wrote *som* (sum), where *son* (son) was obviously intended. The other instance is in the first account on [65].

168. It is unclear if he is the same person as one of the two Indians who were described as "abraham" in the account book; see the notes on [15] and [19].

169. The writer crossed out the number of *kannen* (quarts).

170. This may indicate that the Indian woman took out additional credit, with the same gun as security against the debt.

171. An awkward expression, but correct; the Indian bought half of a quarter of an ell of strouds. One ell sold for 20 guilders.

172. Although the price is somewhat different, this instance is probably identical to the one from the previous note.

173. The author used the symbol for the pound as a currency here, where the abbreviation for the pound weight was called for.

174. It is unclear how the author arrived at this total.

175. Although the bookkeeper used the symbol for pound sterling, there is no indication of any account showing this type of debt. Two hundred twelve pounds would have amounted to about 8,480 guilders.

176. The account of his "wife's sister" appears on [39].

177. See an earlier note on him, note 104 on [27].

178. This section pertains to the third account on the other side.

179. Either the amount of money or the weight of deerskin was entered incorrectly; a skin with that weight would have fetched around 14 guilders.

180. Possibly the Indian borrowed money to pay for repairs to his gun.

181. Probably "his wife" was intended.

182. For this native man, see the appendix: Wappinger, "Kaghqueront."

183. "Marytje Steenbergen" was a witness at a baptism in Kingston on October 18, 1696; *BMK*, 48.

184. This pertains to the second account on the facing page.

185. Considering that the balance to the trader on [51] was 112 guilders and 10 stivers, it is difficult to understand why the Indian had to pay two horses for that amount—especially since a large pig or swine could fetch an Indian 92 or 112 guilders (see [58] and [2]).

186. A reference to the remaining amount on the last account on [51].

187. For this Indian, see the appendix: Wappinger, "Pesewein."

188. An additional small account of this customer is listed below, on the same page.

189. For a note on his father and other relatives, see [17]. His account on [45] also records activities of an individual named "nicklas hofman."

190. The sentence ends in an awkward fashion; it disappears into the binding of the manuscript.

191. The meaning and function of the word *of* (or), possibly meant as *van* (of), remains unclear. It is possible that the bookkeeper began to write the name of the European man who was involved in the transaction (*of* for *h̲of*), realized his mistake, and continued to write the man's name correctly. A "nicklas hofman" is active on the account of an Indian man on [45]; also in that case, trade involved an axe.

192. This entry is repeated from the last account on [43].

193. This pertains to the account of "Joghem," across from this page.

194. He also has an account on [21]; see the note there.

195. For a note on this individual and his relatives, see [2].

196. This charge has been corrected in the original; it now reads "33/-."

197. In this context, *her* is not a known term in Dutch. Possibly the author intended *hey* (him), being "the son" or "hendreck hekan" himself. See also a few lines below.

198. This entry is identical to one that is eight lines above this one.

199. The next two entries pertain to the first account on the opposite page.

200. He provided the same service for the same person one month earlier; see [22].

201. Considering the date of this entry, this could be either Aris A. Steenbergen, who married Beertjen Swart in Kingston on March 11, 1721, or Abraham van Steenbergen, who married Catrina Ploeg in the same town on April 14, 1728. All spouses were registered as living in Kingston; *BMK*, 539, 554. In 1728 both men were listed as freeholders there; *DHNY*, 3:970.

No woman with this surname and a given name starting with an *A* has been located in published sources.

202. The remaining entries on this page pertain to the third account on the facing page, that of "hendreck hekan."

203. As the computation to the right indicates, the author arrived at the amount associated with this reference by taking the balance from [55] and subtracting the total of the debit transactions on this page, 80 guilders. An amount of 10 stivers (0.50 guilder) was not taken into account.

204. A small mistake; the total should have been f180/10.

205. For a note on this "abraham," see note 75 on [19].

206. Both of them, their son, and the woman's sister appear in an account on [63], where his name is given as "pansogh." Taken together, the accounts cover the period between September 1726 and an unknown date in 1727. A son of his, "mack," developed sizeable accounts between 1725 and 1729 on [79] and [99]. See also the appendix: Esopus, "Pansogh."

207. Both are listed in another account on [87]; "pony" has an additional personal account on [77]. He is also recorded fetching goods for "matisso[,] manonck['s] son" on

[107]. Together, these activities were developed between an undetermined date in 1724 and January 1729. See also the appendix: Esopus, "Arropony." For other appearances of Indian women named "Catrin," see the note on [3].

208. The total seems slightly incorrect; perhaps confusion arose from the crossed-out amount.

209. This prominent Esopus Indian developed a sizeable account on [101]; the burial of his child is recorded on [91]. His wife is active on this account; her brother is recorded as paying part of the debt on [58]. On [101], he purchased rum for "manonck's burial." Together, the activities on these accounts cover the period between September 1724 and July 1729. See also the appendix: Esopus, "Andries."

210. The description on [75] indicates that this brother-in-law of "andris" was "Tatteu." He also appears in an account on the next page.

211. For a note on this individual, see note 23 on [5]. Here, he paid off the debt of "pansogh" and "his wife."

212. Presumably for a gun.

213. Pertains to the account above the line.

214. A reference to the account on [57].

215. For this Indian man, see the appendix: Esopus, "Noundawagaeron." He is the same individual as "sundagh" on [77].

216. See the appendix: Esopus, "Quick."

217. Evidently the customer was expected to pay the debt in hops.

218. His debt is also mentioned in an account of "kosoes or kobes[,] hendreck sawagonck['s] son," on [85]. His daughters' accounts are directly below this one. "wiijekaswedie[,] kessa[']s daughter," on [75]–[76] appears to be unrelated to this man.

219. For notes on this woman and her husband, "arent fynhout," see notes 289 and 291 on [71].

220. An earlier amount has been changed into a 0; the account is crossed out.

221. "Theunis Middag" married Catrina Kortregt in Kingston on September 13, 1728. Both were registered as living in Rochester; *BMK*, 555. He does not appear in the list of freeholders in Ulster County in 1728; *DHNY*, 3:969–71.

222. For another occurrence of a "note" in an Indian's account, see [18].

223. In the tax assessment of Ulster County in January 1716–17, "Nicolas Roosa" was recorded as living in Hurley. He acted as one of the fourteen assessors; see UCTAL. He does not appear as such in the list of freeholders in Ulster County in 1728, but a man with the same name is listed in New Paltz; *DHNY*, 3:969–71.

224. He does not reappear in another account; his name is crossed out with two lines in the following account on this page. His wife is active on this account, she is recorded in the last account on [62] as the daughter of the "wife" of "the sawonossie," and is active on the account of "sawannos" on [93]. It is unclear why the name "weghtagkarin" appears immediately beneath that of "gasrit the savage"; it does not appear elsewhere in the account book.

225. For a note on "tamnat" and his brothers, see note 116 on [29].

226. For a note on this individual and his relatives, see note 15 on [2].

227. The origins of this subtotal remain obscure.

228. The meaning of this word remains obscure.

229. The amount appears to have been blotted; it is illegible and has not been entered into the tally to the right.

230. While this name (and many variations) appear often in the account book, we have not been able to construct a coherent profile from these occurrences. For a discussion of "(the) sawanoss(i)e," see the section "Descriptions and Identification of the Native Patrons" in the introduction. He fetches goods for "manonck," for "manonck's wife and son" on [67], for the oldest son of "hend[reck] hekan" on [77], for "hend[reck] hekan" on [91], and for "Jacob[,] gertie[']s husband" on [89]; hendrick hekan trades on his account on [62]. Also on [62], his "wife's daughter" is identified as "gasris['s] wife"; "his wife's son" is also active on this account. On two occasions he is identified as escorting the Indian man "towis"/"touwas" to the trader; see [62] and [93].

231. In this line, the words "for," "skin," and "weighs" have been crossed. No charge was recorded for this transaction.

232. The exact meaning of this verb remains unclear. Probably the axe was mounted on a handle and/or sharpened. The verb does not reappear in the account book.

233. A regular mink would fetch two guilders; see [86].

234. For a note on an Indian with the same name and several others with similar names, see note 92 on [23].

235. For a note on this woman, described here as the wife of "mocka[']s brother," see note 40 on [9].

236. For a note on this individual and his relatives, see note 15 on [2].

237. A double-digit number has been crossed out.

238. He appears as "touwas" on [93], where he is escorted by the same individual.

239. For a note on this individual, see note 230 on [61] and the reference to the introduction mentioned there.

240. For a note on this family, see note 206 on [57]. For the son, see the appendix: Esopus, "Mackeeus."

241. In this line, the words "his," "son," and "remainder" have been crossed out.

242. In this line, the words "by," "son," "on," and "a" have been crossed out.

243. The amount of baize is not specified, but it must have been 1½ ells.

244. "kesegton," more commonly known as Cochecton, was a multiethnic Munsee community located at the Upper Delaware River straddling the New York and Pennsylvania border; see map 1. It is also mentioned on [77], [79], and [97].

245. For a note on this "abraham," see note 75 on [19].

246. This daughter of "sawegonck hendreck" does not reappear recognizably in the account book. Another daughter of his appears in an account on [82] and has her own on

[96]; in the former, she is listed as the wife of "wappaneck[,] kisay's son" and described as "sawagoneck hend[rick's] daughter"; in the latter she is listed as the wife of "mattasson[,] wappeneck['s] son" and described as "hendr[ic]k sawangonck['s] daughter." For a note on this complication, see [96].

This father's name was listed as both "hendr[ic]k sawangonck" and "sawagoneck hend[rick]"—and variations thereof. He is active on the account of "andries the savage" on [101]; his unnamed wife has her own account on [93]; an unnamed son of theirs is mentioned on the credit page of that account, [94]. Two of his sons are listed on [71], "winhas" and "wenagsen." Another son, "kobes" (also listed as "kosoes or kobes") is considerably more active: he has accounts on [65] and [85]–[86]. An unnamed brother, also a son of sawagonck, is active on "Kobes" account on [65]. "kobes" wife "Cattrijn," "kesay's daughter," has her own account on [85] and is active on that of her husband on [65], as is her unnamed brother. The Indian woman "blandine" paid off part of the debt of sawagonck's son "winhas"; see [72]. Taken together, these interlinked appearances cover the period between January 1724 and August 1729.

247. In the tax assessment of Ulster County in January 1716–17, "Barent Newkerck" was recorded as living in Kingston; see UCTAL. He does not appear in the list of freeholders in Ulster County in 1728; *DHNY*, 3:969–71.

248. The account book contains no evidence that this Indian was related to a *dominee*, a Dutch Reformed minister. For a note on this native man, see note 21 on [4].

249. For the same combination of names, see [3] and notes 17 and 18 there.

250. This subtotal relates only to the three entries above it.

251. The keeper of the account book made an error; removing 1 *sch[epel]* ("1 sk[ipple]") makes the sentence comprehensible.

252. He has another account on [83]–[84]. Together, the activities on these accounts span the period between an unspecified month of 1724 and August 1727.

253. The type of colored textile was not specified.

254. On [84] she is listed with the name "maycke." Another of the daughters of the woman "kisay," "Cattrijn," was the wife of "kosoes or kobes[,] hendreck sawagonck['s] son." See the entries on [85]. For a note on "kisay" and her husband, "arent fynhout," see [71].

255. Illegible date.

256. Inadvertently, the writer used *som* (sum) here. The only other instance of this mistake is in the first account on [47].

257. "wappenack" appears as "wappenak" on [66], "wappaneck" on [81], and "wappeneck" on [95]; he is also active on [84], again on the account of his sister's husband. Together, his appearances cover the period between December 1724 and April 1728. For this Wappinger man, see the appendix: Wappinger, "Wappenack."

258. There are insufficient data to conlude that Kobes is the same man as the Indian called "Willemachecane Alias Cobis," who was listed among the native proprietors of lands in Ulster and Albany counties that were deeded on June 6, 1746, to Johannes Hardenberg,

Robert Livingston, and company; UCDB, EE:63; about eight weeks later, he was described as "Capt Kobis[,] Moonhaw['s] brother," among the "Native proprietors & heirs" conveying land in southern Ulster County to the same Europeans; UCDB, EE:63. Therefore, we have listed these men as separate individuals in the appendix: see Esopus, "Kobes," and "Willemachecane."

"Kobes" reappears in the account book as "kosoes or kobes" on [85], and as "kobes" on [86] and [100]. Together, the occurrences cover the period between June 1725 and August 1729.

259. For a note on "hendr[ic]k sawangonck" (also listed as "sawagoneck hend[rick]," and variations thereof) and his relatives, see note 246 on [63].

260. For a note on this woman and her husband, "arent fynhout," see notes 289 and 291 on [71].

261. It is not clear if this is "derck westbroek" who appears on [32], or another individual with the same surname.

262. For a note on this person, see note 257 on [65].

263. This pertains to the second account on the facing page.

264. In this line, the words "for" and "skin" have been crossed out.

265. For a note on this individual and his relatives, see note 1 on [1].

266. For a note on "hendrick hekan" and this son, see note 15 on [2].

267. For a note on this individual, see note 230 on [61] and the reference to the introduction mentioned there.

268. For a note on this individual, see note 23 on [5].

269. For a note on this individual, see note 12 on [2].

270. On [91] he also appears as "kwakesas"; on [15] as "quakesas" (see note 54 there), and on [69] as "abraham or kwakasagh."

271. This is the highest recorded debt in the account book, the second largest being 571 guilders on [44]. See also the account of "manonck" and his kin on [1], resulting in the third largest debt in the account book.

272. He also appears with accounts of his own and in those of others on [68]–[69], [73], [83], and [107]–[108]. Together, these activities span the period between August 1725 and October 1729. His wife "pitternel" appears with her own account on [108], covering the period between an undetermined month in 1728 and October 1729. See also the appendix: Esopus, "Mathesso." For a note on "manonck" and his relatives, see note 1 on [1].

273. His burial is also noted in accounts on [73] and [99].

274. For other appearances of Indian women named "Catrin," see note 18 on [3].

275. This "kattias" was a different individual than "Kattis" on [29], described as "tappose['s] son." He does not reappear in this account book. See the appendix: Esopus, "Kattias."

For a note on "manonck" and his relatives, see note 1 on [1].

276. For a note on this son of "manonck," see note 272 on [67].

277. He appears as "quakesas" on [15] (see note 54 there) and as "kwakesas" on [67] and [91].

278. This instance has not been incorporated into table 7 in the introduction.

279. The origins of this subtotal remain obscure.

280. On [107] and [108] another woman with the name "pitternel" is described as the wife of "matisso," another son of "manonck." For "tatapagh," see note 96 on [23].

281. The last two lines pertain to the second account on the facing page.

282. For a note on this native man, see note 21 on [4]. Apparently his wife was the daughter of "abraham or kwakasagh."

283. A brother of "Winhas" appears further down in the same account. For a note on "hendr[ic]k sawangonck" (also listed as "sawagoneck hend[rick]," and variations thereof) and his relatives, see note 246 on [63].

284. The 10 for stivers was blotted out in the original.

285. Either the bookkeeper erred or a different rate between the pound sterling and the guilder was applied here. In other cases, the rate was 40 guilders to the pound; here it is almost exactly 46 guilders and 3 stivers.

286. He is the same individual as "jacob or nockkehan" on [89]. Together, the accounts span the period between June 1726 and April 1727. For a note on an Indian with the same given name and several others with similar names, see note 92 on [23].

His wife "gerti" (also "gertie") also trades on the account on [89]. Indian women with this Dutch first name also appear in accounts on [85], [90], and [111]. The account in which "gertie" appears on [111] most likely pertains to another woman, as she is described there as the wife of "rokehan." Damage to page [111] makes it impossible to provide dates for that account.

287. Papaconck; see map 1, on the East Branch of the Delaware River. Alternatively, this could be a reference to the residence of "Paponnick," also known as "Arias Japis," an Esopus proprietor who sold lands near New Paltz, New York, on July 23, 1682; see Grumet, *Munsee Indians.*

288. She occurs in the account following this one, either as the "daughter" or the "youngest daughter" of "kisay." She also appears in an additional account of her mother, on [105]. For a note on women in the account book with this Dutch given name, see note 48 on [13].

289. "kisay" herself, her husband "arent fynhout," and their direct kin appear very frequently in the account book. She has an additional account that is put in her name, on [105]–[106], and she is active on the account of her husband on [103] and that of "Waddie[,] hendreck hekan[']s son" on [110]. She occurs with some frequency in the description of her direct relatives who came to trade: "her daughter" in this account; her daughter "sar" in the previous account; "Kobes[,] sawagonck hendreck['s] son," husband of "kisa[']s daughter" on [65]; her son "wappenack" on [81]; her daughter "Cattrijn" on [85]; her daughter "anna-tie" on [106]; and "wieijiekas[,] former husband of kisay['s] daughter" on [59]. Many of her

direct kin trade on her account, that of her husband, and those of others. In the present account, they are "her daughter," "her small daughter," and "her youngest son" and "her youngest daughter"; on [65], her daughter, wife of "Keman the savage[,] or watschap" (later listed with the name "maycke," see [84]); on [72], two of her unnamed daughters and "her daughter[,] winasenck['s] wife"; on [89], "arent fynhout's daughter" and "his children"; on [104], arent fynhout's "son"; on [105], her "young daughter"; and on [106], "her brother," "her daughter[,] wynnes'[s] wife," and "her young son." Taking into consideration also "wiei-jiekas," the "former husband" of one her daughters, and the account(s) of "moskono[,] or wiyiekas['s] daughter margriet" on [59], perhaps a different daughter than the "daughter" also mentioned there, can be added. These occurrences begin at an unspecified date in 1725 and continue until August 1729.

"sar the savage woman" fetched goods for her in 1726, and so did "jawis['s] (or jawi['s]) son" in 1729; see [103] and [105]. It is assumed that she is also listed as "kessa," to identify her daughter "wiijekaswedie" on [75].

290. Pertains to the preceding account.

291. The Indian "arent fynhout" also has accounts on [89] and [103]–[104] and he is active on accounts of other Indians on this page and [81]. For Indians with Dutch given and last names, see note 21 on [4]. Given the context in the accounts, it appears that he is the same man as the individual identified as "arent" on [81] and [89]. As with his wife, "kisay," the occurrences started at an unspecified date in 1725 and continued until August 1729. Together with his wife "kisay" (see note 289) and their kin, they formed one of the most active groups of related Indians in this account book.

A Dutchman, "Arent Fynhouedt," has a small debit account in the first section of this account book, dated August 1711; the bookkeeper had paid 37 guilders "For him" to a "Volunteer[,] who went on The Expedition"; see left side of the page marked 41 (assigned page number 44). Arent Fynhout was baptized in Kingston on June 18, 1671; BMK, 8. No freeholder with that surname was listed in a list of freeholders in Ulster County in 1728; DHNY, 3:969–71.

292. This account book shows that it was very common that natives' debts were outstanding for considerable periods of time; in this particular case, it can be determined that the native woman (or her husband) had already developed the debt ten years earlier.

293. For a note on this woman, see note 40 on [9].

294. This entry pertains to the second account on the facing page.

295. All words and figures in the preceding part of this line were crossed out individually.

296. These last lines pertain to the third account on the facing page.

297. The origins of this total remain obscure; perhaps the small computations at the right extremity of the page are related to it.

298. For an earlier appearance of "debora," see [2].

299. For a note on this son of "manonck," see note 272 on [67].

300. His burial is also recorded on [67] and [99], but dated September 1725. It is conceivable that "abra[ha]m" suddenly died in 1725 while visiting Ulster County, and the instance from this account marks either a ceremony to remove the body for a reburial closer to a Munsee settlement or a "feast of the dead" at the grave; Herbert C. Kraft, *The Lenape-Delaware Indian Heritage: 10,000 BC to AD 2000* (Stanhope, NJ: Lenape Books, 2001), 345–46, 349.

301. The date supplied here for the burial of "kattener," around July 18, 1726, is confusing. On [5] the bookkeeper recorded in Kattener's account the burial of an unspecified person on July 22, 1726, and the burial of this Indian's daughter on September 10 of that year is listed on [87]. Entries on [5] indicate that "Kattener" himself continued to trade after July 1726.

302. "arrons" also appears in an account on [84]; there, he is not described as having "lame arms."

303. Pertains to the preceding account.

304. This transaction did not result in an additional debt.

305. This pertains to the second account on the facing page.

306. This pertains to the third account on the facing page.

307. Alternate spelling of "kisay"/"kisaij."

308. The writer had initially written a capital *C* to start the name, but also wrote a capital *T*. Comparison with the credit side, [76], and page [101] shows that the customer's name was "tatteu"/"tateu"/"tatweu," brother of the wife of the Indian "Andris." See also the appendix: Esopus, "Tateuw," and Marc B. Fried, *Shawangunk Place-Names: Indian, Dutch and English Geographical Names of the Shawangunk Mountain Region. Their Origin, Interpretation and Historical Evolution* (Gardiner, NY: Marc B. Fried, 2005), 46. On [57] he is described as the brother of Andris's wife, a description repeated on [58]. Also, on [101] he appears in an account with evident connections to "andris the savage." Together, his activities cover the period between September 1724 and March 1728. His wife and an unnamed child appear on the next page.

309. "Old" could refer to her age, or it could express her widowhood, as the burial of "abram" is listed earlier. Lacking any date with the present small account, the latter possibility cannot be ascertained.

310. Pertains to the preceding account.

311. This section, and the one above it, pertain to the first account on the facing page.

312. This section pertains to the second account on the facing page.

313. See note 308 with "tatteu," on [75].

314. A few entries in the remainder of the account indicate that the bookkeeper and some Indians later did indeed stay at a mine. A mine is not mentioned in any of the other accounts.

315. He was listed as "Neckarind" on a land deed selling, together with "Tateew" ("tatteu," on whose account he trades here), a tract of land near Napanoch, New York, on June 15, 1728. The deed also entitled the settlers to the use of a mine. See also the appendix: Wappinger, "Nackarend," and Fried, *Shawangunk Place-Names*, 46.

316. The writer rounded off the number with a slight mistake; the total ought to have been 180 guilders and 5 stivers (one-quarter of a guilder).

317. This refers to the subtotal of transactions earlier on this page, starting with the transaction on "march 9[, 1727]" and including the exchanges in the following three lines from "1727/8."

318. For a note on this man and his wife, see note 207 on [57].

319. The same individual as "runup" on [59].

320. He does not appear anywhere else in the account book; his wife is active on the account on the next page. "kasegton," more commonly known as Cochecton, was a multi-ethnic Munsee community located at the Upper Delaware River straddling the New York and Pennsylvania border; see map 1. It is also mentioned on [63], [79], and [97].

321. The Dutch reads *schulp* (most immediate translation: shell). The word can refer to a number of items. Considering the price level of this particular item, a very likely translation is "gorget."

This *schulp* is a different type than the one that appears three times in the *WAB*. There, the purchase of a *schulp* left native customers with a debt of three martens or one beaver; see 107, 115, and 197. In those instances, the word has been translated as "shell(s)."

322. A 22 was changed into 24.

323. This entry and the next one have no related charges in the tally to the right.

324. This may well be the name of "the smith" (*de smet*) who is mentioned on pages [13], [35], and [99].

325. It seems most likely that the "his" refers to hendreck hekan's "oldest son" in the following account.

326. For a note on "hendrick hekan" and his relatives, see note 15 on [2].

327. Probably the Spanish "peso" or "piece of eight." Such coins consisted of eight "reales."

328. For a note on this individual, see note 230 on [61] and the reference to the introduction mentioned there.

329. The amount of 32 guilders has been crossed out.

330. For a note on "hendrick hekan" and this son, see note 15 on [2]. He trades on his father's account on [91] and on his own accounts on [109]–[111].

331. A reference to Cochecton, a multiethnic Munsee community located at the Upper Delaware River straddling the New York and Pennsylvania border; see map 1. It is also mentioned on [63], [77], and [97].

332. The header of this account is crossed out, but either "perraris" himself or his brother ran this account. "perraris" is listed with his own account on [97] as "parraris" and is described as being from "kasegton" [Cochecton; see the previous note]. The debtor's wife is active on this account, and both she and his daughter are listed in the account on [97]. His wife's "accounts" are mentioned on [98]. Together, these activities cover the period between October 1725 and May 1729.

333. For a note on "pansogh" and his son, see [57]. This "mack" continued to develop a sizeable account on [99]. There, his wife "Catryn" is listed with her own account. Together, these accounts cover the period between an unspecified date in 1725 and August 1729. See also the appendix: Esopus, "Pansogh."

334. This subtotal pertains to the preceding account.

335. The entries on the remainder of the page pertain to the second account on the facing page.

336. A reference to the account on [79].

337. She occurs in the account of "arent fynhout the savage" and his wife on [103]. For a note on women in the account book with this Dutch given name, see [13].

338. The charge appears to have been for the beer and one additional guilder.

339. For a note on this Wappinger man, see [65].

340. For a note on this woman and her husband, "arent fynhout," see notes 289 and 291 on [71].

341. See also [67].

342. The same individual as the Indian man named "arent fynhout"; see note 291 on [71].

343. The subtotal is blotted and illegible.

344. From this point on, all entries pertain to the second account on the facing page.

345. For a note on "hendr[ic]k sawangonck" (also listed as "sawagoneck hend[rick]," and variations thereof) and his relatives, see note 246 on [63].

346. Apparently the woman could first obtain a larger quantity of rum at a lower price.

347. For a note on this individual, see note 252 on [65].

348. This entry is repeated from the account of "Keman or watschap" on [65], also dating from 1725.

349. For the identity of his wife, see [65] and [84].

350. That is, "kisay."

351. "arent fynhout."

352. The name pertains to the next account, suggesting that this is what the son of "kampo" was called. The account holder's wife trades on the account on [84].

353. See also note 15. For the location of the native settlement Mamakatin, see map 1.

354. The amount in guilders is heavily blotted.

355. For a note on this son of "manonck," see note 272 on [67].

356. For a note on this individual and his relatives, see note 1 on [1].

357. On the occasion of manonck's burial, this Indian bought either just rum (see this entry) or the list of goods in this part of the account. The rum or set of goods may have been intended as grave gifts. Most of the listed items have not been found in excavated native burial sites in the Northeast, but their presence is suggested by the surviving artifacts in such graves. Some of the rum, for instance, could have been placed in the grave in a "spirit

bottle," and buttons of the shirt would have also survived the elements; see Kraft, *Lenape-Delaware Indian Heritage*, 343, 347, 380–81, 390–97.

358. He has an account on [73]. There he is described as "with the lame arms."

359. Considering the entry on [65], this was most likely "wappenack."

360. On [65] he is listed with his own account, which is headed "Kobes[,] sawagonck hendreck['s] son." The name "kobes" also appears in accounts on [86] and [100].

361. For a note on "hendr[ic]k sawangonck" (also listed as "sawagoneck hend[rick]," and variations thereof) and his relatives, see [63].

362. Most likely a shortened way of writing *eysersterck*; see the glossary.

363. "Tobyas Hoornbeek" married Elizabeth Pietersz Louw in Kingston on February 16, 1729. Both were registered as living in Rochester, where Tobyas was also born; *BMK*, 556. "Tobias Hornebeek" is listed as a freeholder in Rochester in 1728; *DHNY*, 3:971.

364. "kosoes or kobes" had "kesay['s] daughter Cattrijn" as his wife (see the next account); "wiijakas" appears on [59] as the "former husband of kisay[']s daughter." See also note 218 on [59].

365. Another of the daughters of the woman "kesay," "maycke," was the wife of "Keman the savage or watschap." See the entries on [65] and [83]–[84]. For a note on "kisay" and her husband, "arent fynhout," see note 291 on [71].

366. For a note on Indian women with this Dutch first name, see note 286 on [71].

367. Nine guilders were subtracted from the total debt on this transaction.

368. A reference to the total toward the end in the first account on [85].

369. To arrive at a subtotal of 115 guilders, the author had to exclude the debt from the preceding entry.

370. The name "kobes" also appears in accounts on [65], [85], and [100]; see especially note 258 on [65].

371. Apparently the author erred in computing this subtotal; 130 guilders would have been expected.

372. From here on, the entries refer to the second account on the facing page.

373. Apparently the author erred in computing this subtotal; 88 guilders would have been expected.

374. For a note on this woman, see note 40 on [9].

375. For a note on this man and his wife, see note 207 on [57].

376. A word is missing; presumably "wife" was intended.

377. For notes on this individual, see note 23 on [5] and note 301 on [73].

378. The quantity of grease was not specified.

379. No charge was entered for this transaction.

380. Like the first entries, these two lines also pertain to the first account on the facing page.

381. To arrive at this figure, the author had to ignore the payment of 9 guilders.

382. A figure has been changed into a 0.

383. The author erred in writing the entry.

384. For a note on this individual, see [71].

385. This pertains to the preceding account.

386. An incorrect subtotal; 73 guilders would have been the correct amount.

387. Possibly this is a person's name.

388. He is the same individual as "Jacob the savage[,] gerti's husband at paponeck" on [71]. For a note on an Indian with the same Dutch given name and several others with similar names, see note 92 on [23].

389. This total pertains to the preceding account.

390. Elsewhere in this account book, the name is given as "kisay," "kisaij," "kesay," and "kisa" (and presumably "kessa"). For notes on this woman and her husband, "arent fynhout," see notes 289 and 291 on [71].

391. For a note on this Indian woman and others with this Dutch first name, see note 286 on [71].

392. For a note on this individual, see note 230 on [61] and the reference to the introduction mentioned there.

393. The same individual as the Indian man named "arent fynhout"; see note 291 on [71].

394. Whereas the entry gives a price of 12 guilders for the rum, it is listed here as 10 guilders.

395. A 7 has been changed into a 0.

396. These entries pertain to the second account on the facing page.

397. All entries on this page are part of one account.

398. For a note on this individual and his relatives, see note 15 on [2].

399. For a note on this individual, see note 230 on [61] and the reference to the introduction mentioned there. He reappears in this account, a few entries below this one.

400. For a note on "hendrick hekan" and this son, see note 15 on [2]. He has additional accounts on [78] and [109]–[111].

401. "Mary Paling" was married to Thomas Van Keuren in Kingston, on April 11, 1730. Their places of residence were not specified but they were described as "both of Ulster Co"; BMK, 559. In 1728, no Van Keuren with that first name appeared on the list of freeholders in Ulster County; DHNY, 3:969–71.

402. For a note on this "sar," see note 48 on [13]. For notes on her, her husband, and other relatives, see [2].

403. He appears on [15] as "quakesas," see note 54 there, on [67] as "kwakesas" and on [69] as "abraham or kwakasagh."

404. Correct; see [91].

405. The total charge for this transaction is 9 guilders. Since one bar of lead would cost only 2 or 3 guilders, the remainder reflects a charge for "borrowing" the peltry.

406. For a note on "hendr[ic]k sawangonck" (also listed as "sawagoneck hend[rick]," and variations thereof) and his relatives, see note 246 on [63].

407. For a note on this individual, and the reference to the introduction mentioned there, see note 230 on [61]. He reappears three lines below this entry and in an entry at the bottom of the page.

408. For the additional element in this woman's identification, see note 239 on [62].

409. This is either a mistake for 36 guilders, or the author involved other elements in this calculation.

410. He appears on [62], as "towis." Also in that instance he was escorted, by the same Indian man.

411. He also appears on [103] as "mattison" and on [105] as "matteson." In both cases he fetches goods for others. Together, his activities cover the period between an undetermined month in 1726 (in or before November) and April or a later undetermined month in 1728.

He is a different individual than "mattiso"/"matisso," a son of "mannonck."

412. For a note on this Wappinger man, see note 257 on [65].

413. A mistake for _karten_ (cards).

414. This is either a mistake for 71 guilders, or the author involved other elements in this calculation.

415. In the tax assessment of Ulster County in January 1716–17, "Pietter Tappen" was recorded as living in Kingston; see UCTAL. He appears as "Peter Tappen" in a list of freeholders in that locality in 1728; *DHNY*, 3:969. For an Esopus man "Allameetahat" (and variations) with similar aliases, Peter Tap (and variations), active in land dealings and diplomacy between 1746 and 1772, see: 1746, UCDB, EE:63–65; 1751, Deed Mss., Senate House State Historic Site, Kingston, New York; 1764, *PWJ*, 11:62, 66–67; 1767, UCDB, GG:8–9, and Affidavit, Martin Van Bergen, Mss., 6812, NYSL; 1772, GTM-PC, box P26, folder 14. In the 1772 document, he is identified as the son and nephew of Nawoghquarry and Schawenackie, respectively, Esopus men clearly noted in the Ulster County trader's accounts. For the latter two men, also see the appendix: Esopus. We have a full profile of "Allameetahat" available.

416. All entries on this page pertain to the one debit account on the facing page.

417. The accounts on [81]–[82] identify a daughter of "hend[rick] sawagoneck" as the wife of "wappaneck[,] kisay['s] son." It seems more than likely that the woman who appears here as "his wife" and "hend[rec]k sawagonck['s] daughter" is the wife of "wappeneck"; not the wife of "mattasson."

For a note on "hendr[ic]k sawangonck" (also listed as "sawagoneck hend[rick]," and variations thereof) and his relatives, see note 246 on [63].

418. A reference to Cochecton, was a multiethnic Munsee community located at the Upper Delaware River straddling the New York and Pennsylvania border; see map 1. It is also mentioned on [63], [77] and [79].

419. The nature of this transaction remains unclear. It can not be established if "salomon" is a colonist or a native customer.

420. This total pertains to the preceding account.

421. For a note on this individual and the locality, see note 332 on [79].

422. If the customer were charged for the full amount here, fourteen guilders would have been the expected amount.

423. A main distinction was made in two types of peltry: freshly trapped, cleaned, and prepared furs were referred to as parchment beaver (French, *castor sec*), whereas hides that had been used and worn by Indian suppliers were known as coat beaver (French, *castor gras*). The latter were of considerably higher value. See Ann M. Carlos and Frank D. Lewis, "Property Rights and Competition in the Depletion of the Beaver: Native Americans and the Hudson's Bay Company, 1700–1763," in *The Other Side of the Frontier: Economic Explorations into Native American History*, ed. Linda Barrington (Boulder, CO: Westview Press, 1999), 134, 144, 147n3.

424. The meaning of this term remains obscure.

425. In the tax assessment of Ulster County in January 1716–17, "Pieter Louw" was recorded as living in Rochester; see UCTAL. He appears as "Peter Low" in a list of freeholders in that locality in 1728; *DHNY*, 3:971.

426. This name was used for various types of rats living in and near water, such as the American muskrat.

427. This is the largest payment recorded in the account book.

428. No amount of her debt was given.

429. For a note on this individual and his relatives, see note 1 on [1].

430. The burial of "abra[ha]m" had occurred in September 1725; see [67] and [73].

431. For notes on "pansogh" and his son "mack," see note 206 on [57] and note 333 on [79].

432. Originally "10/-" was entered here.

433. A person identified as "the smith" also appears on [13] and [35]; see also note 324 on [77].

434. This entry records the purchase of a raccoon by a native customer.

435. Based on this description, it may be assumed that this "Catryn" was the wife of "mack.". For other appearances of Indian women named "Catrin," see note 18 on [3].

436. From here on, the entries pertain to the second account on the facing page.

437. The name "kobes" also appears in accounts on [65], [85], and [86]; see especially note 258 on [65].

438. From here on, the entries pertain to the third account on the facing page.

439. The burial of "manonck"; see the next account and on [83].

440. For a note on this Indian man, see note 209 on [57].

441. For a note on this individual and his relatives, see note 1 on [1].

442. The burial occurred in January 1727; see [83].

443. For a note on "hendr[ic]k sawangonck" (also listed as "sawagoneck hend[rick]," and variations thereof) and his relatives, see note 246 on [63].

444. For a note on this individual, also pointing to a clear connection with "Andris," see note 308 on [75].

445. The entries pertain to the second account on the facing page.

446. A reference to Minisink, a multiethnic native community at the Delaware River; see map 1. It also appears on [18] and [42].

447. For a note on this individual, see note 291 on [71].

448. She also occurs in an account on [80]; see also note 337 there.

449. Originally, the amount entered was f 119/10.

450. For a note on this individual, see note 411 on [95]. He also appears a few entries below this one.

451. The following debit and credit account pertain to the account of "arent fynhout" on the facing page.

452. In the tax assessment of Ulster County in January 1716–17, Johannis Vernoy was recorded as living in Rochester. He acted as one of the fourteen assessors; see UCTAL. He appears with the same name in a list of freeholders in that locality in 1728; *DHNY*, 3:971. In June 1712, "Paijemham the Indian," an Esopus sachem, complained to the Ulster County justices that "Capᵗ Johannis Vernooy" owed him some duffels and that the latter refused to pay his debt; see Scott and Baker, "Renewals of Governor Nicolls' Treaty of 1665 with the Esopus Indians at Kingston, N.Y." *New-York Historical Society Quarterly* 37 (1953): 261.

An Indian man named "Pecghakagharin/Pceghakaharin Alias Hans Vernoy" was among the native proprietors of lands in Ulster and Albany counties that were deeded on June 6, 1746, to Johannes Hardenberg, Robert Livingston, and company; see UCDB, EE:63–65. In Dutch, Hans was and is a common diminutive of Johannes.

453. For *an* (on).

454. He is listed as "arons hagkie" on the credit page. See the note at the account of his parents, on [7]. See also the appendix: Esopus, "Aroensack."

455. The total amount for this transaction has been entered incorrectly.

456. Pertains to the previous account. The writer made a slight error in writing this total.

457. For notes on this woman and her husband, "arent fynhout," see notes 289 and 291 on [71].

458. She also appears in her mother's accounts on [71]; see also note 288 there. For a note on Indian women who appear in the account book with this Dutch given name, see note 48 on [13].

459. The trader erred in writing this entry.

460. Note that this description can also be read as "by jawi['s] son."

461. For a note on this individual, see note 411 on [95].

462. The trader erred in writing this entry.

463. All entries below relate to the account of "kisay" on the facing page.

464. Note that this description can also be read as "wynnes['s] wife."

465. An amount that was entered originally has been changed to 00.

466. For a note on this son of "manonck," see note 265 on [67].

467. Apart from this word, the line is empty.

468. Probably a mistake for *martervel* (marten skin).

469. For the same combination of names, see [3] and the note there.

470. For a note on her husband "matisso," a son of "manonck," see note 272 on [67]. See [70] for another woman with the same Dutch first name.

471. For a possibly meaning of this activity, see the introduction, "Trading Practices" section.

472. For a note on "hendrick hekan" and this son, see note 15 on [2]. He has additional accounts on [78] and [110]–[111].

473. For a note on this individual and his relatives, see note 15 on [2].

474. Such total does not appear on the facing page and the only other account with a total of 414 guilders is not related to this one; see [22].

475. For a note on "hendrick hekan" and his relatives, see note 15 on [2].

476. No similar (sub)total in terms of debt can be found on the surrounding pages. The subtotal for *credit* transactions on the second account on [108] is unrelated to this account of "waddie" and/or his father, "hendreck hekan."

477. For notes on this woman and her husband, "arent fynhout," see notes 289 and 291 on [71].

478. This subtotal is incorrect; the transactions resulted in a debt of 378 guilders.

479. The remaining entries on this page pertain to the second account on the facing page.

480. Binding sheaves.

481. This subtotal is incorrect; it is crossed out.

482. For a note on Indian women with this Dutch first name, see [71].

483. For the appearances of "Sander," the brother of "Lendert," and their relatives in this account book, see note 52 on [15].

484. There is no correlation with the only other extant account of an individual with this name, on [21].

485. This reference remains obscure, as the accounts of "waddie" on [109] and [110] show no relevant (sub)total. It is possible that this refers to an account on a subsequent page that is no longer part of the manuscript.

Appendix

Bibliography

Index

Natives' Profiles

Note to the Appendix

THE LIST OF INDIVIDUAL profiles that follows identifies Esopus and Wappinger Indians appearing in the Ulster County account book and other records spanning the years from 1682 to 1785 in total. The profiles, compiled from land deeds, court minutes, and other sources, many appearing in print here for the first time, provide a glimpse into the lives of individual Munsee Indians in the mid–Hudson River Valley.

The years in which individuals are active in records is indicated by the abbreviation fl., for file length. Some native people were additionally noted in documents after their deaths; these years are indicated by the abbreviation pm., for postmortem references. Careful attention has been made to include all spelling variations found to date that are believed to be associated with a particular individual. These differing orthographic conventions, representative of the highly fluid and variable spellings found in colonial records, also occur in both Dutch and English names, but are particularly evident in the recording of Indian names whose sounds were unfamiliar to the European ear but were nonetheless written down in a European-style script. Multiple orthographic conventions found within the same document are also included. These multiple spellings are found most frequently in land deeds. The first orthography listed in a given entry represents the variant next to which that individual placed their mark or signature, generally at the end of the document. Other named orthographies that follow represent spelling variants found in the deed text. Cross-indexing the different spelling of names found in records allows for attribution to specific individuals over time. References to page numbers in the translation of trade accounts with named Indians in the current book are enclosed in brackets.

Esopus Cohort

List of Main Names, Dates, and Page numbers in Appendix:

Kattkies (fl. 1682–1722)

June 23, 1682: Katkis

Listed among "Esoopus" Indian grantors appearing before the Kingston Court who declare to have sold to William Fisher and Jacob Rutgers land along the Rondout Creek extending from "Koxsinck . . . till the Boundaries of the Nieuwe Pals [Patent]" (TDRK, book 2:629–30).

June 24, 1682: Katkis

One of the "Esoopus Savages" appearing before the Kingston Court and declaring they had sold the tract named "Mogowaersinck" to Henry Beekman Sr., extending from the lands of William Fisher and Everdt Pel "till the limits of the Pals [New Paltz Patent]" (TDRK, book 2:632–33).

April 18, 1683: Katakis

Listed among the Indian grantors conveying land to Jacob Rutgersen "situated at Kahakamis . . . under the condition that Jacob Rutgerson remit all the debt which Harmon Hekan owes" to him (TDRK, book 3:43–44).

September 10, 1684: Kattkies

One of the Esopus "Indian Natives and Inferious owners," conveying land to English Governor Thomas Dongan from the New Paltz tract to the "Murders Kill" Creek on the Hudson River (NYBP, 5:82–84).

April 15, 1685: Katskoes/Katchkoes

One of the "Indian Proprietors" conveying land to English Governor Thomas Dongan from the "Dancing Chamber . . . Southward alongst said [Hudson] River to the South side of the Highlands and the North side of the Land Called Heaverstraw" (NYBP, 5:108–11).

April 10, 1702: Kattakis

"kattakis and [ ]apennou wife of Mettanwaen [and] several other Indians of Said Esopus" appear before Ulster County justices Jacob Aertsen and Jan Heerman, "and Declare Nimim" under whom Martys De Mott had land at "Shawonkonck" surveyed, "was a stranger and no Esopus [Indian]" (New York Colonial Manuscripts–Governor's Council Papers, Secretary of State, 45:92— document badly burned, but indicates that Mettanwaen was also not an Esopus Indian).

February 24, 1703: Kattees

One of the "native Indyans of Esopus in ye County of Ulster" receiving an additional payment of 1,000 guilders from Jacob Rutgersen, for land he purchased earlier on September 8, 1699, "Called by ye name Sakenisinck or Toquapogh and [originally] patented by John Knight" on the Rondout Creek in the present town of Wawarsing (UCDB, AA:336).

April 1, 1703: Catties

One of the "Indian Proptiotors" conveying lands in Ulster County to Henry Beekman Sr., for 150 pounds, called "Wasschawassinck Eghho[nck] [Magtig-kenigkonk, Saminawawwagkink, Ragawaak] Schowarawasehonck . . . Matagh-konck Mahwaghke [and] Tapoensis" and incorporated on June 25, 1703, as part of the Rochester Patent (Deed ms., Kingston Papers, CV 10181 TA, New York State Archives, Albany. See NYCM-LP, 4:169, for spellings of Indian place-names in brackets; see also CFLP, box 9, folder 17, item 116, for a 1772 copy of an undated map (see map 3) depicting Indian flats or meadowlands along the upper Rondout Creek lying north of Honk falls called Wasawasink, Eghouck, Mattogheuigkeak, Tawaiwewawaghnik, Ragawaack, and Schowarawasekonk, and other meadows along the tributaries of the Mombaccas and Mattaconks kills, called Mattag-houck, Maheuaghe, and Tepoeuanilg).

August 18, 1705: Hiesjern or Kathees

A member of the "Kitsepraw" (Kettsypowy or Kettsapray) family or kin group confirming the location of "a Certaine place . . . Called negpogkaw" on the Neversinck River in a land sale made to Henry Beekman Sr., in the Rochester Patent (UCDB, AA:352).

March 28, 1721, to July 20, 1722: Kattis

"tappose[']s son[,] Kattis" develops a small account with the anonymous Dutch trader active in Ulster County from 1712 to 1732. Purchases totaling 58 guilders recorded of "[various] goods and rum for which his trap is a security" ([29]).

Tautapagh (fl. 1683–1727)

September 20, 1683: Tatapagus

An Indian witness to the proposal made by "Kagakapou alias Jochem" to sell "his land back of Siawaenkonck, the land named Getatauwhackky but all subject to the Heer governors approval. and also the land named Aquapachwach and Pakanesinck" (TDRK, book 3:240).

May 25, 1688: Tatapaw

One of three "Esopus Indian" grantors conveying land to John Knight at Wawarsink along the "Roundout Creek or Kill Lying on ye west or South west of Jacob Ruchsion Land [and] ye Est or nore Est of Ann Beneke So great as it lay as from mountain to mountain Called by ye Indian Name[s] Sakenishing

[and] quapohunge" and that "ye Indians must plant half of ye Land [for] 6 years" (UCDB, AA:74).

February 24, 1703: Tatepagh

One of the "native Indyans of Esopus in ye County of Ulster" receiving an additional payment of 1,000 guilders from Jacob Rutgersen, for land he purchased earlier on September 8, 1699, "Called by ye name Sakenisinck or Toquapogh and [originally] patented by John Knight" on the Rondout Creek in the present town of Wawarsing (UCDB, AA:336).

April 1, 1703: Tatapay/Tatepay

A participant listed among the "Indian Proptiotors" conveying land associated with the Rochester Patent to Henry Beekman Sr. for 150 pounds currency (Deed mss., Kingston Papers, CV 10181 TA, NYSA).

August 18, 1705: Tatapagh

One of the "Indyan proprietors in ye County of Ulster" conveying to Henry Beekman Sr. "all ye Certaine tract of land Situate Lying & being in ye bounds of Rochester [Patent] . . . on both sides of a Certaine Creeke or River . . . Called by ye Indyans nawesinck [Neversink] beginning by a Certaine place Called honck [falls] and so Runs to a Certaine place belonging to ye Kitsepraw Indians . . . Called negpogkaw" (UCDB, AA:352).

1719 to 1725: Tatapagh

"tatapagh['s] wife" develops a small account with the Ulster County trader. She takes "4 kan rum" with her to sell in the trader's name. She receives a credit of 16 guilders against her debt "for 4 days cutting twigs" ([23–24]).

January 1, 1721: Tatepagh

Tatepagh is listed with a small debt by the trader; purchases are recorded of 2 shirts (1 fine), rum, and "his brother [on] a comb" ([45]).

1721 to February 1, 1728: Tatepagh

"Willam Krom[,] tatepagh['s] so[n]" develops an ongoing account with the trader; "his wife" is also active on the account. The trader reports that lead and gunpowder were fetched for him "by y[our] H[onor's] mother." Other purchases are recorded of strouds, baize, 2 duffel blankets, 2 coarse blankets, gunpowder, lead, flintstones, rum, 1 knife, and 4 awls. Payments of 1 elk skin, 6 lbs beaver, and "11 skins not dressed," and credit "for 1 sch[epel] grits and ½ sch[epel] small beans" are noted to reduce the debt ([47–48]).

March 14, 1725 to July 27, 1727: Tatapagh

"tatapagh['s] daughter[,] pitternel" is noted by the trader as an active client on the account of her husband "kattias[,] manonck[']s son." She purchases a colored shirt, 1 coarse blanket, stockings, "a pair of dutch shoes," and rum; she receives "Cred[it] for 1 day of harvesting flax" at 16 guilders and "she remains indebted [at] 40 guild[ers]" on the account ([69–70]).

July 25, 1727: Tautapagh/Tatapagh

Colonel Jacob Rutgersen conveys 120 acres of land to Manuel Gonsalis Jr. that he purchased earlier, in 1713, from "Tautapagh, a medicine man" (i.e., shaman) near Mamakating lying 100 chains west of "the Indian Tatapagh's wigwam" (*Olde Ulster*, 3:175–76).

Crawamogh (fl. 1685–1722)

March 13, 1685: Creawamugh/Creawamucgh

One of four "Esopus Indians and owners of ye Klyn Esopus vly" in Ulster County conveying "the Said Fly or meadow" to Thomas Chambers and Henry Beekman Sr. of Kingston (UCDB, AA:33).

August 13, 1685: Crawman

"Weskennard Indian Sachem [and] Crawman his brother" are listed with the Indian grantors conveying land to Fredrick Phillipse "running along Hudsons River to a Certaine Creeke or River called Kichtawan [Croton River] and called by the Indians Sinksink" in Westchester County (NYBP, 5:90–93).

June 8, 1686: Krewemuch

One of three "Esopus Indians" conveying to Gerrit Artsen, Arien Rosa, and Jan Elton "a certain parcell of land lying upon the east shore [of the Hudsons River] right over against the mouth of the Redout [Rondout] creek, bounded between a small creek [Landsman's Kill] and the [Hudson] river," in the present town of Rhinebeck, Dutchess County (UCDB, AA:42).

April 21, 1688: Crawam

One of four Indian grantors selling land to Thomas Bundell and Michael De Mott along the Esopus Creek in Ulster County (UCDB, CC:205).

August 13, 1702: Cramatacht

One of eight grantors, "native Indians and Proprietors of sundry Tracts of land in Dutchess County," confirming the boundaries of Adolph Philipse's Upper or Highland Patent extending to the Connecticut border (PGP, P14, #56).

February 24, 1703: Crawamo

One of the "native Indyans of Esopus in ye County of Ulster" receiving an additional payment of 1,000 guilders from Jacob Rutgersen, for land he purchased earlier on September 8, 1699, "Called by ye name Sakenisinck or Toquapogh and [originally] patented by John Knight" on the Rondout Creek in the present town of Wawarsing (UCDB, AA:336).

March 27, 1703: Cramawa

One of seven "Indyan proprietors" conveying to Col. Henry Beekman Sr. of Kingston "all that tract or parcell of Land Seituate Lying and being in Dutchess County Betwist the Land of Coll. Peter Schuyler and ye Land of Henry pawling" incorporated earlier as the Rhinebeck Patent in 1697 (Deed mss., Livingston Papers, CO280, box 158, folder 4E., Firestone Library, Princeton, NJ).

March 20, 1711: Crawamogh

One of the "Sachimes of the Native Esopus Indians" renewing peace before Ulster County justices at Kingston and reporting that a message was sent by the Minisinks to the sachem young Ancrop "In order to warne them that the Shetterrayres [or Tutelo] Indians Intend with the french to come and destroy them" (UCCS, 1706–12, mss.).

June 2, 1712: Crawamogh

One of the "Sachimes of the Esopus Indians," renewing peace with Ulster County justices at Kingston and reporting a request made by the "Shawonnos [Shawnees]" to settle among them as "Subjects under Ancrop" (UCCS, 1712–20, mss.).

April 17, 1719: Krwamo

"Krwamo['s] daughter sar[,] hendreck hekan's wife" develops an account with the Ulster County trader; purchases are recorded of lead, gunpowder, penneston cloth, and 1 stroud blanket. Payment of a bear hide and 1 fisher, and credit "for [the] remainder on a skin" are noted ([13–14]).

November 2, 1719, to March 24, 1722: Karwamo

"quakesas[,] karwamo['s] son" (reported elsewhere as "Kwakesas," and as "Abraham or Kwakasagh"; [67], [69–70], [91]) and "his wife" are noted with an account by the trader; "he" escorts an unnamed Indian woman. Purchases are recorded of strouds, blue textiles, a duffel blanket, beads, a hat, gunpowder, lead, molasses, and rum. Payment of a pig and "Cred[it] by his wife for beavers" are listed toward their debt ([15–16]).

Doesto (fl. 1696–1722/pm. 1785)

April 2, 1696: Dostou

"The Second day of April 1696: then appeared Dostou & Maretnim two Indyan Woman [*sic*] — Owners of a Certaine tract of Land to the south of the

Rondout kill in the County of Ulster and Doe Declare before Coll: Henriuis Beeck-man, Major Jacob Rutse & Leftennt: Jacob Aartse Justices of ye peace y^t: For and In consideration of a Certaine Summe of Monny to Corpowaan Late Deceased, Brother of the s^d: Dostou & Maretnim in hand payd by Nicolas Anthony Late of Kingstowne in Said County Deceased, hath sold a Certaine tract of Land Lying & being in y^e: County of Albany and now in y^e: possession of Jacob Lookerman of Albany afores^d: And in Lieu of said Land being y^e: s^d: Jacob Loockerman hath y^e: first grant for s^d: Land, they the s^d: Dostou and Maretnim have given y^t: afores^d: Tract of Land Scituate Lying & being to y^e: South of the Rondout kill or Creeke unto y^e: Children of Said Nicolas Anthony, And pray his Excell: the Captn generall to Confirm the Same unto s^d: Children" (NYCM-LP, 2B:226).

April 19, 1700: Dostou

"Dostou, Amoseren and Nenechonoas Natives of the County of Ulster for and in consideration of a certain [unspecified] sum of money" convey to "Engeltia Gasherie wife of Stephanus Gasherie Esqr. [High Sheriff of Ulster and Dutchess counties, 1699–1700] . . . a Certaine tract or parcel of vacant Land scituated lying & being in the County afores^d., on the South Side [of] the Roundout kill or kreeke beginning by a small Run of water to the West of the Land of Kochsinck called by the Indian name Wiggawappog & from thence alongst said Roundout kill to a small run of Water Called by the Indian name Warramininck & so alongst said run of Water to another small Runn unto the Woods that Waters out at Kochsinck and opposite to the land of angeneta keyser and Peter Lambertsen and as also a Certaine Fall named mentioned called & nominated by the Indians & their nomi-nation [as] Sanchatisinck being adjacent unto said Land from a certaine marked tree there unto annexed." Incorporated as part of the Marbletown Patent in 1703 (NYCM-LP, 2B:276).

March 5, 1715: Doesto

"Doesto an Esopus Indian woman & one of the Sachimests of the said Indi-ans in the County of Ulster & awarawat & Ochperawim her two sons & Asuc-twichtogh her Daughter Lawfull owners of several Tracts of Land Lying in the County of Ulster" endorse a deed to Stephanus Gacherie for a "tract of Land situ-ate Lying & being in the bounds & Limits of the Township of Marbletown in the County aforesaid On the South side of the Rondout Creek or Kill Beginning by said Rondout Creeke opposite to the mouth of a Certain small Creek that waters out in said Rondout at the northeast end of the Clearland of mr. Moses Dupuis Called the Kegseryck from thence Runing Southeasterly to a Certain fall on Cock-sinck Creek or kill by the mouth of a small Run of Water thence Runing along said

Cocksinck Creek including all the turnings & windings of the same to the bounds of the Township of Rochester then along the same to the said Rondout Creek then along the same including all the turnings and windings there of [to] the first Station" (UCDB, BB:380–81).

May 2, 1715: Dorso

"Sawis[,] dorso['s] son" is noted with an account by the Ulster County trader; he is reported as having a "debt from older times." Purchases are recorded of strouds, baize, "flinnen," 1 stroud blanket, gunpowder, lead, shot, wine, and rum. Payments of 3 bear hides and 6 raccoons, and "Cred[it] by his mother" are listed to reduce the debt; "Jores meddagh" (Marbletown justice, 1713–18) is noted as paying an elk skin on his account ([25–26]).

August 18, 1722: Doostoo

Ulster County justices renewing peace with Ankerop and other "Sopus Indians" note, "The pretence of Doostoo concering land at Coxsing is refferred till the next meeting and also the land lying between the bounds of Frederick Hossie & Company and the little Esopus Creek" (GTM-PC, box P26, folder 14).

1785: Dosto

Identified in a memorandum relating to the Hardenberg Patents western boundary as "Dosto an old squa the Daughter [of] Ameltas & mother of Nisinas who was the father [of] John Pauling. Sappan was the son [of] Pawaqhkaqua who was a Daughter [of] Dosto. Dosto informed both Sappan & John Pawling that the Mohawks had given to her & her Children all the Land to [the West Branch of] Delaware River to the Sopus Indians. They always hunted there [and] lived on the West side of the pawpackton [or the East Branch of the Delaware] River and had their Hunting Houses on the Westermost Branch called Slaugecqhta: and [that the] Five Nations never lived on any of those Lands. Cocok [or Cook House] is a place on that Branch called so from the Hooting of owls" (CFLP, box 6, folder 6, #94).

Arropony (fl. 1700–1729)

June 3, 1700: Arropony

One of four Indian signers conveying land in Ulster County to William Titsoord [Tietsort] "at Maugaukemeck commonly called by the name of Schackhaeckeninck" (UCDB, AA:229–30).

September 1, 1724, to March 8, 1725: Pooni/Ponij

"pooni[,] Catrin['s] husband" and "his wife" develop an account with the Ulster County trader. Purchases are recorded of white baize, a coarse blanket, 1 colored shirt, gunpowder, lead, flintstones, and rum; a charge of 13 guilders, 10 stivers, is noted "for repairing 1 [flint]lock." Payments in dressed skins, bear hide, beaver, and raccoon are listed; he earned credit on his account by doing fieldwork during "his days on the farm" ([57–58]).

October? 1724: Pony

The trader notes that "pony" made partial payment "at balancing the account remains indebted" at 60 guilders; he receives 8 guilders "Cred[it] for remainder on deer meat." The trader also lists the incurred debt of 12 guilders on October 10 for "4 kan rum [he] fetched for sundagh" ([77]).

July 13, 1725, to January 16, 1729: Pony

Pony and "his wife Catrin" are noted with an ongoing account by the trader. Purchases are recorded of strouds, baize, 1 stroud blanket, 2 duffel blankets, 2 knives, gunpowder, lead, rum, and "1½ ell of cotton for Kettene[r's] dead child" (1726). Payments of 2 bear hides, 3 raccoons, 20 martens, 1 skin, a pig, and grease are listed to reduce the debt. He receives credit toward his debt "for 5 days on the farm" ([87–88]).

1727: Ponij

"ponij" appears on the account of "matisso[,] manonck['s] son"; he fetched "6 kan rum" and probably a colored shirt on the latter's account ([107]).

Nanisinos (fl. 1700–1734/pm. 1785)

April 19, 1700: Nenechonoas

"Dostou, Amoseren and Nenechonoas Natives of the County of Ulster" convey land to Engletje Gacherie lying "West of the Land of Kochsinck" and incorporated later as part of the Marbletown Patent in 1703 (NYCM-LP, 2B:276).

July 31, 1706: Nisinos/Nesinos

"Nesinos one of the Chiefest sachems" grants to Jacob Rutsen for 200 pounds currency a right of purchase to lands lying "northwest (nearest) of the Township of Marbletown Called or known by the Indian names of Moghogwagsinck, Kawiensinck, Pahataghkan, Menaghanonck being a great Island, Matagherack, Oghkananteponck & Passigkawanonck, which said Land tracts & parcels of Land Lye upon the fish kill or [Delaware] River that Runs towards Menesinck" (UCDB, AA:400).

March 22, 1707: Nanisinos

"Nanisinos an Esopian native Indian one of the sachems Rightful Lord owner and proprietor" conveys to Johannis Hardenbergh for 60 pounds currency "all that tract of Land Lying and being in the County of Ulster aforesaid Running from

Certain hills (that Lye on the Southeast Syde of the Meadow or Cow land that Lyes on the fish Creek River or kill to the northwest of Marbletown bounds and are the north west parts of the hills and Mountains that Range from the blew hills [Catskill Mountains]) North west ten miles & stretches northeasterly on the brows of said hills as they Range to the bounds of the County of Albany and southeasterly on the brows of said hills as they range to opposite the west Corner of Marbletown bounds and still further southwesterly with the full breadth from the northeast boundaries of Rochester . . . southeast . . . to a Certain fall in the Rondout Creek Called by the Indians hoonckh which is the northwest bound of the Land Called Nepenach." Incorporated as the Hardenbergh Patent in 1708 (NYCM-LP, 4:92).

March 5, 1715: Awarawat

One of two sons of the Esopus woman and Indian "Sachimests" Doesto, conveying land to Stephanus Gacherie on the Rondout and Cocksinck creeks in Marbletown (UCDB, BB:380–81).

May 13, 1725: Nenison

The Indian man "Jan palin[,] nenison[']s son" is noted with a small debt by the Ulster County trader; credit purchase is recorded "On 1 girdle . . . [and] his brother on 1 knife" ([15]).

October 10, 1732: Nenesine

One of four native witnesses to a land sale of 15,000 acres made by "River Indians [and] Native Proprietors" to Daniel Kettlehuysen and company for 130 pounds New York currency "Lying and being in the County of Albany on the East Side of Hudsons River near and about a Certain Tract of Land Called Ho[o]sick" (NYCM-LP, 11:49B).

August 7, 1734: Nesie

Listed among the "Native Indians" selling 4,000 acres of land to Daniel Denton bordering the Hardenbergh Patent in Albany County lying "on the West Side of Hudsons River and on [the] West Side of the Bluw Hills of [the] Catts kill [Mountains] Bounded along Each Side of Chawtickignank krick [present Batavia Kill] to the Schowherres krick and then along on each side of the aforesaid Schowherres krick to the nearest falls to Schowharres for & in Consideration of the sum of forty four pound Eight Shillings" (NYCM-LP, 11:104).

August 7, 1734: Nesie

Listed among the "Native Indians" selling 2,000 acres of land to Michael Dunning bordering the Hardenbergh Patent in Albany County lying "On the West Side of Hudsons River and on ye West Side of the Bluw Hills of [the] Cats Kill[s] Bounded along Each Side of Chawtickagnack Krick to the Schowherres

Krick and then along on Each Side of the Afore Said Schowherres Krick to the nearest fall to Schowherre for & in Consideration of the sum of forty four Pound Eight Shillings" (NYCM-LP, 11:105, see also 11:120, for survey notes describing this and the above-mentioned land purchase).

August 1734: Nesie

Mentioned in a petition by "the Sachems or Chiefs of the Schoharie Mohawk" to the governor of New York as one of seven "River Indians" who they claimed had sold 6,000 acres of land near their lower "Castle" on the Schoharie Creek reserved to them for their "own use in Hunting & Raising Corn." The Mohawk sachems further declared that "the River Indians are Thieves and will steal any bodys Land they can. That if your Petitioners Cannot Enjoy their own Lands and have the Disposal of them themselves They Shall be Obliged to do themselves Justice upon the River Indians to prevent their stealing their Lands from them for the Future" (NYCM-LP, 11:106).

1785: Nisinas

Noted in Chancellor Robert Livingston's legal argument supporting Hardenbergh Patent proprietors against the claims made by heirs of Colonel John Bradstreet as "Nisinas an Indian Sachem in Ulster County" who had originally sold the lands to Johannis Hardenbergh in 1706 (NYCM-LP, 41:13, see page 24).

1785: Nisinas

Identified in a memorandum relating to the Hardenbergh Patent's western boundary as "the father [of] John Pauling" and the son of "Dosto an old squa the Daughter [of] Ameltas" (CFLP, box 6, folder 6, #94).

Quick (fl. 1703–1725)

February 24, 1703: Quick

One of the "native Indyans of Esopus in ye County of Ulster," receiving an additional payment of 1,000 guilders from Jacob Rutgersen, for land he purchased earlier on September 8, 1699, "Called by ye name Sakenisinck or Toquapogh and [originally] patented by John Knight" on the Rondout Creek in the present town of Wawarsing (UCDB, AA:336).

November 14, 1724, to August 13, 1725: Queck

"runup[,] the husband of queck['s] daughter" and "his wife" develop an account with the Ulster County trader. Purchases are recorded of cotton, strouds, "1 box of [paint]," and rum. They receive credit of 20 guilders "for hops" against the "remainder on one coarse blanket." Payment of "1½ lb dressed skins" is also listed to reduce the debt ([59–60]).

Kwakasagh/Old Abraham (fl. 1703–1725/pm. 1727–1751)

April 1, 1703: Ruwekeseg/Ruwakasegh

A participant listed among the "Indian Proptiotors" conveying land associated with the Rochester Patent to Henry Beekman Sr. for 150 pounds currency (Deed mss., Kingston Papers, CV 10181 TA, NYSA).

August 18, 1705: Ruwagkaseg alias Abram

The principal signer and "Metmahes Sunn of y[e] afores[d] Abram" are listed among the "Indyan proprietors in ye County of Ulster" conveying to Henry Beekman Sr. "all ye Certaine tract of land Situate Lying & being in ye bounds of Rochester [Patent] . . . on both sides of a Certaine Creeke or River [that] Runs towards Waggackemek [or Menissing Patent] in s[d] County Called by ye Indyans nawesinck [present Neversinck River] beginning by a Certaine place Called honck [falls] and so Runs to a Certaine place belonging to ye Kitsepraw Indians (to Witt) Hiesjern or Kathees etc. Called negpogkaw Including all ye Low Land on both sides of sd [Neversinck] Creeke or River, as also a Certaine Island Lying in sd River Called memahenonck" (UCDB, AA:352).

November 2, 1719, to March 24, 1722: Quakesas (Kwakesas)

"quakesas[,] karwamo['s] son" (reported elsewhere as "Kwakesas"; [67], [91]) and "his wife" are noted with an account by the Ulster County trader; he escorts an unnamed Indian woman. Purchases are recorded of strouds, blue textiles, a duffel blanket, beads, a hat, gunpowder, lead, molasses, and rum. Payment of a pig and "Cred[it] by his wife for beavers" are listed toward their debt ([15–16]).

July 8, 1721, to April 15, 1722: Abraham

"Young Abraham[,] Abraham's son" develops a small account with the trader. Purchases are made of 1 dozen buttons, gunpowder, lead, and rum totaling 14 guilders. He pays off the debt with "1 elk skin," also valued at 14 guilders ([19–20]).

March 23, 1722: Abramhan

"abramhans['s] daughter menckesonghua" is noted with a small account by the trader, listed with an "old debt" at 20 guilders. She leaves a gun and a wampum belt "as security" for new transactions on strouds and rum ([47]).

April 28, 1725: Abraham or Kwakasagh

The trader reports that Abraham or Kwakasagh made new purchases of a shirt, 1 knife, 1 coarse blanket, gunpowder, lead, and rum. Payment of 1 otter and 1 marten is listed; "his daughter[,] Jan Ros[a's] wife" pays part of his debt ([69–70]).

1725: Abraham

The trader reports that "Abraham son of Abraham" was indebted for 16 guilders "on remainder on a 1 [*sic*] coarse blankets" ([81]).

May 15, 1725: Kwakesas

The trader reports that the wife of the Indian man "manonck" bought "2 ells of cotton for kwakesas['s] son" ([67]).

September 28, 1725: Abram

"abram['s] burial" is reported by the trader in the accounts of Manonck and his relatives ([67], [73]).

1727?: Abraham

"abraham's old wife" develops a small debt with the trader; purchase is recorded "on 1 dufels blanket" at 28 guilders ([75]).

1728: Kwakesas

The trader reports that "Sar[,] Hendreck hekan[']s wife" ("Krwamo['s] daughter"; [13]) was indebted for 33 guilders "on kwakesas['s] account[,] her part" ([91]).

October 10, 1751: Old Abram

A map by Jacob Hoornbeek depicting the lands of Henry Beekman Sr., based on "His Indian purchase and Deed" (in 1705), notes the location of the "place called By the Indians Nawesinck" on the southwest boundary line of the Rochester Patent or otherwise the "Low Land att Neawesinks Between the [cre]ek and the Hills" and also "the Island By the appel tree where ould [*sic*] abram the Indian Did formerly live on" (Wilson Family Papers, Map Division, William L. Clements Library, University of Michigan).

Norman (fl. 1703–1729)

April 1, 1703: Noorma/Noorman/Noormah

One of the "Indian Proptiotors" conveying land associated with the Rochester Patent to Henry Beekman Sr. for 150 pounds currency (Deed mss., Kingston Papers, CV 10181 TA, NYSA).

January 23, 1719: Norman de Wielt

Norman is noted with an account by the Ulster County trader. He is indebted for 6 guilders "on [the] remainder on a coarse blanket [fetched] by antony" ("hester's son"; [9]) and also 33 guilders "on his son's account"; purchases "Anew" are recorded of "1 kan rum" and various lengths of strouds, linen, and ribbon, totaling a debt of 107 guilders. Credit of 72 guilders is recorded "for 1 skin" and "8 lb beaver" toward his account, and he remains indebted at 35 guilders ([21–22]).

June 4, 1721, to May 25, 1722: Norman

The trader lists the payment of 35 guilders "at balancing the account" and records additional purchases of textiles, lead, and rum. Payment in bear hides, raccoon, and "5 lb beaver" is noted. The Indian "meckeck" (May 30, 1721) buys cotton and lead on the account ([31–32]).

July 20–21, 1729: Norman

The trader records payment "at balancing the account" and additional purchases of 2 stroud blankets, lead, and rum; "derck westbroek" (of Rochester) is noted as paying part of his debt ([31–32]).

Pansogh (fl. 1703–1751/pm. 1785)

April 1, 1703: Pensog/Pensegh

A participant listed among the "Indian Proptiotors" conveying land associated with the Rochester Patent to Henry Beekman Sr. for 150 pounds currency (Deed mss., Kingston Papers, CV 10181 TA, NYSA).

August 18, 1705: Pensogh

One of the "Indyan proprietors in ye County of Ulster" conveying to Henry Beekman Sr. "all ye Certaine tract of land Situate Lying & being in ye bounds of Rochester [Patent] . . . on both sides of a Certaine Creeke or River . . . Called by ye Indyans nawesinck [Neversink] beginning by a Certaine place Called honck [falls] and so Runs to a Certaine place belonging to ye Kitsepraw Indians . . . Called negpogkaw" (UCDB, AA:352).

December 16, 1721: Natasough

One of five Indians (Anckeroop, Werangagh, Quagquepan, . . . and Manhawee) testifying before Poughkeepsie Justice Barent Van Kleeck of Dutchess County that "Such Indians In thare Life time Named Viz Aracogh and Guttecgtenonck and Rackawoounck did a bout one or two and Twenty Years agoo Sell unto Late Mr Robert Sanders, for himself and others a Certain tract of Land in Ulster county beginning at a fall in the river called the wall kill or Palls Creek" (*BSDC*, book 1:47–48).

August 18, 1722: Reconsough

Listed among the "Sopus Indians" renewing peace with Ulster County justices at Kingston and complaining about settler encroachment on lands near Chechunck, Coxsing, Mammekotton, and the Little Esopus Creek (GTM-PC, box P26, folder 14).

September 1, 1724: Pensogh

"pensogh's wife" is noted by the Ulster County trader with a debt of 30 guilders "on 12 kan rum and 1 small cask"; the debt is "paid by Kattener" ([57–58]).

December 27, 1724, to 1727: Pansogh

"pansogh's wife and son" and he are listed with an account by the trader; "her [his wife's] sister" is noted as being from "kesegton" [Cochecton] and buys "duffels and colored textiles" on their account. Purchases are recorded of cotton, white and blue baize, stockings, gunpowder, lead, rum, and knives. Payments of a bear hide, beaver, marten, and "1 leg and 1 piece of rump meat," and credit "for harvesting flax" are noted to reduce the debt. His son also has a credit of 21 guilders "on his bill," which the trader "paid with 1 colored shirt" ([63–64]).

1725 to 1729: Pansogh

"mack[,] pansogh['s] son" develops a sizeable account with the trader; the Indian woman "sar the savage woman" fetches gunpowder for him. Other purchases are recorded of cotton, strouds, colored textiles, 1 coarse blanket, 1 duffel blanket, a colored shirt, gunpowder, lead, a knife, and rum. Payments in deerskin, beaver, 10 raccoons, and 1 bear hide are listed. He performs fieldwork on two occasions for eight and seven "days on the farm" to reduce the debt ([79–80]).

March 8, 1729, to August 1, 1729: Pansogh

"mack[,] pansogh['s] son" and "his wife[,] Catryn" are noted with ongoing accounts by the trader; "½ sch[epel of] bran" and "½ ell of cotton" were fetched for him "by y[our] H[onor's] sister"; a "kan" of rum was fetched by the Indian man kobes. Mack makes purchases of cotton, strouds, 1 stroud blanket, a colored shirt, gunpowder, lead, beer, rum, "1 sch[epel of] bran," and ½ bread. His debt also includes "1 small skin for the smith." Payments of 1 raccoon, 8 martens, a skin, and credit "for 10 days on the farm" are listed to reduce his debt. Catryn purchases duffels; cotton; 1 stroud, 1 duffel, and 2 coarse blankets; 2 knives; a kettle; gunpowder; and rum. Payments of 17 lbs skins and "10 lb fat" are noted toward her debt ([99–100]).

May 1, 1751: Pansog/Pansocgh

Listed among the twenty-three Indian signers receiving 102 pounds 16 shillings for confirming the boundaries of the Hardenbergh Patent (Deed mss., Senate House State Historic Site, Kingston, NY).

December 26, 1785: Spansough

The deponent Johannis Bevier Jr. (age sixty-two) testifies "[t]hat he could hold a Common Discourse with the Indians in there [sic] Language That when he was about 15 or 16 years of age he heard, Spansough, & Henry Hekon Two old grayheaded Indians Discoursing with the Deponents father about the Rivers back where they lived — That the Indians said the mahak Lamas[,] that is the Big fish[,] went into the [West Branch of the Delaware] River that came from [the Indian village of] Cookhouse[,] and that the Chanelies Lemas[,] that is little fish[,] went up the papahunk kill [or East Branch of the Delaware River.] That the Creek from Cookhouse was the Right fish kill [or head of the Delaware River] . . . &

[the] Reason was because it keep the Righest Course and had the Deepest watter" (CFLP, box 6, folder 9, #121).

Schawenackie (fl. 1703–1754/pm. 1767)
March 27, 1703: Shawanagkies
   One of seven "Indyan proprietors" conveying to Col. Henry Beekman Sr. of Kingston "all that tract or parcell of Land Seituate Lying and being in Dutchess County Betwist the Land of Coll. Peter Schuyler and ye Land of Henry pawling" incorporated earlier as the Rhinebeck Patent in 1697 (Deed mss., Livingston Papers, CO280, box 158, folder 4E., Firestone Library, Princeton, NJ).
August 5–6, 1714: Shawanachkie
   Listed among the Esopus Sachims renewing peace with Ulster County justices at Kingston and citing concerns about a rumor "that the Christians did intend to make warr against the Indians" (MJC, 1714–41, folder 1).
December 8, 1719: Sawenakies
   Sawenakies, "his wife," and "his son" are listed with an account by the Ulster County trader; purchases are recorded of strouds, white baize, 1 stroud blanket, 1 duffel blanket, 2 pairs of stockings, a hat, a cap, "1 string of beads," and 2 knives. Payment in bear hide, fisher, raccoons, and "34 lb deerskins" are noted toward their debt ([17–18]).
[July 8, 1721?]: Sawanagkis
   The trader records a small purchase made by "Sawanagkis['s] son on 2 lb gunpowder and lead and bread" totaling 20 guilders ([19]).
January 1, 1721, to March 21, 1724: Sawangh
   "sawangh['s] son" is listed with an ongoing account by the trader. He purchases duffels, strouds, 1 stroud blanket, 2 shirts, gunpowder, lead, rum, "1 small box with paint," and 1 bread; "nicklas hofman" is listed as fetching a small axe for him. Credit "for 2 deer" and 72 pounds "raw skins" is listed toward his debt ([45–46]).
May 5, 1723: S:jawanegkie
   The "Chieef Indian of Pawlings [Patent, who] was Seekoremaw & ye Chieef of ye Land of Beekmans [Rhinebeck Patent] S:jawanegkie" are noted in a deposition reporting that "Both parties of Indians [have] mett in Dutchess County, to Shew the Land [purchased] by Pawlings, And what purchased by Beekman[s] . . . & They agreed the Division Lyn bettween their fourfathers was by a Small Run of water Called nanotanapenen. The Land to the Southerd Should belong to proprietors [ceded?] to the Pawlings, & to ye north to ye Beekman. Butt the Indians on

the Pawlings Syd Coming to a plain confession, they aknowledge they had land from a stooney Point, Called Korenagkoyosink Sum 8: or : [10] Chains to ye North ward of sd Kill, which Bears East from the Point of the Klyn [little] Esopus fly [or vly, present Esopus Meadows Point on the west side of the Hudson] which we Took to be the place Intended which if ever ther has been a marked tree must have been there about and to Run from that place of Hudsons River East onye Strik near to ye midle of the meadow Called Pawlings fly" (Livingston Papers–NYSL, MF, reel #28).

September 26 to October 29, 1723: Sawanagh

"Joghem[,] Sawanagh['s] son" makes an additional purchase from the trader of "4 ell of fine colored cotton-yarn." Niklas "hofman" is listed as fetching another axe for him. Payments in raccoons and beavers, and credit for working "on the farm" against the "remainder on 1 dufels blanket" are noted to reduce the debt ([53]).

October 13, 1730: Shawanachko

One of twenty grantors confirming the boundaries of the Great Nine Partners Patent in Dutchess County ("only excepting still the Whrits of some North Indians") in a new Indian deed presented to the Nine Partners Company "Sealed and Delivered by Shawanachko and Shawasco [or Schawash, the Mohican sachem of Shekomeko]" (William P. McDermott and Clifford Buck, *Eighteenth Century Documents of the Nine Partners Patent, Dutchess County, New York* [Baltimore, MD: Dutchess County Historical Society, 1979], 110–12).

February 9, 1733: Schawenackie

"Nacapin, Schawenackie, Tatakeem and Mameitageeck Indian Inhabitant[s] In the County of albany" convey to Johannis Halenbeeck for 17 pounds 10 shillings "one Certain Tract of Land Lying and being In the County and Province aforeSaid at or upon a Certain Creek Called and known by the Name of Caterskill and beginning by the Grote Vals kill and the Land Lying on boath Sides of the Caterskill Containing by Estimation Three hundred Acres" (Cadwallader Colden, *The Letters and Papers of Cadwallader Colden*, vol. 6, 1761–1764 [New-York Historical Society *Collections* 55, 1923], 2:87–88).

May 12, 1733: Shawanachke

Noted among seven Indians listed in a memorandum confirming the sale to Johannis Halenbeeck made on February 9, 1733, for "the Island on the Cateracks Kill Lying on the West Side of Trin Clos Platts and of the falls" (Colden, *Letters and Papers*, 2:88).

November 4, 1737: Shawenah

Proprietors of the Great Nine Partners Company of Dutchess County report that "two Indians being come to town [New York City] Shawash & Shawenah with letters from the Partners on the premises showing they were real owners. Shawash owning the greatest part of ye [unsold] land & not yet paid [for their rights reserved in 1730]. We met them at Cap A. Rutgers agreed & gave them for their right and to execute ye Indian deed which was executed accordingly" (McDermott and Buck, *Eighteenth Century Documents*, 15).

November 4, 1737: Shawanachko

Phillip Cortlandt of the New York Council reports the appearance of "Shawanachko and Shawasquo, two of the Indians within named, and acknowledged the within Deed, to be their and each of their Voluntary Act and Deed, and that they executed the same for the uses therein mentioned; and also confessed and declared that they had respectively received the goods following, to witt, the said Shawanachko three striped Blanketts, three Dufills Blankets, four Dozen of pipes, ten knives, two Hatchets, one Strouds Blankett, six pounds of powder, ten pounds of lead, two white shirts, and One Gunn. And the said Shawasquo seven striped Blanketts, seven Duffills Blanketts, eight Dozen of pipes, twenty knives, five hatchets, one Strouds Blankett, eighteen pounds of powder, eighteen pounds of lead, and one good gun, four white shirts, and one half barrel of strong beer" (McDermott and Buck, *Eighteenth Century Documents*, 112–13).

July 31, 1743, to April 23, 1754: Schabanash/Schabanach called Jephtha

Appears in Moravian records under his given baptismal name Jephtha a "Sopus Ind" baptized at the Mohican town of Shekomeko in northern Dutchess County on July 31, 1743. A widower, wife (unnamed) died of alcoholism in April 1744. He relocated to Bethlehem, Pennsylvania, in August 1745 to be with his son Thomas (a "Sopus Ind" baptized under that name at Shekomeko on August 22, 1743, and officially accepted "as worker among the heathen" — Jephtha's deceased wife was his stepmother; he died in November 1747 at Bethlehem). Jephtha moved to Nazareth, Pennsylvania, in September 1747 and made several trips to the Mohican town of Wechquadnach in northwestern Connecticut in 1749 before settling at Gnadenhutten, Pennsylvania, in 1750. The "Sopus Ind" Lazara, "daughter of Jeptha," was baptized March 16, 1749, at Wechquadnach and died there November 19, 1749. Jephtha is listed as the father or stepfather of Magdalena and Josua; Josua's mother was Jeptha's deceased wife. He also had a granddaughter at the

Mohican town of Stockbridge in Massachusetts. Noted as a "visitor at Menio-lagomekah" in August 1752 and as a brother of another visitor earlier in May; Jephtha died April 23, 1754, at Gnadenhutten after a long illness (Wheeler, "Living Upon Hope: Mahicans and Missionaries, 1730–1760" (PhD diss., Yale Univ., 1999), 320–21; MOA, box 3191, folder 1; box 111, folder 2; box 112, folder 2; box 117, folder 3; box 122, folder 3).

October 17, 1743: Shawvonock now Jeptha

One of six signatories to a petition claiming that the Mohican sachem "Sha-was" (or Abraham of Shekomeko) had not been paid for his rights to the "Second [or "Little"] Nine partners land" in northern Dutchess County (MOA, box 113, #10).

May 1, 1751: Sowanck

A participant noted among the Indian signers receiving 102 pounds 16 shillings for confirming the boundaries of the Hardenbergh Patent (Deed mss., Senate House State Historic Site, Kingston, NY).

September 3, 1767: Schawenack

Identified as the uncle of the Indian informant Allameetahat or Piet Tap in testimony delineating the boundary between the Esopus and Catskill Indians; he is also likely a brother or brother-in-law of Newachquary noted as the father of Piet Tap (Affidavit, Martin Van Bergen, mss., 6812, NYSL).

Metmahes/Young Abraham (fl. 1705–1726)

August 18, 1705: Metmahes

"Metmahes Sunn of y[e] afores[d] Abram [or Ruwagkaseg]" is listed among the "Indyan proprietors in ye County of Ulster" conveying to Henry Beekman Sr. "all ye Certaine tract of land Situate Lying & being in ye bounds of Rochester [Patent] . . . on both sides of a Certaine Creeke or River . . . Called by ye Indyans nawesinck [Neversink] beginning by a Certaine place Called honck [falls] and so Runs to a Certaine place belonging to ye Kitsepraw Indians . . . Called negpogkaw" (UCDB, AA:352).

July 8, 1721, to April 15, 1722: Young Abraham

"Young Abraham[,] Abraham's son" develops a small account with the Ulster County trader. Purchases are made of 1 dozen buttons, gunpowder, lead, and rum totaling 14 guilders. He pays off the debt with "1 elk skin" valued at 14 guilders ([19–20]).

January 1, 1724, to April 12, 1725: Abraham

"Eijsack[,] Abraham['s] son" develops a small account with the trader; "his mother" and "his wife[,] sawegonck hendreck['s] daughter" are also active on the account. The trader reports a debt of one of the Indians with "barent nieuw kerck" for 2 goatskins. Purchases are recorded of 1 coarse blanket, gunpowder, lead, and rum. Payment of a "bear hide and grease for the coarse blanket" and "his wife'[s] Cred[it] for hides" are listed toward the debt ([63–64]).

September 1, 1724, to July 8, 1729: Abraham

"Abraham['s] Youngest daughter" develops an account with the trader. Purchases are recorded of strouds, rum, and "1 duffels blanket [fetched] by her father" (1726). Part of the debt is paid off with pieces of silver and copper. Payment of a bear hide, a fox skin, and 1 other skin is also listed ([57–58]).

1725: Abraham

The trader reports that "Abraham son of Abraham" is indebted for 16 guilders "on remainder on a 1 [sic] coarse blankets" ([81]).

November 15, 1726: Abraham

"Abraham's burial" is reported by the trader in the accounts of Manonck and his relatives ([99]).

Hendrick Hekan (fl. 1707–1751/pm. 1770–1785)

March 22, 1707: Kakawaramin

"Kakawaramin an [sic] Native Indian of Esopus" conveys to Johannes Hardenbergh Sr., for 30 pounds New York currency, "all that tract of Land Lying and being in Said County of Ulster Extending from the Northwest boundaries of the township of Marbletown northwesterly to a Certain place Called Kawienesinck [a hill north of the Bushkill Creek] and stretching northeast to a Certain Creek or kill Called by the Indians Anquathkonckkill and southwesterly to the west Corner of said boundaries of Marbletown." Incorporated as part of the Hardenbergh Patent in 1708 (Deed ms., privately owned).

March 20, 1711: Kakaweremin

One of the "Sachimes of the Native Esopus Indians" renewing peace before Ulster County justices at Kingston and reporting that a message was sent by the Minisinks to the sachem young Ancrop "In order to warne them that the Shetterrayres [or Tutelo] Indians Intend with the french to come and destroy them" (UCCS, 1706–12, mss.).

June 30, 1712: Keatawerremm

One of the "Sachimes of the Esopus Indians" called to appear at Kingston "who were sent for by the Justices On The Occasion that Rumors were spread in this County that the Indians would Rise against the Christians" (UCCS, 1712–20, mss.).

August 5–6, 1714: Kakawaremin

Listed among the Esopus Sachims renewing peace with Ulster County justices at Kingston, and citing concerns about a rumor "that the Christians did intend to make warr against the Indians" (MJC, 1714–41, folder 1).

April 17, 1719: Hendreck Hekan

"Krwamo['s] daughter sar[,] hendreck hekan's wife" develops an account with the Ulster County trader; purchases are recorded of lead, gunpowder, penneston cloth, and 1 stroud blanket. Payment of a bear hide and 1 fisher, and credit "for [the] remainder on a skin" are noted ([13–14]).

August 18, 1722: Takawarement

Listed among the "Sopus Indians" renewing peace with justices at Kingston, and complaining about settler encroachment on lands near Chechunck, Coxsing, Mammekotton, and the Little Esopus Creek (GTM-PC, box P26, folder 14).

January 10, 1724: Hend Hekan

"hend Hekan's son" is noted by the Ulster County trader with a debt of 7 guilders on gunpowder and lead; recorded in the accounts of "manonck the savage" and his relatives ([2]).

September 1, 1724, to July 13, 1726: Hendreck Hekan

Hendreck Hekan develops an account with the Ulster County trader; "his son" and "his wife" and "his younger son" are all active on the account; "his wife is indebted from older times" at 38 guilders. Purchases are recorded of strouds, cotton, a coarse blanket, 1 fine shirt, linen, a knife, gunpowder, lead, flintstones, a kettle, 1 goatskin, beer, rum, and 1 bread. Payments of 3 martens, 1 otter, and "42 lb Elk skins" are listed ([55–56]).

November 1, 1724: Hendrick Hekan

The trader records in the accounts of "mocka[']s brother" the purchase "on 1 gun for 20 martens[,] hendrick hekan is his guarantor for the gun" ([61]).

February 18, 1725: Hend Hekan

Reported by the trader as paying part of the debt incurred by "the sawanos" [Shawnees?], he pays with 6 martens valued at 13 guilders ([62]).

March 14, 1725: Hendreck Hekan

"hendreck hekan's boy[,] kryn" satisfies his debt of 7 guilders on gunpowder and lead with the trader, recorded in the accounts of "manonck and his wife and son" ([67]).

November 4, 1725, to February 27, 1727: Hendreck Hekan

"hendreck hekan['s] oldest son" ("wadde"; [78]) develops an account with the trader; "his brother" and "hend [hekan's] youngest son" (or his boy kryn?) are also active on the account; an Indian man called "sawannes" fetches flintstones. Purchases are recorded of strouds, a coarse blanket, a duffel blanket, 2 shirts (1 fine), a knife, gunpowder, lead, flintstones, and 1½ bread. An additional item of debt is recorded as "on [the] remainder on cotton by y[our] H[onor's] brother." Payments of 1 bear hide, an elk skin, 2 skins, martens, a fisher, and 1 beaver are noted to reduce the debt ([77–78]).

August 20, 1726, to October 15, 1728: Hend Hekan/Hendreck Hekan

He and his wife Sar are noted with ongoing accounts by the trader; "his son waddie" fetches a coarse blanket for them; "mary pawling" fetches gunpowder. The Indian called "sawannos" (or "sawanos") also fetches goods. Purchases are recorded of duffels, strouds, cotton, gunpowder, lead, flintstones, 1 kettle, rum, and a bucket of cider. "Sar[,] hendreck hekan['Js wife" is reported as having had an "old account in Kingston" and a debt of 33 guilders "on kwakesas['s] account[,] her part." She makes new purchases on "1 shirt of linen" and "1 duffels blanket for her son"; the purchase "on 1 kan rum at [the] bur[ial] [of] Andries['s] child" is also listed on her account. Payments of 2 elk skins, ½ lb dressed skins, 3 skins, a marten, and 1 pig are listed toward their debts ([91–92]).

1727 to July 5, 1729: Hendreck Hekan

"Waddie[,] hendreck hekan['Js son" is noted with an ongoing account by the trader; "his father" and the Indian woman "kisay" are mentioned on the account. Purchases are recorded of strouds, cotton, band, fabric, 2 stroud blankets, a duffel blanket, 1 shirt, gunpowder, lead, flintstones, swan shot, 2 knives, ½ turkey, 1 "schepel" of Indian corn, rum, cider, and 1 gun at 320 guilders. Payments in elkskins, a bear hide, deer meat, skins, and martens are noted toward his account ([109–111]).

1727 to August 8, 1729: Hend Hekan

"magh[,] hend hekan['Js son" develops an account with the trader; "his younger brother" is also active on the account. Purchases are recorded of cotton, gemp (fabric edging), 2 stroud blankets, a duffel blanket, 1 shirt, gunpowder, flintstones, lead, ½ "schepel" of Indian corn, ½ bread, and rum. Payments of 2 small skins, a bear hide, 1 marten, and credit "for 8½ days" and "10 days binding on the farm" and two more days "for cutting in the meadow" are listed to reduce the debt ([109–110]).

April 21, 1730: Kahawelemin/Kahawalemin alias Hendrick Heakan

Noted among Indian signers appearing before the Kingston Court to claim land at Mamecatten (or Memekitton) lying between Nepenaack and Assewayke-mak, and accepting a gift confirming an earlier Indian sale of the tract on June 8, 1696 (GTM-PC, box P26, folder 14).

September 7, 1741: Hakawaremin

An Esopus "under Shachim," renewing peace with county justices and precinct supervisors at Kingston (GTM-PC, box P26, folder 14; *PWJ*, 1:15–16).

August 27, 1743: Kakawaremen alias Hendrick Hekan

One of the Esopus "under Sachims" meeting with Ulster County justices at Kingston as representatives of "four Tribes [or families], to witt, ye Kighshepaw, Mahew, Mogewehogh, [and] Kaghkatewees" and accepting a present to permit a survey of the Hardenbergh Patent (GTM-PC, box P26, folder 14).

May 7, 1745: Hendrick Hekan

An Esopus sachem noted during a renewal of the Nicolls Treaty at Kingston desiring the regulation of prices by county justices on exchanges of native produce and European trade goods (UCCS, 1737–50, mss.).

June 6, 1746: Cacawalemin alias Hendrick Hekan

A "Sopus Indian" and principal signer (including his "two sons . . . Tamacapawain & paskhelind") conveying land to Johannes Hardenbergh Sr. and company in the Hardenbergh Patent straddling Albany and Ulster counties, "beginning at papaconck at the [East Branch of the Delaware] River and running Down the Said River as farr as to the bounds of the Cashichton Indians including half the River and Islands as farr as aforesaid then along the bounds of the Land of the Cashichton Indians to the bounds of Rochester pattent then beginning again at Papaconck aforesaid and Running up Said River including half the River and half the Island as aforesaid to Pacatachkan and so up to the head [of the East Branch of the Delaware River] thereof [and] from thence with a Straight line to the head of Cateria Kill [Kaaterskill] (the Mohack [Mohawk] Claim [to the north] allwaies Excepted) from thence to the bounds of Kingston and so all along the bounds of Kingston Hurley Marbletown and Rochester as our Right goes (Excepting the Land which the Said Moonhaw or Ancrop now hath in his possession under the Patent of Rochester)." Noted as being too ill to confirm his signature acknowledging receipt of payment for the lands totaling 7,000 Dutch guilders or 175 English pounds in currency (UCDB, EE:63–65).

August 2, 1746: Kakalerreme/Kakalarimme

The principal signer listed among the "Native proprietors & heirs of Proprietors of Cashichton and Sundery Other tracts" accepting 125 English pounds in currency from Johannes Hardenbergh Sr. and company for land within the Hardenbergh Patent in southern Ulster County, "Beginning at a Certain plase in Ulster County aforesaid Called the Great Hunting house or Gagh house lying to the North East of the Land Called Bashes Land thence to run west by North untill it meets with the Fish Kill or Main bransh of Delaware River then Crossing the said kill or River west four English Miles into the woods then Northerly parallel with Said Fish Kill as far as the Said Cashichton or Menissink Indians [and] their right or Claim then Easterly four Miles to the late purches of the Sopus Indians bearing date [June 6, 1746] on Said River then along Said purchais as they run to the Northeast Corner of Rochester pattent then South Easterly along Said Rochester pattent to the Land or pattent of Capt John Evans and all along Said John Eveness pattent till it meets with the North East Corner of the [Minisink] pattent of [E]benearar [Ebenezer] Willson & Dirck Vandenburgh and Company and from thence to the first Station" (UCDB, EE:61–63).

May 1, 1751: Henderyik Heckkan

"Amoucht [and] Wesanep both sons of Henderyik Heckkan Descsed" along with twenty-three Indian signers, receive 102 pounds 16 shillings from Johannes Hardenbergh Jr., for confirming the boundaries of the Hardenbergh Patent "begining at a Certain pleace Called Schokeakena and so runing along the west side of the Fishkill or Delaware River to the head thereof and from the head thereof to the head of Cartrights Kill [Kaaterskill] and so along the Cartwrights kill to the bounds of Kingston and all along the bound of Kingston to the bounds of Hurley and then along the bounds of Hurley to the bound of Marbletown then along the bounds of Marbletown and the blue [or Catskill] Mountains to bounds of Rochester then all along the high mountains Commonly Called the blue mountains and the bounds of Rochester to the bound of capt John Evens [Evans Patent] and from thence running to the land granted to Ebenezer Willson and other[s Minisink Patent] then all along the land to the land sold by the Indians of Cassekegkton to Major Johannes Hardenbergh [Sr.] In co[m]ppany and so along [their] purchases to the first station" (Deed mss., Senate House State Historic Site, Kingston, NY).

June 3, 1751: Hendrickhokeau

Mentioned in a deed made by twenty-two "Indian proprietors" receiving 149 pounds 19 shillings for their rights to lands "between the Fish-kill and Papagonck river" in the Hardenbergh Patent (Jay Gould, *History of Delaware County and Border Wars of New York* [Roxbury, NY: Keeny & Gould, 1856], 242).

December 10, 1770: Hendrick Hegan

The "Indians Sander their Chief Sachem & Hendrick Hegan" are noted in Colonel John Bradstreet's argument before the New York Council against the Hardenbergh Patent proprietors' claims to lands lying between the East and West Branches of the Delaware River. "This Hendrick several of our Opponents say lived on the West side of the Popaghtonk Branch where he had an orchard" and had attended a "Treaty" concerning these lands on August 27, 1743 (Charles H. Lincoln, *Manuscript Records of the French and Indian War* [Worcester, MA: American Antiquarian Society, 1909], 118).

January 21, 1771: Hendrick Heikan

Jacob Wesfal (or Westfal, age seventy-seven) testifies before Justice Abraham van Aken "that he has lived at [colonial] Menissink above sixty years & was well acquainted with the Indians at Delaware & up the fishkill [branch] to the head thereof (To Witt Hendrick Heikan, Menonck, & a Great number of others who lived up the fishkill at Kishiston [Cochecton] and further to the head thereof) that this deponent allways understude by these Indians that the Branch or river which comes from the northeast was allways called by the name of Papakonk river and that the northwest Branch or river was called by the Indians Lamass Seaposs which is fishkill and further this Deponent saith that Dischoursing with the above Indians as long as he can Remember hi never heard of any Mohacks [Mohawks] or any other Indians that ever claimed any right to any Part of the above mentioned Land" (NYCM-LP, 28:71).

January 21, 1771: Hendrick Heckan

Trader Pieter Kuykendal (or Peter Kockindal, age seventy-two) testifies before Abraham van Aken "that he hath lived all his Days at Menissink and was well acquainted with the Indians who lived along the fishkill or Delaware [River] & up the same to Keshiston & from that to Shohakana [Shehaken] & so to kookhoush-ackke [Cookhouse] & colletie and up the other Branch to Papakonk & Paghkatag-kan [—] that a Number of Indians who said, they Lived at Papakonk, on the west side of the Papakonk river, who Traded with this Deponent, and often Invited him to come to their houses at Papakonk to Drink Sider with them, This Deponent fur-ther asked the said Indians where they had the Sider to Drink, which they Replyd at Papakonk on their Own Lands [—] that among these Indians was Hendrick Heckan their Chief Chesham [i.e., sachem] & many others — — — And further this Deponent Saith that Dischoursing with the Above Indians as long as he can remember he Never heard of any Mohacks or any Other Indians to claime any right to any Part of the abovementioned Lands or any Part there of" (NYCM-LP, 28:72).

January 21, 1771: Hendrick Hekan/Hendrick Heckhan

Wellem Kudbeck (or William Cuddebeck, age sixty-seven) testifies before Abraham van Aken "that he is born & brought up at Peenpack that he was well acquainted with Hendrick hekan the Chief Chesham of the Dallaware & Esopus Indians who Lived at Papakonk, that the above said Hendrick Heckhan offten told this Deponent that he Lived at Papakonk on the west side of that river Between the fish kill & the Papakonk river, and that he had a Large [apple] Orchard where he Lived, and Invited this Deponent to come and Drink Sider with him at his house [—] that the Indians offten told him that the North west branch was all-ways Called by the Indians Lames Seapose which is fish kill and the North East branch the Papakonk river and this Deponent further sayth he never heard of any Mohacks that Ever made any Pretance to the Land Between those two rivers" (NYCM-LP, 28:73).

January 21, 1771: Hendrick Hekan/Hendrick Heckhan

Gerardus van Inwegen (age sixty) testifies before Abraham van Aken "that he is born and brought up at Peenpack that he was well acquainted with Hendrick hekan the Chief Chesham of the Dallawares & Esopus Indians who Lived at Papa-konk and that the abovesaid Hendrick Heckhan offten told this Deponent that he Lived at Papakonk on the west side of that River Between the fish kill and the Papakonk river and that they had a Large Orchard where he Lived [—] this Depo-nent further saith that the Indians offten told him that the Northwest branch was allways Called by the Indians Lamass Seaposs which is fish kill and the North East branch the Papakonk river and this Deponent further Saith he never heard of any Mohacks that Ever made any Pretance or had any right to the Lands Between those rivers" (NYCM-LP, 28:74).

1785: Hendrick Hekan

Noted in Chancellor Robert Livingston's legal argument supporting Harden-bergh Patent proprietors against the claims made by heirs of Colonel John Brad-street as one of the "Native Indians" who sold land to Johannis Hardenbergh and Company in 1746 (NYCM-LP, 41:13, see page 37).

December 26, 1785: Henry Hekon

The deponent Johannis Bevier Jr. (age sixty-two) testifies that he was "Born at Nepenack . . . That he could hold a Common Discourse with the Indians in there [sic] Language That when he was about 15 or 16 years of age [1738 or 1739] he heard, Spansough, & Henry Hekon Two old grayheaded Indians Discoursing with the Deponents father about the Rivers back where they lived — That the Indians said the mahak Lamas[,] that is the Big fish[,] went into the [West Branch of the Delaware] River that came from [the Indian village of] Cookhouse[,] and that the Chanelies Lemas[,] that is little fish[,] went up the papahunk kill [or East Branch of the Delaware River]. That the Creek from Cookhouse was the Right fish kill [or head of the Delaware River] . . . & [the] Reason was because it keep the Righest Course and had the Deepest watter" (CFLP, box 6, folder 9, #121).

Andries (fl. 1709–1729)

September 7, 1709: Andries

Ulster County justices at Kingston report that "one andries an Indian has assaulted Jan Midda[u]gh, tennant of s^d Coll Rutse[n], and y^t Coll Beekman hath issued out his warr[an]^t to ye Constable of rochester [Precinct] for ye apprehending of s^d andries" (UCCS, 1706–12, mss.).

August 18, 1722: Andries

"Andries the Indian" is listed among the "Sopus Indians" renewing peace with Ulster County justices at Kingston and complaining about settler encroachment on lands near Chechunck, Coxsing, Mammekotton, and the Little Esopus Creek (GTM-PC, box P26, folder 14).

September 29, 1724, to August 4, 1726: Andris de Welt

Andris, "his wife," and "his wife's brother [Tatteu]" are noted with an account by the Ulster County trader; purchases are recorded of strouds, baize, cotton, a white shirt, gunpowder, lead, knives, "1 kettle from Catharina," and pipes. Payments in otter, fox, a pig, and "skins by her brother" are listed to reduce the debt ([57–58]; see [75] for "tatteu[,] andris['s] wife's brother").

October 15, 1728: Andries

The trader records the purchase "on 1 kan rum at [the] bur[ial] [of] Andries['s] child" in the accounts of Hendrick Hekan and his wife Sar ([91–92]).

February 2, 1726, to July 27, 1729: Andris de Welt

Noted with an ongoing account by the trader; "tateu" fetches cotton and rum for him; the Indian man "Sawagonck" fetches gunpowder and a pipe. Other purchases are recorded of strouds, cotton, "colored textile[s,]" a stroud blanket, "1 shirt for his [other?] child" (1729), gunpowder, lead, and a bottle of rum; he also buys "½ gall rum at manonck['s] burial." Payments in skins, dressed skins, bear hides, and a fisher are listed ([101–102]).

Ankerop II/Tackawaghkin (fl. 1711–1728)

March 20, 1711: Tackawaghkin alias Young Ancrop

"Tackawaghkin alias yo[u]ng Ancrop Chief Sachim" and other "Sachimes of the Native Esopus Indians" (Arameghtan, Kegtagkaes, Kakaweremin, and Crawamogh) renew peace before justices of the Ulster County Court of Sessions at Kingston. "The Justices demanded of said Sachims by Ariaantie Tappen Interpretess: Whether any Christians had broke any of the articles of peace agst the Indians they answered: none of the said articles (by their knowledge) were broke by the Christians & presented — A bush of String'd Wampum a small beare skin

& a beaver Lap [*cutting*: remnant or piece of . . .] In acknowledgement & Renewing the peace — The Chief Sachim presented also a small bush of wampum with desire to be hence forward termed & called by the name of Ancrop & promised if he hears any bad news from any parts ag^st the Christians that he give notice & advertise them of the same and desires the Christians may do the same Which the Justices promised to do — And sayd Sachim further sayth that the Menesinck Indians have sent him a string of wampum In order to warne them that the Shetterrayres [or Tutelo] Indians Intend with the french to come and destroy them — The Justices Informed them that they was glad to heare that no Christians had Injured them & told them nott to lett theire people threaten any hurt to the Christians They promised to hind^er that to the utmost of theire power — The Justices Ordered that there be given unto the said Indians as a present 3 Cloths of Duffills three shirts 3 gall Rum & one barrell of beer[,] which they took with thankfulness" (UCCS, 1706–12, mss.).

June 2, 1712: Ancrop

"Ancrop Chiefe Sachime" and other "Chiefe Sachimes of the Esopus Indians" (Keataghcage, Aramochtan, Crawamogh, and Paijemhanck) renew peace with Ulster County justices at Kingston. "The said Sachimes produced to the Justices the said article of peace In writing delivered to them in Coll. Nicols time and presented a String of Wampum in acknowledgement of Renewing said peace & say they hope it may Continue — The Justices perused the said article of peace & told the Sachimes they were glad to see them fullfill the same in Renewing said peace & hoped that the Indians might give no occasion of breaking the same — The Sachimes further Say we are all brethron and what befalls one shall befall the other & promised to give notice of & Assist ag^st any Riseing or Invation [invasion] of any Indians or Other Enemy and in token of theire fedillity p[re]sented Six beaver Skines one Elk ditto two beare ditto one fox ditto & one [pine] Martin ditto — The Justices Received the Same with Satisfacation & told them if any of the Common Enemy should assault them that they should be welcome to shelter themselves under the Christians and that then we would protect them and made them a present to theire great Sattisfaction — Paijemhanck the Indian Complains that Capt. Johannis Vernooy owes him a Cloth of Duffells & denyes to pay him and that Jurian Quick owes him a pound of powder & a Shirt & also denyes to pay him — The Justices told the Sachims to take Care to Inquire into the premises & if his demands be Just to do him Justice — The Said Sachimes [also] informed the Justices that there is about Six hundred Indians called Shawonnos [Shawnees] who Cannot live at peace in theire own native Country & begged the Said Sachimes that they Might Settle among them to the west or north west of the blew hills [Catskill Mountains] in Ulster County where said Esopus Indians now Reside and that they will become Subjects under Ancrop the Chiefe Sachime of the Esopus Indians And the Said Sachimes ask leave of the Justices to settle said Indians Among them — The Justices Answered that such things was above theire power to grant & that it did belong to his Excell^cy the governor who they ought to Request for the same — The Sachimes thereupon desired the Justices to Represent the desire of the said Indians & them to his Excell^cy and to desire his Answer thereon — The Justices promised to do the Same" (UCCS, 1712–20, mss.; see also New York Executive Council Minutes, NYSA, 11:116, for the July 3 resolution by Governor Robert Hunter and the Council, noting they had received a letter from Kingston dated June 26, informing them "that ye Sachims of the Esopus Indians desired to settle some others among them Whom its believed are some of those Who are in Warr with North Carolina and also a Report from ye Justices of Ulster County Signifying that they have renewed their Friendship with the Esopus Indians who desire that about six hundred of the Shawanos who Cannot live among them [of North Carolina] becoming subjects to their Chiefe Sachim — It is the opinion of this Board that a Letter be written to the Justices of ye peace of Ulster County acquainting them that if these Indians who desire to settle beyond the Blew hills under ye subjection of the Esopus Sachim have Left their Country because they would not be engaged in the Warr against the people of North Carolina, that then they may Settle there, under that Subjection and promise not to Intermeddle in that Warr and offer assurances of fidelity [but] if they are a part of those Indians that were actually engaged in that Warr and have by the people of Carolina been driven out of their Country and are desirous of Composing that difference then this Board will endeavor to dispose the people of Carolina to make peace with them and to Restore them to their antient [sic] Settlements again, and in the meane time they Continue where they are among the Esopus Indians beyond the Blew Hills").

June 30, 1712: Ancrop

"Ancrop: Chiefe Sachim" and other "Chiefe Sachimes of the Esopus Indians" (Keataghcage, Aramochtan, Orochkanienjo, Keatawerremm, and Meaquarrape) appear before the Ulster County Court in Kingston "who were sent for by the Justices On The Occasion that Rumors were spread in this County that the Indians would Rise against the Christians . . . The Justices Informed the Sachimes that from Poghkepsinck there was a Letter written to his Excell^cy the governor

Importing that there had been three strange Indians & brought a band of Wompum to Signifie & warne the Indians to make Ready to fight against the Christians & demanded of them if they knew any thing of it — the sachaimes declared they knew nothing of what was Reported — the Justices further Implyed to them that they were Informed that Some Indians go against North Carolina & desired them if any Indians did Intice any of them to go against Any of the Queens Subjects that they deny the same & give notice thereof to the Christians — They promised to do yᵉ same — The Sachimes [further] said they was sorry to undʳ stand that it was Entered in the Renewing the peace the second day of this [month] Instant that it was about six hundred Indians that would settle among them And Affirme it was but one Sachime & about thirty or forty Souls & desire that it may be Represented to his Excellency accordingly & that it are [Shawnee] Indians that have Lived about Menesinck above twelve yeares" (UCCS, 1712–20, mss.; see also New York Executive Council Minutes, NYSA, 11:103, for provincial council minutes on May 16, 1712, reporting that Governor Robert Hunter "His Excellᶜᵉʸ Communicated to the Board a Letter from Baltus Van Cleake [or Kleeck, from Poughkeepsie] a Justice of the peace of Dutchess County of the 14ᵗʰ Instant acquainting him that the Katskill Indians had sent a belt of wampum to the Indians in Dutchess County warning them to prepare for Warr and that nine Days after the Date of the Letter the Sinni [Senecas] and Shawanas [Shawnees] would fall upon the Inhabitants along Hudsons River").

August 5–6, 1714: Ancrop

"Att a meeting of Justices and Sachems & others of the Esopus Indians to Renew the peace & discourse about some mo[re consid]eratio[ns] that is by the Indians &c — this 5ᵗʰ day of August 1714 — present . . . Ancrop [and] Aremetan — An Indian boy being Examined what he knew about what Gerritt the Negro man of Jacob Hassbrouck did say Concerning that the Christians did Intend to warr against the Indians — The Said Indian Ladd did Say that the Said Negro man did Call him aside and Asked him where the most of the Indians Lived and further told Said Indian boy that the Christians did intend to make warr against the Indians — the Negro denyes It Stiffly — Saverall [other] discourses being Referred untill tomorrow morning — the Justices offered to the Indians to Influ[ence] what punishm[en]t &c had on the negro — August the 6ᵗʰ mett according to adjournment . . . present Sachimes — Ancrop Chiefe Sachim — Aremetan — Keatachkaugs — Kakawaremin — Maquarape — Orakaniensjo — Shawanachkie — and some Indian Ladds — the articles of peace Read & All demands And Controversies heard & debated and full Sattisfaction to [the] Content being Given on

both sides:x parted with Content & the peace according to said Articles Renewed"
(MJC, 1714–41, folder 1).

1716/1717?: Ankerop

Ankerop and "his wife" are noted with a small account by the Ulster County
trader. Credit purchases are recorded of 1 bar lead, textiles, strouds, beer, and
wine ([7]).

December 16, 1721: Anckeroop

One of five Indians (. . . Werangagh, Quagquepan, Natasough, and Manhawee) testifying before Poughkeepsie Justice Barent Van Kleeck of Dutchess
County that "Such Indians In thare Life time Named Viz Aracogh and Guttecgtenonck and Rackawoounck did a bout one or two and Twenty Years agoo Sell
unto Late Mr Robert Sanders, for himself and others a Certain tract of Land in
Ulster county beginning at a fall in the river called the wall kill or Palls Creek"
(BSDC, book 1:47–48).

August 18, 1722: Ankerop

Ulster County justices at Kingston report they have "mett in order to make
propositions to the Sopus Indians and to renew peace as has been usual according
to the articles of peace made by Governor Nickolls late Gover– of this Province
. . . [present] Ankerop Chif Sachim[,] Renap — Takawarement — Warangaagieng
— Andries the Indian, Reconsough, and several others — Arriantie Tappe[n]
Interpretes[s] — it was told the Indians that it has been Custemary when the Indians
meet the Justices to renew the peace, to examine and inform one another wheather
the peace has in any way been broken, Ankerop says that they have been sent for
and Expects the Justices to inform them the reason thereof, and sayes they are come
to hear the same, upon which they presented one Beaver Skin, one Drest Dear Skin
and a string of Wampong. Then the Justices told Ankerop the Chiefe Sachim, and
the rest of the Indians, that they have heard that one of our Young men last Tuesday
met one of your young men carrying Rom, and drew his sword and offered Vio-
lence to your Young Indian, which we highly Condemne and shall take care that
the said Young man, be punished accordingly[.] The Justices told the Indians that
they were informed that some of the Indians had inticed severall Negroes to fight
against the Christians, They answer that they know nothing of it, and promised
when they hear that any of their people are mischiefeously inclined they promise
to acquaint the Christians with it, The Indians make pretence that the land to the
Southwest of Neskotack [in Evans Patent] to a certain fall or ford nigh by Chechunck [an Indian plantation] in the Palls break [on the Wallkill River] are by several
people Inhabitted without having purchased the Same, and it appears by a coppy

of an Indian Deed of sale by the Indian proprieters to Coll. Thomas Dungan late Govr of this Province bearing date the tenth day of September 1684, that the said Tract is included in the said Indian Deed of sale, and the Indians say that the said Tract is not purchased upon which, the Justices promiss the Indians that they will acquaint his Ex.^{cy} the Governor with it, The pretence of Doostoo concerning land at Coxsing [in Marbletown] is refferred till the next meeting and also the land lying between the bounds of Frederick Hossie [Hussey] & Company and the little Esopus Creek [or present Saw Kill], The pretence which the Indians made for the land of Jacob Freer [of New Paltz] is purchased and paid for as appears by an Instrument signed by severall Indian Proprietors, Against the pretence for Mammekotton Coll Ruttse produced an Indian purchase for the same vizt from Ashewagkomeek to the land of Nepanagh, The Indians demand six hundred Guilders of Alders Roos for the land of Waghkonk [or Awaghkonk, in present Woodstock] which is referred as above [near the Little Esopus Creek]. Ordered that Major Hardenbergh give to the Indians to the Vallue of five pounds eleven Shillings and six Shillings to Arreantie the Interpretes[s]" (GTM-PC, box P26, folder 14).

December 19, 1722: Ancrop

"Ancrop the Indian" (accompanied by Ulster County justices, Joseph Hasbrook, John Hardenburgh, and Roseft Elting) confirms a corner boundary location of the New Paltz Patent at a "High Mountain which he named Maggenapogh at or near the foot of which hill is a small run of water and a swamp which he Called Moggonck and the S[aid] Indian Ancrop afirms itt to be the Right Indian names of the said places" (UCDB, CC:205).

January 29, 1723: Ankerop

Ulster County justices at Kingston report they have met with, "at the request of the Indians, . . . the Chief Schachims and other Esopus Indians who came to renew the peace according to articles of peace made between said Indians — and Coll. Richard Nicholls late Gent[leman] of this Province, who were viz.th present — Ankerop — Moghweekaghkingh — Weeraghkaghwinck — Roondaghnaer — Shachims — and severall other Indians, The Indians acquainted the Justices with the death of Peter, and that they have put Roondaghneere in his room, The Indians present, 6 Racoon Skins — 5 Beaver Skins [and] 1 Otter, to the Justices, As a token of their being well pleased with our Garb they give 3 Beaver Laps, and complain that severall Christians settle on their land without having purchased the same near Shawangong in [John] Evens [Evans] Patent . . . Ordered that Maj.^{r} Hardenbergh give the Indians to the Vallue of three pounds, and six Shillings to Areaantjie Tappen [Interpretess]" (GTM-PC, box P26, folder 14).

January 3, 1727: Ankeron

Ulster County supervisors record the expenditure of 1 pound 4 shillings made "To Major [Johannes] Hardenbergh" for the bounties he paid to "Christysen Depou for one wolfe" and "ankeron ye Indian one woelf" (BSUC, 1:39).

May 15, 1727, to July 21, 1728: Ankerop

"arronshagkie or ankerop[']s son" is noted with an account by the Ulster County trader. Purchases are recorded of various lengths of strouds, "floret (silk) garters" and baize, 1 stroud blanket, a colored shirt, flintstones, gunpowder, lead, and rum. Payments in elk skins, deerskins, otters, and credit of 27 guilders "for 4 days on the farm" are listed toward his debt ([105–106]).

June 22, 1728: Ankerop

Ulster County justices report "on a Complaint Lately made to Coll. Gasbeck [Chambers] that one Indian Called James is Suspected to have Committed felony with Jacob ten Brook esq. who thereupon Issued out Huean[d]crys [neighborhood alerts] to have him apprehended and after ward Issued out a special warrant to have him apprehended but it being thought fitt first to acquaint the Indian Sachims of the matter pursuant a treaty of peace made with the Indians by Govr Nicolls late Govr of this province. And Mr. Roleff Elting now acquaints the Justices that he has acquainted ankerop the Chief Sachim and Renop another Chief Indian and they Said that the Said James was none of their Indians and that they would not protect him. Ordered that the said warrant be executed" (Minutes, Court of Justice of the Peace, 1719–44).

Achpalawamin/(Old) Suwies (fl. 1715–1746)

March 5, 1715: Ochperawim

One of two sons of the Esopus woman and Indian "Sachimests" Doesto, conveying land to Stephanus Gacherie on the Rondout and Cocksinck creeks in Marbletown (UCDB, BB:380–81).

May 2, 1715: Sawis

"Sawis[,] dorso[']s son" is noted with an account by the Ulster County trader; he is reported as having a "debt from older times." Purchases are recorded of strouds, baize, "flinnen," 1 stroud blanket, gunpowder, lead, shot, wine, and rum. Payments of 3 bear hides and 6 raccoons, and "Cred[it] by his mother" are listed to reduce the debt; "Jores meddagh" (Marbletown justice, 1713–18) is noted as paying an elk skin on his account ([25–26]).

May 13, 1725: Sawis

"Sawis[']s son" [unnamed] fetches "2 ells of cotton" from the Ulster County trader on the account of the Indian man "Jan palin[,] nenison[']s son" ([15]).

June 6, 1746: Ahpalawamin/Achpalawamin alias Suwies

A "Sopus Indian" conveying land on the Upper Delaware River within the Hardenbergh Patent straddling Albany and Ulster counties (UCDB, EE:63–65).

Nawoghquarry (fl. 1717–1726/pm. 1767)
August 1717: Nanoghquarij

"Nanoghquarij" and "his wife" are noted with an account by the Ulster County trader; his wife is reported as having a "debt of older times." Purchases of various lengths of penneston cloth and 1 kettle are recorded. Payment of 2 bear hides and "Cred[it] for various" unlisted items are noted toward their debt ([5–6]).

October 25, 1717: Nawoghquarry

Noted with an additional purchase by the trader; credit recorded is on "1 string of beads" at 6 guilders. "Remains indebted at balancing the account," 67 guilders ([13]).

September 27, 1726: Nawaquay/Nanoghquary/Nawoghquary

The principal signer "Nanoghquary and divers other Native Indians of Esopus and Albany County" confirm past payments made by Johannes Hardenbergh amounting to 111 pounds paid to them at various times up to March 1707, for lands in the Hardenberg Patent bounded on the northeast by the Sawyers and Kaaterskill creeks and "extending westwart to the woods and land at Delaware River" (Deed mss., Senate House State Historic Site, Kingston, NY).

September 3, 1767: Newachquary

Identified as the father of the Indian informant Allameetahat or Piet Tap in testimony delineating the boundary between the Esopus and Catskill Indians; he is also likely a brother or brother-in-law of Schawenack noted as the uncle of Piet Tap (Affidavit, Martin Van Bergen, mss., 6812, NYSL).

Mannonck (fl. 1717–1727/pm. 1729–1771)
August 21, 1717, to September 2, 1724: Manonck de Wielt

"manonck the savage" develops the third largest recorded account with the Ulster County trader; "his son" and/or "his son Jacob" and the Indian woman "debora" including "her oldest son" are also active in the exchanges. "hend hekan's son" purchases gunpowder and lead on the account. Other purchases are recorded of fabric, strouds, duffels, blue textiles, baize, white baize, silver ribbon, 1 duffel blanket, 2 stroud blankets, 3 coarse blankets, 1 coat ("to his son"), a shirt and 2 pairs of buttons (and "1 shirt for his son Jacob"), 2 pairs of stockings and a pair of children's stockings, 2 boxes with paint, 1 axe, 2 small axes, 2 knives, gunpowder, lead, rum, slices of meat, and "1 gun for 5 pieces-of-eight if he keeps it." The trader reports that "his son still has 1 stroud blanket coming to him that he has paid." Payments of 7½ lb beavers, 7 deerskins, 11 lb dressed skins, 3 skins, a pig, and 12 guilders "Cred[it] by debora in addition," and 4 lb beavers by "her oldest son" and including "Cred[it] for beaver" made by "their [Manonck's] son Jacob" are listed toward the debt. Dutch settler Jan van Kampen (senior or junior of Marbletown or Rochester) pays 120 guilders on the account ([1–2]).

September 12, 1724: Manonck

The trader reports that "manonck's son" fetched 4 "kans" of rum for the Indian man Kattener ([5]).

March 14, 1725, to July 25, 1726: Manonck/Mannonck

"manonck and his wife and son" are noted with an ongoing account by the trader, resulting in the highest recorded debt in the account book. "[H]is son Jacob" and "his son mattiso" are also named on the account; "his son's wife" pays the remaining debt on a shirt. Strouds are purchased for "Cattener," and "his [Manonck's] wife" buys "cotton for Kwakesas['s] son." The Indian man called "the sawanosse" fetches a duffel blanket for them. The Indian woman "Catryn" buys rum on the account. New purchases are recorded of strouds, cotton, 2 stroud blankets, 2 duffel blankets, 3 coarse blankets (1 for "his wife"), 1 fine shirt, 5 colored shirts (2 for "his son Jacob"), 1 sheath knife, a kettle, 2 lb tobacco, gunpowder, cider, rum, and service rendered "for repairing his [flint] lock." Payments of 8½ lb beavers, 1 beaver weighing 2 lb, 7 pigs, skins, and 6 lb skins, and credit "his son has paid for cotton by going [to] Kingston" are listed to reduce their debt ([67–68]).

March 14, 1725, to July 27, 1727: Manonck

"kattias[,] manonck[']s son" develops an account with the trader; "his mother" and "his wife" and the Indian man Mattiso "fetched" various goods for him. His wife is listed as "tatapagh['s] daughter[,] pitternel." Purchases are recorded of cotton, strouds, stockings, gunpowder, lead, rum, a coarse blanket, "a fine [colored] shirt," and "1 pair of dutch shoes"; payments of 2 bear hides and "8 lb dressed skins" are noted. He also receives credit "for 4½ [days] mowing" to reduce the debt. His wife receives "Cred[it] for 1 day of harvesting flax" toward her account ([69–70]).

August 28, 1725, to December 3, 1726: Mannonck

"mattiso[,] mannonck[']s son" develops an account with the trader; "his father" is active on the account and fetches gunpowder and lead. Other purchases recorded of strouds, 1 stroud blanket, a colored shirt, 1 "dobelstin" shirt, gunpowder, lead, and rum. The trader also reports that he bought "4 kan of rum at [old] abram[']s burial" and had repairs done "on his [flint] lock" at 2 guilders. Payment of "2 dressed skins" and credit "for 3 days on the farm" and "for 1 deer by his mother" are listed toward the debt ([73–74]).

November 15, 1726: Manonck

Manonck remains indebted to the trader for 72 guilders "at balancing the account" and makes new purchases of a coarse blanket, 1 fine shirt, gunpowder, cider, and rum, accruing a total debt of 192 guilders; he receives "Cred[it] for remainder on skins" at 10 guilders. The trader also reports that he bought "rum at [young?] abraham's burial" ([99–100]).

January 3, 1727: Manonck

The trader records the purchase of goods "for manonck['s] burial" including strouds, a fine shirt, gunpowder, and later "rum at the burial of manonck"; all are listed in the account of "kampo's son" ([83]).

January 4, 1727: Manonck

The trader lists purchases of rum in the accounts of the Indians Makwas and Andris "at the burial" dated January 4, and "at manonck['s] burial [undated]" ([101]).

1727 to June 8, 1729: Manonck

"matisso[,] manonck['s] son," is noted with an ongoing account by the trader; "his wife[,] pitternel[?]" and "her mother[']s account" are also mentioned. The Indian man Ponij buys rum and a colored shirt on the account. One ell of strouds is fetched "by y[our] H[onor's] mother" at 16 guilders. New purchases are recorded of strouds, cotton, 1 colored and 1 "dobelstin" shirt, a knife, gunpowder, lead, flint-stones, cider, and rum. Payments of 4 lbs beavers, 18½ lbs skins, 1 beaver, 1 fox, and "2 cats," and credit "for 1 day shooting fire" are noted to reduce his debt ([107–108]).

January 21, 1771: Menonck

Jacob Wesfal (or Westfal, age seventy-seven) testifies before Justice Abraham van Aken "that he has lived at [colonial] Menissink above sixty years & was well acquainted with the Indians at Delaware & up the fishkill [branch] to the head thereof (To Witt Hendrick Heikan, Menonck, & a Great number of others who lived up the fishkill at Kishiston [Cochecton] and further to the head thereof)" (NYCM-LP, 28:71).

Walengaghkin (fl. 1717–1746)

August 21, 1717: Warangau

"Warangau[,] samtie's daughter's husband" develops a small account with the Ulster County trader. Credit purchases are recorded of strouds, beer, rum, gunpowder, and lead at 48 guilders. He is noted as receiving 10 guilders "Credit for Specie" and remains indebted for 38 guilders ([7–8]).

July 8, 1721: Matekie or Hans Jacob

The trader records payment totaling 38 guilders toward the debt of "Matekie or hans Jacob at balancing the account" ([19]).

December 16, 1721: Werangagh

One of five Indians (Anckeroop, . . . Quagquepan, Natasough, and Manhawee) testifying before Poughkeepsie Justice Barent Van Kleeck of Dutchess County that "Such Indians In thare Life time Named Viz Aracogh and Guttecgtenonck and Rackawoounck did a bout one or two and Twenty Years agoo Sell unto Late Mr Robert Sanders, for himself and others a Certain tract of Land in Ulster county beginning at a fall in the river called the wall kill or Palls Creek" (*BSDC*, book 1:47–48).

August 18, 1722: Warangaagieng

Listed among the "Sopus Indians" renewing peace with Ulster County justices at Kingston and complaining about settler encroachment on lands near Chechunck, Coxsing, Mammekotton, and the Little Esopus Creek (GTM-PC, box P26, folder 14).

January 29, 1723: Weeraghkaghwinck

Noted among the Esopus Indian "Shachims" renewing peace before justices of the Kingston Court and complaining about settler encroachment "on their lands . . . near Shawangong in [John] Evens [Evans] Patent" (GTM-PC, box P26, folder 14).

September 7, 1741: Walagagkin (Walagaghin)

An Esopus "under Shachim," renewing peace with Ulster County justices and precinct supervisors at Kingston (GTM-PC, box P26, folder 14; *PWJ*, 1:15–16).

August 27, 1743: Walengaghkin alias Mattakie

One of the Esopus "under Sachims" meeting with Ulster County justices at Kingston as representatives of "four Tribes [or families], to witt, ye Kighshepaw, Mahew, Mogewehogh, [and] Kaghkatewees" and accepting a present to permit a survey of the Hardenbergh Patent (GTM-PC, box P26, folder 14).

June 6, 1746: Waligcaghin/Waligkagin alias Kip

A "Sopus Indian" conveying land on the Upper Delaware River in the Hardenbergh Patent straddling Albany and Ulster counties (UCDB, EE:63–65).

August 2, 1746: Walansyak

One of the "Native proprietors & heirs . . . of Cashichton" or Menissink Indians selling land within the Hardenbergh Patent in southern Ulster County (UCDB, EE:61–63).

Kattener (fl. 1719–1730)

September 16, 1719, to September 10, 1726: Kattener

He and "his wife" develop a small account with the Ulster County trader; he buys "4 kan rum [fetched] by manonck's son" (1724). He makes other purchases of strouds, colored textiles, gunpowder, lead, "a bottle," and additional rum; receives credit "on 1 knife and shot" in exchange "for skins" valued at 6 guilders. His wife buys stockings, a colored shirt, and rum. The trader also records the purchase of 1 stroud blanket and 4 "kans" of rum "at his daughter's burial" on July 22, 1726, and later on "sep^t 10 then balanced accounts with him . . . and his wife" ([5–6]).

September 1, 1724: Kattener

The trader notes that the debt of "pensogh's wife" for 30 guilders "on 12 kan rum and 1 small cask" is "paid by Kattener" ([57–58]).

May 15, 1725: Cattener

The trader reports that Manonck and his relatives have purchased "½ ell of strouds for Cattener" ([67]).

July 18, 1726: Kattener

The trader lists the purchase "on 1 p^t rum by y[our] H[onor's] brother at the burial of kattener['s daughter]" in the accounts of "mattiso[,] mannock['s] son" ([73]).

1726: Kettene[r]

The trader records the purchase by the Indian man "pony" of "1½ ell[s] of cotton for kettene[r']s dead child" ([87]).

1727: Ketternar

The trader notes that "Catrijn[,] nanondo['s] daughter" has purchased "1½ ell[s] of cotton for ketternar['s other?] child" ([107]).

April 21, 1730: Katinner/Cattinner/Catenner/Cattenar/Catanner

Ulster County justices at Kingston report that "Maj.^{r} Hardenbergh, Capt Nottingham Capt Rutsen & Mr Nicholas Rosa Executors of Coll Jacob Rutsen deceased, Complain of Cattinner an Indian for that the said Catenner has disturbed Manuel Gunsalsdeek Jun[ior] in his possession of a certain Tract of land called Mamecatten & burned his Plow & Harrow and drove him away from ye land & distroyed the Wheat of the said Manuel, The said Catenner and severall Indians being present, the s^d Catenner denies the burning of the Plow and Harrow, but says that he told ye said Manuel, that the land did belong to him and if the s^d Manuel sowed that[,] the Wheat was his & says that he told the s^d Manuel to goe from his land, The Justices told the s^d Cattenner in the presence of the rest of the Indians, that it appears to ye Justices that ye land he claimed was sold by the Indians Thirty four years ago, and that he ought not to disturb the s^d Manuel & that they expect that he should for the future be at rest, But if the s^d Executors would give them anything they might, but if they doe he must take it as a gift but not as a Consideration, Maj.^{r} Hardenbergh in behalf of himself & the rest of the Executors aforesaid doe of their own accord by the recommendation of ye Justices Volantary give to the said Cattenar one Blanket 3 Gallons of Rum one Barrel of Strong Bear & eighteen quarts of rum as a free gift and the said Catanner [with] all the Indians present vizt Noundawagaeron, Chief Shachim alias Renniap, Kahawalemin alias Hendrick Heakan & Seaveral other Indians present doe acknowledge that the land where s^d Manuel settled on is part of the lands called Memekitton is Justly bough.^{t} of the Indian Proprietors on the eight day of June 1696, & is included in the said Deed from the land called Nepenaack to a small run of water called by the Indians Assewaykemak, and so along ye said run of water & the land of Hansjoor ye Indian & they promise that they will not claime any land between the land called Nepenek to the said Creek called Assewakemak, In Testimony whereof & to prevent any other Indians to make any claime to the Premisses afore mentioned, we ye s^d Indians have hereunto sett our hands & seals this Twenty first day of Aprill anno Dom, 1730[, which,] — Katinner — Noundaugaron — Kahawelemin [and] Wittnesses in ye present of ye Justices — Abel — Telemahawogh — Kateas" (GTM-PC, box P26, folder 14).

Sander/Nachnawachena (fl. 1719–1751/pm. 1770)
1719: Sander

"Kawahym[,] Sander[']s mother" develops an account with the Ulster County trader; "her son" is also active on the account. Purchases are recorded of ribbon, textiles, strouds, floret (silk ribbon), stockings, a girdle, 1 cap, a hat, a jackknife, 1 pair of scissors, shot, molasses, and rum. "Cred[it] for 1 dressed skin" at 24 guilders is noted toward the debt ([15–16]).

November 22, 1719, to May 1, 1721: Sander de Wielt

Develops one of the largest accounts with the trader; "his brother's daughter" is also mentioned on the account. Purchases are recorded of blue textiles, strouds, cotton, red penneston, 1 coarse blanket, 3 stroud blankets, a girdle, a shirt, a cap, buttons, lead, gunpowder, beer, rum, 1 small glass bottle, and 1 "schepel" of Indian corn. Payments of dressed skins, deer meat, bear hide, martens, raccoon, and a canoe are listed. Sander makes "1 trip to manesenck [Minisink]" and another "to namesinck [Nawesinck] with [the Indian man] herij" to earn credit, and receives credit "for his note for moses du pri [of Rochester.]" The trader also reports that 5 guilders are paid on the account "by benyamen du pri" ([17–18]).

January 1719 to June 24, 1728: Sander

"Lendert [or Lendart] the savage[,] Sander's brother" develops an account with the trader; "his mother's" debt is also mentioned. Purchases are recorded of strouds, baize, colored woolen, 2 duffel blankets, 3 shirts, a girdle, "1 pair of buckles," a string of beads, a knife, awls, gunpowder, lead, rum, and a gun at 240 guilders. The trader notes that Lendert "returned the gun[,] the stock brok[en]" and received credit of 200 guilders. Payments of 3 bear hides, 10 martens, 1 katlos (lynx), "20 dressed deerskins," and 2 deer are listed. He receives credit against his debt for dressing skins, "for going to Nawesingh," and "for 5 day[s] mowing" ([21–22], [111]).

1720–1727: Sander de Wielt

Sander is noted with an ongoing account by the trader; "his youngest brother" and "his mother" and "his wife" are active on the account. They make purchases of linen, 1 stroud and 3 duffel blankets, stockings, gunpowder, lead, "1 lb pepper," and rum. Payment of 4 deerskins is listed; "His brother is cred[itor] for 2¼ deer meat." Sander receives additional credit for a canoe, for preparing skins, "for 1 trip to Menisenck [Minisink]," and "for 4 days working at southfield" ([41–42]).

June 24, 1728, to July 20, 1729: Sander

"sander['s [youngest?] brother willam" is noted with an account by the trader; he makes purchases of strouds, ribbons, colored shirts, "3 ells of stocking garter," a duffel blanket, "2 ells of band and awls," gunpowder, lead, flintstones, an axe, "4 lb sugar," and rum. "Cred[it] for 1 beaver," "for 10 days mowing on the farm," and "for cutting the meadow" is noted toward his debt ([41–42]).

September 7, 1741: Nachnawachena alias Sanders

Ulster County justices and precinct supervisors report the appearance at Kingston of "The Esopus Indians haveing desired a Meeting of the Justices — Nachnawachena alias Sanders, Chief Sachim together with Hakawaremin, Qualaghquininjon, Walagagkin — under Shachims and 23 Indians more besides Squas & Children — The Indians being asked what they had to offer to the Justices, and made answer that they Came only to Shak-hands & Renue the friendship, and gave three Small deer Skins Eight [musk] Rats & two minks, and further Said they were a poor people & had no better present to make, and they Expected that Each ought to assist the other, The Justices answered that they were Glad that they Came to Renue the peace which has been kept all along by the ancestors, and shall on the part of the justices and their children be kept as long as the world stands, And the Justices told them that if they should come by the knowledge of any Enemys to hurt the Christians that they shall acquaint us with it, as wee Shall doe to them, if wee know of any Enemy to hurt them, to which they all agreed, The Sachims Shewed the Articles of peace made in Writting by our ancestors, which they promised to observe on their part, & the Justices promissed also to observe on their part, The Indians Said they Intended to Come next Spring to Renue the peace again, and they, were answered that when they wanted to speake with the Justices — that they ought first to Send a messenger to know when it would Suit the Justices that they might acquaint The Justices that live Remote, The Justices and Supervisors give the Indians a present of Eight pounds Eight Shillings & Six pence, Ordered that the Indians have a Copy of these proceedings" (GTM-PC, box P26, folder 14; *PWJ*, 1:15–16).

August 3, 1743: Sander

Ulster County justices report "On [the] Complaint of Maj.ʳ Hardenbergh [Sr.] in behalf of himself and partners proprietors of a certain Tract of land in the said County, That the Esopus Indians hindered the Surveyor [Henry Wooster] appointed by the said proprietors to run the out lines of said Tract, desires that yᵉ Justices will be pleased to order that the Sachim of the Indians be desired, that he and the Indians under [him] come here in Kingston, To meet the Justices concerning the Premisses, and that the Sachem acquaint eight days before he intends to meet them, ordered that Capᵗ Hoorebeek be desired to acquaint the Sachim with this order, and that a copy of this order be sent by the Clerk to Capᵗ Hornbeek, . . . Capᵗ Hornebeek sent a letter dated the 18ᵗʰ August signed by Sander the Sachim wherein he signifies that he and the Indians intends to meet the Justices on Saturday the 27ᵗʰ, August 1743, and desires that the [white] People may not sell any strong Liquors to the Indians about that time" (GTM-PC, box P26, folder 14).

August 27, 1743: Nachnawachena alias Sanders

Ulster County justices report the appearance of "The Esopus Indians having mett according to the time appointed by the Sachim, viz.ᵗ — Nachnawachena alias Sanders, Chief Sachim, together with Kakawaremen alias Hendrick Hekan[,] Quaalaghquainyou alias Abeel, Walengaghkin alias Mattakie, Mamarekamek alias Malluijink[,] yᵉ under Sachims and several other Indians, Squaes & Children — the Indians being asked why they hindered the Surveyor to run the out lines of Maj.ʳ Hardenbergh & Company — Hendrick Hekan answered that the reason was because they had no notice given them of the Measuring, if they had, had notice given them, they would not have hindered the Surveyor, Maj.^{r} Hardenbergh in behalf of himself and Company desires that the Justices acquaint the Indians that he desires only to run the out lines of his Patent in order to find out the true owners of the land, and that the measuring shall not take away their land, that after it is measured, he will not claim any of their land, without first, agreeing and paying the particular owner of each Tract except what is already purchased of some of the Indians, The Indians Agree that the Maj.^{r} and Company shall have priviledge to Survey round their Patent and up the River Papakonk and the land already purchased, and also to divide their land but not to claim any right to the soil before it is purchased from the Indian owners, and they ask what the Maj.^{r} will give them for the privileage of measuring as aforesaid, Maj.^{r} Hardenbergh desired that the Indians would ask what they thought reasonable for that libertie, and the Indians desire the Maj.^{r} that he would give them six gallons Rum to which the Maj.^{r} agrees, and desires that they will name the Indians, that own land from the right of the Minissink Indians and so Northward as far as the Esopus Indians Claim, The Indians answer that it belongs to four Tribes [or families], to witt, ye Kighshepaw, Mahew, Mogewehogh, [and] Kaghkatewees, The Maj.^{r} promisses in the presence of the Justices and Sachims that he and Company will not buy any lands but what shall be in the presence of the Justice and Sachims, The Maj.^{r} desires that the Indians will help him to carry his baggage and give their Cannoes when wanted for payment, to which they agree, The Indians being asked, if they had anything to offer, they answered that they were glad that they were so well agreed, they for their part were very well satisfied, ordered that a copy of these proceedings be given by the Clerk to the Chief Sachim, 27 August 1743. The Indians gave 2 Deer Skins one String of Wampon 8/5 in pennys 1/28th Silver & 3 [Musk] Ratts . . . Ordered Three Duffell Blankets One Stript Blanket [and] Four Hatts to be given to ye Indians" (GTM-PC, box P26, folder 14).

May 7, 1745: Sander

Ulster County justices report the arrival of "Sander Chief Sachim of the Esopus Indians" accompanied by "Hendrick Hekan[,] Renuade ye Sachims and Severall other Indians — — — by Abell their Interpreter brings in Court a Beaver and four Strings of Wampon and they Said They gave that to Confirm the Peace formerly Made by our Ancestors and Theirs — They gave also a Dear Skin and five Minks to Shake hands in friendship — They gave Seven [Musk] Ratts, they Complain that there are So many Taverns, which is a great Reason of their Poverty and Desire that they may be Remedied — They gave 2 [Musk] Ratts one Dear Skin

& 23 Pennys and Complains that their Produce is too Cheap and the Commodities which they want from the Christians to Dear, and therefore they Desire that their produce may be Dearer and the Christians Commodity Cheaper — They were told they Shall have their answers in the afternoon — The Answer of the Justices to the Indians: 1ˢᵗ The Justices take it very well of them to renew the Peace made by both the ancestors, and that the Same be kept in friendship on both Sides as long as the sun and moon Shines. 2ⁿᵈ The Justices Join heartly in Shaking hands with greatest friendship. 3ʳᵈ As to the Taverns the Justices Cannot Lesson the number of them and advise you to Sobriety and to mind their Hunting to Maintain their Familys, But if any white People Defraud or Cheat them . if they Complain and it appearing so . the Justices will See them Justice Done. 4. As to the Price of goods on both Sides must be Regulated according as Parties on both Sides Can agree. The Justices Ordered to be given to the Indians 5 gall. Rum, [a] Barrll Beer and 3 Loaves of Bread, 4 lb Powder, 2 lb Lead, [a] Calfe, 5 lb Bacon, t[w]o Strouds [and] 6 Hatts" (UCCS, 1737–50, mss.).

June 6, 1746: Corpoaan/Corpaaen/Corpoane alias Sander

A "Sopus Indian" conveying land on the Upper Delaware River within the Hardenbergh Patent straddling Albany and Ulster counties, and one of three principal signers acknowledging receipt of payment for the lands (UCDB, EE:63–65).

June 3, 1751: Sandervatheverander

The Indians "Sandervatheverander, Anough, Hendrickhokeau, Swathekeen, Able, Renp, Shenck, Mounau, Jacobus, Mathesso, Benjamin, and others, All lawfull owners and proprietors" convey to Johannes Hardenbergh Jr. for 149 pounds 19 shillings "all that certain tract or parcel of land, situate, lying and being, between the Fish-kill and Papagonck river, in the county of Ulster and Albany, Beginning at the head of the Fish-kill, and from thence running with [a] direct line, to the head of Catricks-kill [Kaaterskill], and from the head of Catricks-kill with a direct line to the head of Papagonck river, and thence down the east side of the said river Papagonck to a certain place called Shokakeen, where the Papagonck river falls in the Fish-kill, and then up the said Fish-kill, including the same, to the head thereof or the place of beginning" (Gould, *History of Delaware County*, 242).

December 10, 1770: Sander

The "Indians Sander their Chief Sachem & Hendrick Hegan" are noted in Colonel John Bradstreet's argument before the New York Council against the Hardenbergh Patent proprietors claims to lands lying between the East and West Branches of the Delaware River, and who attended a "Treaty" concerning these lands on August 27, 1743 (Lincoln, *Manuscript Records of the French and Indian War*, 118).

Lewahlauqua (fl. 1719–1751)

November 8, 1719, to July 1724: Jurewen

"the son of Sar[,] Jurewen's sister" develops a small account with the Ulster County trader; "he" (Jurewen, "indebted" for 34 guilders) and "his wife" are also active on the account. Purchases are recorded of 1 stroud blanket, 1 coarse blanket, a cap, 1 knife, gunpowder, lead, shot, rum, and a pair of shoes. Payments of 4 skins, 2 deer quarters, 2 beavers, a raccoon, "1 fat sow or pig," and "4 sch[epels] cranberies" are listed against the debt. Jurewen receives credit on the account "for 4 days on the farm [and] 4 days for his wife" ([19–20]).

1721: Juren

"Juren and [his wife] hanna" are noted with an account by the trader; they make purchases of strouds, baize, penneston, "Cotton for their daughter," 1 duffel blanket, gunpowder, lead, and rum. They receive 36 guilders "Cred[it] for spinning" and an additional 10 guilders "For 5 days spinning" to reduce their debt ([35–36]).

May 1, 1751: Lewahlauqua or Jurryan

Listed among the twenty-three Indian signers receiving 102 pounds 16 shillings for confirming the boundaries of the Hardenbergh Patent (Deed mss., Senate House State Historic Site, Kingston, NY).

Allamaaseeit (fl. 1721–1761)

1721 to February 1, 1728: Willam Krom

"Willam Krom[,] tatepagh['s] so[n]" develops an ongoing account with the Ulster County trader; "his wife" is also active on the account. The trader reports that lead and gunpowder were fetched for him "by y[our] H[onor's] mother." Other purchases are recorded of strouds, baize, 2 duffel blankets, 3 coarse blankets, gunpowder, lead, flintstones, rum, 1 knife, and 4 awls. Payments of 1 elk skin, 6 lbs beaver, and "11 skins not dressed," and credit "for 1 sch[epel] grits and ½ sch[epel] small beans" are noted to reduce the debt ([47–48]).

December 2, 1745: Lamiut

Major Jacobus Swartwout of colonial Minisink (present-day Port Jervis) writes to New York Governor Clinton during King George's War informing him of a report made by the Indians Lamiut and Roghso "about the 10th of November last" that the French and their Indian allies on the Mississippi River intended in the winter "to destroy Albany, Soapus [Kingston] and Minisink, and likewise the Frontiers of [New] Jersey & Pensylvania" (*NJHS*, 4:288–89).

June 6, 1746: Lamaseet/Lamaseeth alias William Crom

A "Sopus Indian" conveying land on the Upper Delaware River in the Hardenbergh Patent straddling Albany and Ulster counties (UCDB, EE:63–65).

August 2, 1746: Alamaseak/Aleamset

One of the "Native proprietors & heirs . . . of Cashichton" or Menissink Indians selling land within the Hardenbergh Patent in southern Ulster County (UCDB, EE:61–63).

December 10, 1750: Capt Allamouse

The Pennsylvania Colonial Council receives an affidavit reporting the "Obstruction made by some AEsopus or Mohiccon Indians to Edward Sculls' surveying Lands within the New Purchase" at the forks of the Lechawacksein Creek several months earlier on October 28, by "Cap^ts Allamouse and Clitches, who . . . were sent by their King Tattanhiek" or Tattanhick (*MPCP*, 5:489–90).

May 6, 1755: Allaamaseeitt/Allaamaseitt/Allamaaseeit/Allomooseeitt/Allemasaitt

The principal signer listed among the "Sachems and chiefs of the Antient [*sic*] Tribe and Nation of Indians Called Ninneepauues otherwise and in English known by the name of the Delaware Indians" conveying to Connecticut setters for 500 Spanish dollars land on the Upper Delaware River in Pennsylvania and New York, extending north from the Lackawach River to the Neeconnocking (or Pankatooma) River and west to Moshooetoo mount or Moshetoo (mosquito) hill. Also listed among the four "Ninnepaues Sachems" and principal "grantors" signing a memorandum in behalf of the rest confirming the sale (*SCP*, 1:260–72).

February 17, 1761: Attamesick

Noted by the Pennsylvania Colonial Council as one of the Delaware Indian signers to purchases made by Connecticut settlers on the Upper Delaware River "about Six years ago; That afterwards a second purchase was made . . . from the said Indians, either as a farther purchase in extent, or in confirmation of the former" (*MPCP*, 8:563–66).

April 11, 1761: Allamesick

Noted by the Pennsylvania Council as a Delaware signer to "Indian Purchases" of land made by settlers "under the Charter of Connecticut" (*MPCP*, 8:598–600).

Noundawagaeron (fl. 1722–1751)

August 18, 1722: Renap

Listed among the "Sopus Indians" renewing peace with Ulster County justices at Kingston and complaining about settler encroachment on lands near

Chechunck, Coxsing, Mammekotton, and the Little Esopus Creek (GTM-PC, box P26, folder 14).

January 29, 1723: Roondaghnaer/Roondaghneere

Esopus Indian "Shachims" renewing peace before the Kingston Court "acquainted the Justices with the death of Peter, and that they have put Roondaghneere in his room" (GTM-PC, box P26, folder 14).

October 10, 1724: Sundagh

The Ulster County trader lists the incurred debt of 12 guilders "on 4 kan rum fetched for sundagh" by the Indian man "pony" ([77]).

November 14, 1724, to August 13, 1725: Runup

"runup[,] the Husband of queck['s] daughter" and "his wife" develop an account with the Ulster County trader. Purchases are recorded of cotton, strouds, "1 box of [paint]," and rum. They received credit of 20 guilders "for hops" against the "remainder on one coarse blanket." Payment of "1½ lb dressed skins" is also listed to reduce the debt ([59–60]).

June 22, 1728: Renop

Mr. Roleff Elting informs Ulster County justices "that he has acquainted ankerop the Chief Sachim and Renop another Chief Indian" about the felony commited against Jacob ten Brook by the Indian James, "and they Said that the Said James was none of their Indians and that they would not protect him" (Minutes, Court of Justice of the Peace, 1719–44).

April 21, 1730: Noundaugaron/Noundawagaeron alias Renniap

The "Chief Shachim" noted among Indian signers appearing before the Kingston Court to claim land at Mamecatten (or Memekitton) lying between Nepenaack and Assewaykemak, and accepting a gift confirming an earlier Indian sale of the tract on June 8, 1696 (GTM-PC, box P26, folder 14).

May 7, 1745: Renuade

An Esopus sachem noted during a renewal of the Nicolls Treaty at Kingston desiring the regulation of prices by county justices on exchanges of native produce and European trade goods (UCCS, 1737–50, mss.).

December 2, 1745: Roghso

Major Jacobus Swartwout of colonial Minisink (present-day Port Jervis) writes to New York Governor Clinton during King George's War informing him of a report made by the Indians Lamiut and Roghso "about the 10th of November last" that the French and their Indian allies on the Mississippi River intended in the winter "to destroy Albany, Soapus [Kingston] and Minisink, and likewise the Frontiers of [New] Jersey & Pensylvania" (NJHS, 4:288–89).

June 6, 1746: Noondawiharind/Noondauwcharind alias Rinnip

A "Sopus Indian" conveying land on the Upper Delaware River in the Hard-enbergh Patent straddling Albany and Ulster counties (UCDB, EE:63–65).

May 1, 1751: Rynnip

A participant noted among the Indian signers receiving 102 pounds 16 shil-lings for confirming the boundaries of the Hardenbergh Patent (Deed mss., Sen-ate House State Historic Site, Kingston, NY).

June 3, 1751: Renp

Noted among the twenty-two "Indian proprietors" receiving 149 pounds 19 shillings for their rights to lands "between the Fish-kill and Papagonck river" in the Hardenbergh Patent (Gould, *History of Delaware County*, 242).

Tatteu (fl. 1724–1728)

1724 to May 22, 1726: Tatteu

"tatteu[,] Andris['s] wife's brother" develops an account with the Ulster County trader; "his sister" fetches strouds for him. Other purchases of cotton, gunpowder, lead, a knife, rum, and beer are recorded ([75]).

February 2, 1726: Tateu

Listed by the trader as fetching "1½ ell of cotton and 1 bottle rum" for the Indian man "andris the savage" ([101]).

1727 to 1728: Tatweu

Tatweu, "his wife," and "his child" are noted with an account by the trader; the Indian woman "Catharina" fetches a shirt for them. Purchases are recorded of strouds, white baize, cotton, a coarse blanket, 1 duffel and 1 stroud blanket, 2 colored shirts, gunpowder, lead, flintstones, a pipe, rum, and 1 bread; "his wife's account" contains a purchase of 1 shirt and strouds for stockings. Tatweu is reported as buying "8 kan rum to drink at his si[s]ter's grave" (in 1727). Payments in bear meat, 1 bear hide, martens, 2 raccoons, and 2 skins are listed toward their debt ([75–76]).

March 9, 1728: Tateu

Noted by the trader as having "had 5½ kan [rum] on the promise to show a mine in the spring" ([76]).

June 15, 1728: Tateew

"Tateew, Ochangues and Neckarind Indians and the Native owners and proprietors" convey to Cornelius Hornebeck and Frederick Schoonmaker for 10 pounds currency, "a Certain Mine . . . Lying and being within Rochester [Precinct] . . . on the South Side of the Sandbergs kill near to a Certaine place

Called Nepenagh [Napanoch] together with the Quantity of four hundred acres of Land." Affirmed on June 19, 1728, in a memorandum by Abraham Gaasbeek Chambers, a judge of the Ulster County Court of Common Pleas (UCDB, DD:6–7).

Mackeeus (fl. 1724–1762)
December 27, 1724, to 1727: Unnamed

"pansogh's wife and son" and he are listed with an account by the Ulster County trader; "his son" purchases cotton, blue baize, stockings, 1 knife, a shirt, and rum on the account. Their son also has a credit of 21 guilders "on his bill," which the trader "paid with 1 colored shirt" ([63–64]).

1725 to 1729: Mack

"mack[,] pansogh['s] son" develops a sizeable account with the trader; the Indian woman "sar the savage woman" fetches gunpowder for him. Other purchases are recorded of cotton, strouds, colored textiles, 1 coarse blanket, 1 duffel blanket, a colored shirt, gunpowder, lead, a knife, and rum. Payments in deerskin, beaver, 10 raccoons, and 1 bear hide listed. He performs fieldwork on two occasions for eight and seven "days on the farm" to reduce the debt ([79–80]).

March 8, 1729, to August 1, 1729: Mack

"mack[,] pansogh['s] son" and "his wife[,] Catryn" are noted with ongoing accounts by the trader. "½ sch[epel of] bran" and "½ ell of cotton" are fetched for him "by y[our] H[onor's] sister"; a "kan" of rum is fetched by the Indian man kobes. Mack makes purchases of cotton, strouds, 1 stroud blanket, a colored shirt, gunpowder, lead, beer, rum, "1 sch[epel of] bran," and ½ bread. His debt also includes "1 small skin for the smith." Payments of 1 raccoon, 8 martens, and a skin, and credit "for 10 days on the farm" are listed to reduce his debt. Catryn purchases duffels, cotton, 1 stroud, 1 duffel and 2 coarse blankets, 2 knives, a kettle, gunpowder, and rum. Payments of 17 lbs skins and "10 lb fat" are noted toward her debt ([99–100]).

August 2, 1746: Machcatin/Makokin

One of the "Native proprietors & heirs . . . of Cashichton" or Menissink Indians selling land within the Hardenbergh Patent in southern Ulster County (UCDB, EE:61–63).

December 20, 1754: Mactkka

Reported among the "Sachems of the Anchant and Renowned . . . Delaware nation" endorsing a deed to Connecticut settlers for the "Eastern Lands" on the

Delaware River in New York south of the Hardenberg Patent for 108 "Spanish mill Dollars" (*SCP*, 1:196–200).

May 6, 1755: Mackeus/Makeus/Mackeeus

Listed among the Ninneepauues or Delaware Indian signers conveying land to Connecticut setters on the Upper Delaware River in Pennsylvania and New York, and one of the four "Ninnepaues Sachems" and principal "grantors" endorsing a memorandum in behalf of the rest confirming the sale (*SCP*, 1:260–72).

October 29, 1755: Mackeus/Macheus

"Mackeus Kalestias Wescollong [and] Mechokenous Sachems and chiefs of the Tribe and Nation of the Indians Called Ninnepauues otherwise and in English Known by the Name of the Delaware Indians" convey to Connecticut setters for 110 Spanish dollars and English trade goods land on the Upper Delaware River in Pennsylvania extending south from the Lackawaak River to the Delaware water gap and "west To the Mohawk Terretorys on Mosheetoo hill or mount" (*SCP*, 1:308–14).

February 17, 1761: Mayhios

Noted by the Pennsylvania Colonial Council as one of the Delaware Indian signers to two land sales "made about Six years ago" to Connecticut settlers on the Upper Delaware River (*MPCP*, 8:563–66).

April 11, 1761: Maykeos

Noted by the Pennsylvania Council as a Delaware signer to "Indian Purchases" of land made by settlers "under the Charter of Connecticut" (*MPCP*, 8:598–600).

June 22, 1762: Mackcuwas

One of the Indian sachems of the "Delawares, Mohiccons, and Opings" endorsing Teedyuscung's complaint to Sir William Johnson about his refusal to appoint a clerk to record discussions regarding land claims during a treaty conference at Easton, Pennsylvania, from June 18 to 28 (*PWJ*, 3:762–71).

Tanksetackin/Young Suwies (fl. 1725–1746)

May 13, 1725: Unnamed

"Sawis['s] son" fetches "2 ells of cotton" from the Ulster County trader on the account of the Indian man "Jan palin[,] nenison[']s son" ([15]).

June 6, 1746: Tanksetachin/Tanksetackin alias Charles Brodhead alias Young Suwies

A "Sopus Indian" conveying land on the Upper Delaware River within the Hardenbergh Patent straddling Albany and Ulster counties (UCDB, EE:63–65).

Kobes (fl. 1725–1751)
June 7, 1725: Kobes

"Kobes[,] sawagonck hendreck['s] son who has kisa[']s daughter" develops an account with the Ulster County trader; "his wife" and "her brother" are also active on the account; [derck?] "westbrock" (of Rochester) fetches rum for them. Purchases recorded of white baize, 1 stroud blanket, a coarse blanket, 1 coat, a colored shirt, a white shirt, a knife, gunpowder, 1 bread, rum, beer, and cider. Payment of "4 lb beavers" and a skin is listed ([65–66]).

December 30, 1725, to 1728: Kosoes or Kobes

"kosoes or kobes[,] hendreck sawagonck['s] son" and "his wife[,] kesay['s] daughter Cattrijin" are noted with ongoing accounts by the trader; they make payment "on the debt of wiijakas" ("former husband of kisay['s] daughter"; [59]) and "escorted" an Indian boy. The Indian woman "Gertie" fetches gunpowder for them. A small debt of 6 guilders is listed with "tobyas Hornbeck" (of Rochester). Purchases are recorded of strouds, cotton, a coarse blanket, a shirt, gunpowder, flintstones, lead, 1 kettle, a knife, 1 jackknife, pipes, 1 bread, rum, and cider. Payments of 4 bear hides, 62 lbs elk skins, 12 lbs dressed skins, 7 lbs skins, raccoons, martens, and 2 minks are listed to reduce their debt ([85–86]).

August 1, 1729: Kobes

The trader notes that "kobes" fetched 1 kan of rum for "Mack[,] pansogh['s] son" ([99–100]).

May 1, 1751: Cakosoes

A participant noted among the Indian signers receiving 102 pounds 16 shillings for confirming the boundaries of the Hardenbergh Patent (Deed mss., Senate House State Historic Site, Kingston, NY).

Mathesso (fl. 1725–1751)
August 21, 1725: Mattiso

This man, son of manonck, appears with a small debt for "½ gall[on] rum" on his father's account with the Ulster County trader ([67]).

August 28, 1725, to December 3, 1726: Mattiso

"mattiso[,] mannonck['s] son" develops an account with the Ulster County trader; "his father" is active on the account and fetches gunpowder and lead. Other purchases are recorded of strouds, 1 stroud blanket, a colored shirt, 1 "dobelstin" shirt, gunpowder, lead, and rum. The trader also reported that he bought "4 kan of rum at [old] abram[']s burial" and had repairs done "on his [flint] lock" at 2 guilders. Payment of "2 dressed skins" and credit "for 3 days on the farm" and "for 1 deer by his mother" are listed toward the debt ([73–74]).

July 21, 1726: Mattiso

The trader reports that Mattiso fetched cotton for "kattias[,] manonck[']s son" ([69]).

1727 to June 8, 1729: Matisso

"matisso[,] manonck['s] son" is noted with an ongoing account by the trader; "his wife[,] pitternel[?]" and "her mother[']s account" are also mentioned. The Indian man "ponij" buys rum and a colored shirt on the account. One ell of strouds was fetched "by y[our] H[onor's] mother" at 16 guilders. New purchases are recorded of strouds, cotton, 1 colored and 1 "dobelstin" shirt, a knife, gunpowder, lead, flint-stones, cider, and rum. Payments of 4 lbs beavers, 18½ lbs skins, 1 beaver, 1 fox, and "2 cats," and credit "for 1 day shooting fire" are noted to reduce his debt ([107–108]).

June 3, 1751: Mathesso

Noted among the twenty-two "Indian proprietors" receiving 149 pounds 19 shillings for their rights to lands "between the Fish-kill and Papagonck river" in the Hardenbergh Patent (Gould, *History of Delaware County*, 242).

Kattias (fl. 1725–1761)

March 14, 1725, to July 27, 1727: Kattias

"kattias[,] manonck[']s son" develops an account with the Ulster County trader; "his mother," "his wife," and the Indian man Mattiso "fetched" various goods for him. His wife is listed as "tatapagh['s] daughter[,] pitternel." Purchases are recorded of cotton, strouds, stockings, gunpowder, lead, rum, a coarse blanket, "a fine [colored] shirt," and "1 pair of dutch shoes"; payment of 2 bear hides and "8 lb dressed skins" is noted. He also received credit "for 4½ [days] mowing" to reduce the debt. His wife received "Cred[it] for 1 day of harvesting flax" toward her account ([69–70]).

April 21, 1730: Kateas

A witness noted among Indian signers appearing before the Kingston Court to claim land at Mamecatten (or Memekitton) lying between Nepenaack and Assewaykemak, and accepting a gift confirming an earlier Indian sale of the tract on June 8, 1696 (GTM-PC, box P26, folder 14).

August 2, 1746: Carichtsias/Caches

One of the "Native proprietors & heirs . . . of Cashichton" or Menissink Indians selling land within the Hardenbergh Patent in southern Ulster County (UCDB, EE:61–63).

December 10, 1750: Clitches

The Pennsylvania Colonial Council receives an affidavit reporting the "Obstruction made by some AEsopus or Mohiccon Indians to Edward Sculls' surveying Lands within the New Purchase" at the forks of the Lechawacksein Creek several months earlier on October 28, by "Cap^ts Allamouse and Clitches, who . . . were sent by their King Tattanhiek" or Tattanhick (*MPCP*, 5:489–90).

December 20, 1754: Cark

Reported among the "Sachems of the Anchant and Renowned . . . Delaware nation" endorsing a deed to Conncticut settlers for the "Eastern Lands" on the Delaware River in New York south of the Hardenberg Patent for 108 "Spanish mill Dollars" (*SCP*, 1:196–200).

May 6, 1755: Kalestias

Listed among the Ninneepauues or Delaware Indian signers conveying land to Connecticut setters on the Upper Delaware River in Pennsylvania and New York, and one of the four "Ninnepaues Sachems" and principal "grantors" endorsing a memorandum in behalf of the rest confirming the sale (*SCP*, 1:260–72).

October 29, 1755: Kalestias

One of four Ninnepauues or Delaware sachems selling land to Connecticut setters west of the Delaware River in Pennsylvania (*SCP*, 1:308–14).

February 17, 1761: Christias

Noted by the Pennsylvania Colonial Council as one of the Delaware Indian signers to two land sales "made about Six years ago" to Connecticut settlers on the Upper Delaware River (*MPCP*, 8:563–66).

April 11, 1761: Christias

Noted by the Pennsylvania Council as a Delaware signer to "Indian Purchases" of land made by settlers "under the Charter of Connecticut" (*MPCP*, 8:598–600).

John Pauling (fl. 1725–1771/pm. 1785)

May 13, 1725: Jan Palin

The Indian man "Jan palin[,] nenison[']s son" is noted with a small debt by the Ulster County trader; credit purchase is recorded "On 1 girdle" and "his brother on 1 knife" ([15]).

June 6, 1746: Mathalane alias Jan

A "Sopus Indian" conveying land on the Upper Delaware River in the Hardenbergh Patent straddling Albany and Ulster counties (UCDB, EE:63–65).

May 1, 1751: Matheheian

A participant noted among the Indian signers receiving 102 pounds 16 shillings for confirming the boundaries of the Hardenbergh Patent (Deed mss., Senate House State Historic Site, Kingston, NY).

June 3, 1751: Jan Palling

"Suppau, Jan Palling . . . and twenty other Indian proprietors" receive 149 pounds 19 shillings for their rights to lands "between the Fish-kill and Papagonck river" in the Hardenbergh Patent (Gould, *History of Delaware County*, 242).

1771: John Paulin

"John Paulin and Sapan, two Esopus Indians" show surveyor William Cockburn the location of Indian place names on the Upper Delaware River and its tributaries in the Hardenberg Patent (Cockburn, "Hardenberg Patent Survey Map," 1771).

1785: John Pauling/John Pawling

Identified in a memorandum relating to the Hardenberg Patent's western boundary as the son of Nisinas (CFLP, box 6, folder 6, #94).

Aroensack (fl. 1727–1751)

May 15, 1727, to July 21, 1728: Arronshagkie/Arons Haghkie

"arronshagkie or ankerop[']s son" is noted with an account by the Ulster County trader. Purchases are recorded of various lengths of strouds, "floret [silk] garters" and baize, 1 stroud blanket, a colored shirt, flintstones, gunpowder, lead, and rum. Payments in elk skins, deerskins, and otters, and credit of 27 guilders "for 4 days on the farm" are listed toward his debt ([105–106]).

May 1, 1751: Aroensack

A participant noted among the Indian signers receiving 102 pounds 16 shillings for confirming the boundaries of the Hardenbergh Patent (Deed mss., Senate House State Historic Site, Kingston, NY).

Willemachecane (fl. 1728–1746)

June 24, 1728, to July 20, 1729: Willam

"sander[']s [youngest?] brother willam" is noted with an account by the Ulster County trader; he makes purchases of strouds, ribbons, colored shirts, "3 ells of stocking garter," a blanket, "2 ells of band and awls," gunpowder, lead, flintstones, an axe, "4 lb sugar," and rum. "Cred[it] for 1 beaver," for "10 days mowing on the farm," and "for cutting the meadow" are noted toward his debt ([41–42]).

June 6, 1746: Willemachecane alias Cobis

A "Sopus Indian" conveying land on the Upper Delaware River within the Hardenbergh Patent straddling Albany and Ulster counties (UCDB, EE:63–65).

August 2, 1746: Capt Kobis

"Moonhaw['s] brother" and a witness listed among the "Native proprietors & heirs . . . of Cashichton" or "Menissink Indians" selling land within the Hardenbergh Patent in southern Ulster County (UCDB, EE:61–63).

Wappinger Cohort

List of Main Names, Dates, and Page Numbers in Appendix

Kechkenond (fl. 1680–1721)
December 23, 1680: Kakenand

One of the Indian grantors conveying "the land commonly caled the hopp ground" in the town of Bedford, Westchester County (Robert Bolton, *The History of the Several Towns, Manors, and Patents of the County of Westchester, from its First Settlement to the Present Time* [New York: Chas. F. Roper, 1881], 1:13–14).
August 13, 1702: Kechkenond

A participant to the land sale confirming Adolph Philipse's Highland or Upper Patent extending to the Connecticut border (PGP, P14, #56).
? 1715: Kegkenond

"Kegkenond's sister" is listed with a small debt by the Ulster County trader; purchase recorded is of strouds, ½ lb gunpowder, and shot ([11]).
? 1719: Kegkenond

Kegkenond is listed with a modest account by the trader; "his daughter" and "her husband" are also active on the account. Kegkenond has a debt "from older times" and owes 2 guilders "to the smith for the axe." New purchases are recorded of cotton, strouds, baize, 1 blanket, 1 duffel blanket, and 1 pint rum. Payments of deerskins and "1 deer meat" are listed toward his debt ([13–14]).
August 9, 1721: Keghkenond

"Keghkenond[']s daughter" along with "her father" and "her husband" are listed with a sizeable debt by the trader. "Keghkenond['s] daughter" escorts an unnamed Indian woman and makes purchases of white baize, fine colored textiles, 1 duffel blanket, and rum. Her father is indebted for 9 guilders on the "remainder of textiles." Her husband incurs a debt of 31 guilders on strouds and service rendered "for repairing his [flint]lock" ([35]).

Kaghqueront (fl. 1680–1722)
June 15, 1680: Paquetarent

A witness and one of "two Sakamakers" approving a grant of land to Arnout Viele made by "Highland Indians" in the town of Poughkeepsie (Jonathan Pearson and A. J. F. van Laer, trans. and eds., *Early Records of the City and County of Albany and Colony of Rensselaerswijck* [Albany: Univ. of the State of New York, 1869–1919], 2:84–85).

September 3, 1683: Kakeroni/Kakaroni

"Kakeroni [the principal signer and] for his brothers named Hans and Tapowacs" is listed among the "Esoopus or Wappinger" grantors declaring before the Kingston Court in Ulster County that they had conveyed "land situated in the Lange Rack [Long Reach] along the Kill named missinck on the east bank along the [Hudson] river . . . Commencing from the land of the savages named Massany and Packhins [in the City of Poughkeepsie], the land is named Sepasgewack . . . Kakaroni owner of the land declares to be satisfied. But everything must be paid between now and next spring, as per list [of trade goods]." The sale is permitted "but subject to the Heer governor's approval" (Dutch Records, Kingston, book 1, 239–40).

? August 1685: Penarand

One of the "natives and principal owners . . . of Ketchtawong" selling land to New York Governor Thomas Dongan "on the east side of Hudson's river, within the county of West Chester, beginning at Kechtawong Creek [Croton River], and so running along Hudson's river northerly to the land of Stephannus Van Cortlandt['s]" Appamaghpogh and Meahagh purchase of 1683 (Bolton, *History of the Several Towns, Manors, and Patents*, 1:92–93; see 86–87 for 1683 purchase).

April 26, 1688: Kaghqueront

"Kaghqueront and other the Natives by a Lycense of Coll [Thomas] Dongan, some time Governour of this Province," convey to Johannes Cuyler of Albany a tract of "Vacant Land" east of the Casper Creek in the town of Poughkeepsie, "bounded to the North by the Land of said Robert Sanders and Meyndert Harmense [Poughkeepsie or Minnisink Patent] to the East by the Land of said Coll Cortlandt & Company [Rombout Patent] to the South by the Land of said Peter the Brewer and to the West by the Land of said Collonell Schuyler [Patent]" (NYBP, 7:143–45).

September 2, 1697: Kaghqueront

Johannes Cuyler of Albany patents "Certaine Tracts of Vacant Land" east of the Casper Creek in the town of Poughkeepsie, "Purchased from Kaghqueront [on April 26, 1688] . . . as also the Vacant Land and meadow [called Matapan] which Tapuas, the [Highland] Indian, conveyed to Lawrence Van Ale[n] and Gerret Lansing [on May 16, 1683]" (NYBP, 7:143–45).

November 27, 1722: Peghtarend

Peghtarend and "his wife" are listed with an account by the Ulster County trader; a debt of 12 guilders is listed as being owed "to mary Stenbergen" (of Kingston?). Purchases are recorded of strouds, duffels, 2 stroud blankets, stroud stockings, paint, 2 barrels, 1 bread, 3 qt molasses, 1 bar lead, rum, and a saddle. The trader lists payment "for 2 horses settling the account" ([51–52]).

Old Nimham/Sackoenemack (fl. 1696–1744/pm. 1762–1764)

June 24, 1696: Ninham

Ninham, Willem, Mattasiwanck, Quagan, and Rapawees, "Indians, [and] rightful owners," convey to Albany trader Hendrick Ten Eyck "the land and the kil called Aquasing, called by us the Viskil [Fishkill or Crum Elbow Creek]" in the present town of Hyde Park. "This land begins on the north side of the Viskil at the boundary of trees of Pa[w]ling [Patent] . . . [extending southward] with the Viskil to the other kils until Meyndert Harmense's property [Poughkeepsie Patent]; this aforesaid land runs eastward until the Valkil [or Fallkill Creek] of Meyndert Harmense [northern property line] and westward to Hutsons [sic] River . . . This is the amount that has to be paid: 5 kettles, Coverlets 4 and 8 shirts, Blankets 4 and 8 pair of stockings, Duffel cloth 4, Gunpowder 12 lb., Lead 25 staves, Guns 4, Sewant [wampum] 300 guilders of black and white, Axes 12, Knives 20, Tobacco 2 rolls, Adzes 12, 1 barrel of cider, 1 half barrel of good beer, 2 hats, 1 ancker of rum, 2 nice jackets, 2 shirts nice, 2 pair of stockings [nice]." Incorporated as part of the Great Nine Partners Patent in 1697 (Dutch-Indian Deed ms., FDR Presidential Library and Museum).

April 10, 1702: Nimim

"kattakis and [ ]apennou wife of Mettanwaen [and] several other Indians of Said Esopus" appear before Ulster County justices Jacob Aertsen and Jan Heerman, "and Declare Nimim" under whom Martys De Mott had land at "Shawonkonck" surveyed, "was a stranger and no Esopus [Indian]" (New York Colonial Manuscripts–Governor's Council Papers, Secretary of State, 45:92).

October 8, 1712: Nemham/Nimham

"Nimham, Agans, Agtapyhout, Sekomeck & Alotam, proprieters Natives o[w] ners & Indians," convey three thousand acres of land in the towns of Poughkeepsie

and Wappinger to George Clark and Leonard Lewis of New York City, extending from "the Noort of the Land of Franses Rombout, Stavanes Van Cortland &c [Rombout Patent], att a place Coled Matapan [falls], to the South Side thereof, and Soo with a West Line to John Casperses Creeck on the bounds of Coll Pieter Schuyler [Schuyler's Patent] And Soo along Noorderly sd Creeck tell it comes with an East Line oposeit the East Sid of Cuyler Vlakte [flat or plain; Cuyler Patent], and Soo East Runneng tell it Comes About a Mile to the Easterd of the Matapan [Wappinger] Creeck and then Suderly along the Sd Matapan Creeck, keeping a Mile to the East Side tell it Comes with a westerly Line Opossiet the fore Mentioned Matapan [falls], from where it first begins" (NYCM-LP, 5:124; see also 5:90–91 for acreage recorded in the petition and license to purchase the land on April 24, 1712).
September 7, 1721: Nimham

New York Governor William Burnet grants a "Certificate of [Protection] to the Wapingers" stating that "Whereas the Wapinger and Waweytanow [Wawyachtenok or Westenhoek] Indians have formerly obtained of Go[v]. [Robert] Hunter [1710–19] a Certificate of their good & faithfull Behaviour and an assurance of his protection in all their just Rights and Pretentions and whereas ye said Indians by Nimham their Speaker have desired the like assurance from me in Consideration of their true & faithfull behaviour as good Subjects to his M.[ty] K. George [II] — I have therefore thought it desirable to give them this testimonial of my good opinion of them so to an assurance of all New favors & protection so long as they continue to Deserve it by their Peaceable and good deportment Given us" (New York Colonial Manuscripts, Governor's Council Papers, 63:143, NYSA).
September ? to November 14, 1721: Nemham

"Nemham[']s sister" develops an account with the Ulster County trader; "His mother" buys rum on the account. Purchases are recorded of 1 ell of strouds, 2 stroud blankets, 3 coarse blankets, 2 shirts, stroud stockings, 1 pair of black stockings, 1 small box with paint, gunpowder, lead, flintstones, rum, and beer. Payments of 4 deer, 27 lb skins, and 9 lb grease are listed to reduce the debt ([39–40]).
1721?: Minham

"Minhams Wigwam[s]" and the houses of early Dutchess County settlers Jacobus Swartwout, Johannes Buys (Boys or Boyce), and Johannes Terboss at "Weikopieh," are depicted on a survey "Map of [the] North line of [the] Highland Mountains" (PGP, P18, #99, oversized).
August 9, 1722: Nemham

Dutchess County assessment lists record the expenditure of 1 pound 15 shillings made to Fishkill justice of the peace and former South Ward supervisor

(1720) "Major Johannes Terboss for four Wouleves heads That he has Payed [as per dated certificates] one to Johannes Schut [on February 2], [two to Jurian Springsteen and John Montros on April 19] & a nother [on March 18] to Nemham the Indian" (*BSDC*, book 1:52).

April 25, 1724: Naunhamiss

One of the Indian signers selling land to Massachusetts authorities for two townships (Sheffield and Great Barrington) "lying upon Housatonack River, allias Westonook" along the disputed borders with New York and Connecticut for "Four Hundred and Sixty Pounds [currency] Three Barrels of Sider & thirty quarts of Rum" (Henry A. Wright, ed., *Indian Deeds of Hampden County* (Springfield, MA: N.p., 1905), 116–19).

October 13, 1730: Nimham

"Acgans & Nimham, Principal Sachemache and Proprietors, in behalf of all the rest" ("native Indian proprietors of land in Dutche[ss] County") receive "certain sums of money, goods and merchandise, to the value of one hundred and fifty pounds," for endorsing a new "Indian Deed" relinquishing their rights ["only excepting still the Whrits of some North Indians"] to "all the land in full formerly granted by Patent" in 1697 to the Great Nine Partners Company "situate and being on Hudson's river, between the creek called by the natives Aquasing, and by the Christians by Fish Creek [Crum Elbow Creek], at the markt trees of Pawling [including the said Creek] and the land of Meyndert Harmense and Company; then bounded southerly by said Land of Harmense & Company [Poughkeepsie Patent] so farr as their bounds runns; then westerly by said land of Harmense and Company until a southerly line run so farr south until it comes to the southside of a certain meadow wherein there is a white oak tree marked with the letters HT; then bounded southerly by an east and west line to the division line between this province of Newyork and Colony of Connecticuts, and so bounded easterly by the said division line & northerly by said Fish creek as farr as it goes & from the head thereof by a paralell line to the south bounds, running east and west to the said division line" (McDermott and Buck, *Eighteenth Century Documents*, 5:109–13).

February 1, 1743: Nimham

Dutchess County assessment lists record the expenditure of 5 shillings 9 pence for "rum Expended to Nimham a Sachem & other Indians" (*BSDC*, book 3:257).

May 21, 1744: King Nimham

Gottlob Buttner, a Moravian missionary working at the Mohican settlement of Shekomeko in northern Dutchess County, wrote in his diary that "There came

6 Indians from ye Highlands here, & stayed all night, they went to ye Maahacks [Mohawks], who [had] sent for them to treat about some Matters, we heard that they ridiculed our Brothers much, also that their King Nimham, who is a sorceror [i.e., shaman] speaks much against us, & forbids all his People to come into our Meetings" (MOA, box 112, 2:#3).

August 2, 1762: Sasckamuk (Sacekamuk)

Identified in a deposition by Daniel Nimham (fl. 1745–1778), along with "Tawanout or John Van Gilder," as a recipient of lands in Dutchess County granted by "the Indian Nation [of] the Wapingoes" on September 2, 1718 (Kempe Papers, Court Case Records, box 10, folder 9, NYHS).

August 25, 1762: Old Nimham

Identified in Catharyna (Rombout) Brett's complaint to British Indian agent Sir William Johnson about claims to her lands made the previous year by a "Capt. Nimham" (Daniel). Brett alleged that "Old Nimham" had died about twelve years ago. He was permitted to live on land set aside for him near the town of Fishkill. He had two sons, the eldest known by the nickname "One Shake." Brett also claimed that the reserved lands of Old Nimham (at Wei-kopieh/Wickapee/Weekepe/Weakepey/Wiccopee/Wickapy) were sold after his death to Capt. Swartwout for 20 pounds by One Shake and "Seven or Eight more Indians," after they received her permission "to Sell ye Emprovement" (*PWJ*, 10:493–95).

September 20, 1763: old Capt. Nimham

Mentioned in a complaint made by Hendrick Wamash and some of his people to Sir William Johnson, that "Mrs. Brett . . . Coll. Beekman, Verplank, Cortland, & Phillips . . . had not paid his Ancestors vizt. old Capt. Nimham &ca. For a Tract of Land near to ye. Fish Kills." Hendrick receives a pass to travel to New York City and address their complaints to Lt. Governor Cadwallader Colden, "who they hoped & expected would do them Justice in the Affair, as they imagined that He must, (from his Surveying the Same) be well acquainted with the State of the Case" (*PWJ*, 10:853–54).

October 8, 1763: Nimham the Grandfather

Hendrick Wamash appears before Lt. Governor Colden claiming "that several people at Fishkill and Poughkepsey owe him for some pieces of Land in several places," and is told "that near 40 years [1721] since the Indians of Fish-kill and Wappingers were heard by Governor Burnet on a like complaint at the House of Mr. Haskol near the place since called New Windsor [in colonial Ulster County, New York], that then everything was settled to the content of Nimham the Grandfather of this Man & of the other Indians" (Cadwallader Colden, *The Colden Letter Books 1760–1765* [New York: New-York Historical Society, 1877], 1:247–48).

November 17, 1764: Sackoenemack of Dutchess County

Identified as the father of Nimham and grandfather of Daniel Nimham in a document granting Samuel Monroe guardianship over Wappingers land rights in Dutchess County: "Daniel Nimham Son and Heir of Nimham the Son of Sackoenemack of Dutchess County" (Kempe Papers, Court Case Records, box 10, folder 9, NYHS).

John Van Gelder (fl. 1718–1758/pm. 1758–1768)

September 2, 1718: John Van Gilder

"John Van Gilder & an Indian named Sasckamuk" are noted as recipients of lands in Dutchess County granted by "the Indian Nation [of] the Wapingoes" (Kempe Papers, Court Case Records, box 10, folder 9, NYHS).

August 1721: Jan Van Gelder

"Jan van gelder[']s sister" is listed with a small account by the Ulster County trader. She makes purchases of 1½ ells of white baize and 11½ "kans" of rum and various unlisted goods; receives a credit of 10 guilders through a payment by "Coll[.] gasbeek [Abraham Gaasbeek Chambers of Foxhall Manor]" toward her debt ([29–30]).

March 7, 1723: Jan Van Gelder

The trader lists a small debt of 40 guilders in the accounts of "Jores[,] hester's son," from an unspecified purchase made by "his wife[,] Jan van gelder's sister" ([22]).

April 25, 1724: John Van Gilder

One of the Indian signers selling land to Massachusetts authorities for two townships (Sheffield and Great Barrington) "lying upon Housatonack River, allias Westonook" along the disputed borders with New York and Connecticut for "Four Hundred and Sixty Pounds [currency] Three Barrels of Sider & thirty quarts of Rum." The Indians reserve for themselves a tract of land extending from the river to the New York border (Wright, *Indian Deeds*, 116–19).

October 24, 1737: John Van Guilder

"John Van Guilder of Sheffield" is granted rights by John Pophnehaunau-wack (or Konkapot) and others to the southern half of the reserved Indian lands (in Egremont) west of Sheffield, Massachusetts, and extending to the Taconic Mountains (Wright, *Indian Deeds*, 141–42).

June 1, 1756: John Van Gilder

Noch Namos, an "Indian woman now of the Fishkills in Dutchess County in the Province of New York formerly of Housatunnock," conveys the whole of the reserved Indian lands in Sheffield "for the love and affection I have and Do bear unto John Van Gilder . . . and for many other good Causes and Consideration . . . as well as Sundry Sums of money and other presents" (Wright, *Indian Deeds*, 155–57).

September 12, 1758: John Van Gelder

John van Gelder's last will (dated May 22, 1758) and an inventory of his estate (on September 12, 1758) is entered in probate court at Springfield, Massachusetts (Debra Winchell, "The Impact of John Van Gelder: Mohican, Husbandman and Historical Figure," in *Mohican Seminar 3, The Journey: An Algonquian Peoples Seminar, Selected Research Papers, 2003–2004*, ed. Shirley W. Dunn, 127–44 [Albany: Univ. of the State of New York, 2009], 142).

August 2, 1762: Tawanout or John Van Gilder

Identified in a deposition by Daniel Nimham as his "Uncle . . . his Mothers Brother," and one of two sons of the Wappinger Indian chief Awansous (fl. 1680–1707). John inherited the whole of Awansous's land rights in the South Precinct (or Philipse upper Patent) of Dutchess County after the death of his brother Sancoolakheekhing and later passed his rights to Daniel Nimham sometime in 1758 (Kempe Papers, Court Case Records, box 10, folder 9, NYHS).

October ?, 1768: John Van Gelder/Toanunck

Identified by Joseph van Gelder (his son) and others during provincial litigation made against the lower manor of Rensselaerswyck as "John Van Gelder in Indian Toanunck," and reported to have "belonged to the Catt's Kills" (Miscellaneous Manuscripts V[van Rensselaer, John], NYHS).

Pesewein (fl. 1720–1730)

June 3, 1720: Pesewein

Dutchess County assessment lists (January 20, 1724) record the expenditure of 15 shillings made "To Coll Leonard Lewis [judge of the Court of Common Pleas, Poughkeepsie] for Mony Desbursed for the County — To a Woulfs head Payd to an Indian Named Pesewein 5 Shill — To a Woulfs head Payd to John Schoute 10 Shillings" (*BSDC*, book 1:33).

April 1722: Piswijn

The Ulster County trader records a small debt incurred by "piswijn's wife on 1 box with paint" at 4 guilders ([53]).

January 16, 1724: Pesiewein

Dutchess County assessment lists record the expenditure of 5 shillings made to Poughkeepsie justice and former Middle Ward supervisor (1722–23) "Capt Barent Van Kleeck for a Wolf Killed by pesiewein" (*BSDC*, book 2:7).

October 13, 1730: Cocewyn/Pecewyn

One of the "native Indian proprietors of land in Dutche[ss] County," confirming the expanded boundaries of the Great Nine Partners Patent (McDermott and Buck, *Eighteenth Century Documents*, 110–12).

Wappenack (fl. 1724–1732/pm. 1762)

December 1724: Wappenack/Wappenak

The Ulster County trader lists small transactions with Wappenack and his son in the account of "Keman the savage or watschap." Wappenack is the brother of "kisay[']s daughter," the "wife" of Keman. The trader notes "the son of her brother wappenack" bought "1 colored shirt[,] paid" for with a credit of 9 guilders to "Wappenak['s] son for 1 skin" and the debt of "her brother" for 2 guilders against the "remainder on strouds" cloth ([65–66]).

November 29, 1725, to August 18, 1726: Wappaneck

"wappaneck[,] kisay's son" develops an account with the trader; "His wife[,] sawagoneck hend[rick's] daughter" is listed with her own account. "1 sch[epel of] Indian corn" was fetched "by y[our] H[onor's] mother" and "1 kan rum by arent" (the Indian?), "his father" purchases rum on the account. Wappaneck remains indebted "on gunpowder and lead and molasses" and "on a shirt from older times." He makes new purchases of white baize, strouds, 1 coarse blanket, a shirt, 1 sheath knife, a bottle, gunpowder, lead, flintstones, "½ sch[epel of] flour," and rum. Payments of 2 bear hides and unlisted skins are noted toward his debt; he pays "1 marten for 1 stack of cards." His wife purchases rum and makes partial payment with skins ([81–82]).

November ?, 1726, to April 24, 1728: Wappeneck

"mattasson[,] wappeneck['s] son" develops an account with the trader; "his wife" is active on the account and "hendr[ic]k sawagonck['s] daughter['s] debt" is also listed. Purchases are recorded of strouds, cotton, colored textiles, 1 coarse blanket, a duffel blanket, 4 shirts (1 colored), pipes, gunpowder, lead, flintstones, cider, rum, 1 bread, molasses, a stack of playing cards, and "1 gun of pitter tappen" (of Kingston) at 240 guilders. Payments of 2 bear hides, 2 elk skins, 4½ lb skins, 15½ lb dressed skins, 6 lb fat or grease, deer meat, 1 pig, and 9 lb beaver are listed to reduce his debt ([95–96]).

October 13, 1730: Wappenas

One of the "native Indian proprietors of land in Dutche[ss] County," confirming the expanded boundaries of the Great Nine Partners Patent (McDermott and Buck, *Eighteenth Century Documents*, 110–12).

October 10, 1732: Wapanoos

One of four witnesses to a land sale of 15,000 acres made by "River Indians [and] Native Proprietors" to Daniel Kettlehuysen and company for 130 pounds New York currency "Lying and being in the County of Albany on the East Side of Hudsons River near and about a Certain Tract of Land Called Ho[o]sick" (NYCM-LP, 11:49B).

August 2, 1762: Wapenaus/Wappenaus

Identified in a deposition by Daniel Nimham as the deceased father of Mehloss and a cousin of "Nimham the Father." Wappenaus was granted lands by Nimham within the Fishkill Precinct (or Rombout Patent) of Dutchess County and later passed his rights to John Packto, the son of Ahtaupeanhond (Kempe Papers, box 10, folder 9, NYHS).

Nackarend (fl. 1728–1732)

March 9, 1728: Nackarend

The Ulster County trader notes the sale "to nackarend [of] 2½ ells of baize at the mine for martens" valued at 15 guilders; the transaction is recorded on the account of the Indian man "tateu" ([76]).

June 15, 1728: Neckarind

"Tateew, Ochangues and Neckarind Indians and the Native owners and proprietors" convey to Cornelius Hornebeck and Frederick Schoonmaker for 10 pounds currency, "a Certain Mine . . . Lying and being within Rochester [Precinct] . . . on the South Side of the Sandbergs kill near to a Certaine place Called Nepenagh [Napanoch] together with the Quantity of four hundred acres of Land." Affirmed on June 19, 1728, in a memorandum by Abraham Gaasbeek Chambers, a judge of the Ulster County Court of Common Pleas (UCDB, DD:6–7).

August 10, 1729: Nackerin

Dutchess County assessment lists record the expenditure of 10 shillings made to Poughkeepsie justice "Peter Van Kleeck Esqr for a Woulfs head paid to Nackerin an Indian" (*BSDC*, book 3:21).

October 13, 1730: Narcarindt

A participant noted in a land sale confirming the expanded boundaries of the Great Nine Partners Patent in Dutchess County (McDermott and Buck, *Eighteenth Century Documents*, 110–12).

February 2, 1731: Nakarint

Dutchess County assessment lists record the expenditure of 1 pound made to Tryntie Van Cleeck for the bounty "paid to an Indian Nakarint [for] Two Wolfes heads" (*BSDC*, book 3:24).

March 28, 1732: Nockkerin

Dutchess County assessment lists record the expenditure of 1 pound 10 shillings made "To the Hears of the Widdow Trynty Van Kleeck Deceased for Three Woulf heads paid to Indians—Two to Nockkerin & one to nennquin" (*BSDC*, book 3:38).

Bibliography

Unpublished Sources

Columbia University, New York

Philips-Governor Family Papers, Rare Book and Manuscript Library.

Firestone Library, Princeton University, Princeton, NJ

Deed Manuscript, March 27, 1703. Livingston Papers, CO280, box 158.

FDR [Franklin D. Roosevelt] Presidential Library and Museum, Hyde Park, NY

Dutch-Indian deed manuscript for lands in present Hyde Park, New York, June 24, 1696.

Huguenot Historical Society Archives, New Paltz, NY

New Paltz Town Records, 1677–1932.

New-York Historical Society, New York

John Tabor Kempe Papers. Papers pertaining to Daniel Nimham and the Wappinger Indian land claims in Dutchess County, NY, Court Case Records, box 10, folder 9.

Miscellaneous Manuscripts V: van Rensselaer, John. October 1768. "Notes of Evidence with Some Information Filed by the King Against John Van Rensselaer, For an Alleged Intrusion Upon Lands Claimed to be Vacant Between the Manors of Livingston and Rensselaerwick, in the Rear of Kinderhook."

New York State Archives, Albany

Deed Manuscript, April 1, 1703. Kingston Papers, CV 10181 TA.

New York Book of Patents and Deeds. Secretary of State, Collection Series 12943-78, Letters Patents, 1638–1775.

New York Colonial Manuscripts—Governor's Council Papers. Secretary of State, Collection Series A1894, Council Papers, 1664–1781.

New York Colonial Manuscripts—Indorsed Land Papers. Secretary of State, Collection Series A0272-78, Applications for Land Grants, 1642–1803.

New York Executive Council Minutes. Secretary of State, Collection Series A1895, Council Minutes, 1668–1783.

New York State Bureau of Surplus Real Property, Albany

William Cockburn: Survey Map of the Hardenbergh Patent, 1771.

New York State Library, Albany

Livingston Papers. Microfilm.
Moravian Archives. Microfilm Series.

New York State Library, Manuscript and Special Collections

Cockburn Family Land Papers: 1732–1864 (Collection SC7004).
Martin van Bergen, Affidavit, 3 September 1767 (Single Accession Mss., 6812).

Private Collection

Deed Manuscript, March 22, 1707. Land Sale Made by the Esopus Indian Kakawaramin to Johannes Hardenbergh Sr.

Rutgers University, New Brunswick, NJ

George Tappen Manuscript. Philhower Collection, box P26, folder 14 (transcriptions of records in the Ulster County Clerk's Office, 1847), Special Collections and University Archives.

Senate House State Historic Site, Kingston, NY

Deed Manuscripts, September 27, 1726; May 1, 1751.

Ulster County Clerk's Office, Kingston, NY

Dutch Records Kinston: English translations of Dutch Records by Dingman Versteeg, 1896–1899 (followed by appropriate translation book and page number).
Minutes of the Court of Justice of the Peace, 1719–1744.

Minutes of the Justice Court, 1714–1741, folders 1–3.

Minutes of the Ulster County Court of Sessions, 1706–1712, 1712–1720, 1737–1750.

Tax Assessment List, 1716–17. ICN 02-01657, Historic Records-101 box collection. Also available at http://www.co.ulster.ny.us/archives/exhibits/burning/Tax Assessment.html.

Ulster County Deed Books. Vols. AA through EE.

William L. Clements Library, University of Michigan, Ann Arbor

Wilson Family Papers, Map Division: 1751. Map by Jacob Hoornbeck of lands belonging to Henry Beekman Sr. in the township of Rochester, Ulster County.

Published Sources

Banner, Stuart. *How the Indians Lost Their Land: Law and Power on the Frontier.* Cambridge, MA: Harvard Univ. Press, 2005.

Becker, Marshall J. "Anadromous Fish and the Lenape." *Pennsylvania Archaeologist* 76 (Fall 2006): 28–40.

———. "The Lenape and Other 'Delawarean' Peoples at the Time of European Contact: Population Estimates Derived from Archaeological and Historical Sources." *Bulletin of the New York Archaeological Association* 105 (1993): 16–25.

———. "Lenopi; Or, What's in a Name? Interpreting the Evidence for Cultural Boundaries in the Lower Delaware Valley." *Bulletin of the Archaeological Society of New Jersey*, no. 63 (2008): 11–32.

———. "Matchcoats: Cultural Conservatism and Change in One Aspect of Native American Clothing." *Ethnohistory* 52 (2005): 727–87.

Bolton, Robert. *The History of the Several Towns, Manors, and Patents of the County of Westchester, from Its First Settlement to the Present Time.* New York: Chas. F. Roper, 1881.

Boyd, Julian P., and Robert J. Taylor, eds. *The Susquehannah Company Papers.* 11 vols. Wilkes-Barre, PA: Wyoming Historical and Geological Society, 1930–71.

Cantwell, Anne-Marie, and Diana diZerega Wall. *Unearthing Gotham: The Archaeology of New York City.* New Haven, CT: Yale Univ. Press, 2003.

Carlos, Ann M., and Frank D. Lewis. "Property Rights and Competition in the Depletion of the Beaver: Native Americans and the Hudson's Bay Company, 1700–1763." In *The Other Side of the Frontier: Economic Explorations into Native American History*, edited by Linda Barrington, 131–49. Boulder, CO: Westview Press, 1999.

Colden, Cadwallader. *The Colden Letter Books 1760–1765*. Collections 1. New York: New-York Historical Society, 1877.

———. *The Letters and Papers of Cadwallader Colden*. Vol. 6, *1761–1764*. Collections 55. New York: New-York Historical Society, 1923.

Donck, Adriaen van der. *A Description of New Netherland*. Edited by Charles T. Gehring and William A. Starna. Translated by Diederik Willam Goedhuys. Foreword by Russell Shorto. Lincoln: Univ. of Nebraska Press, 2008.

Dunn, Shirley W. *The Mohican World, 1680–1750*. Fleischmanns, NY: Purple Mountain Press, 2000.

Fernow, Berthold, comp. *Calendar of Council Minutes, 1668–1783*. *New York State Library Bulletin* 58. Albany: Univ. of the State of New York, 1902.

Folts, James D. "The Westward Migration of the Munsee Indians in the Eighteenth Century." In *The Challenge: An Algonquian Peoples Seminar*, edited by Shirley W. Dunn, 31–47. *New York State Museum Bulletin* 506. Albany: Univ. of the State of New York, 2005.

Fried, Marc B. *Shawangunk Place-Names: Indian, Dutch and English Geographical Names of the Shawangunk Mountain Region. Their Origin, Interpretation and Historical Evolution*. Gardiner, NY: Marc B. Fried, 2005.

Goddard, Ives. "The Historical Phonology of Munsee." *International Journal of American Linguistics* 48 (1982): 16–48.

Gould, Jay. *History of Delaware County and Border Wars of New York: Containing a Sketch of the Early Settlements in the County, and a History of the Late Anti-Rent Difficulties in Delaware, with Other Historical and Miscellaneous Matter, Never Before Published*. Roxbury, NY: Keeny and Gould Publishers, 1856.

Grumet, Robert S. "Esopus." In *The Encyclopedia of New York State*, edited by Peter Eisenstadt, 527. Syracuse, NY: Syracuse Univ. Press, 2005.

———. *Historic Contact: Indian People and Colonists in Today's Northeastern United States in the Sixteenth through Eighteenth Centuries*. Norman: Univ. of Oklahoma Press, 1995.

———. "The Minisink Settlements: Native American Identity and Society in the Munsee Heartland, 1650–1778." In *The People of the Minisink: Papers from the 1989 Delaware Water Gap Symposium*, edited by David G. Orr and Douglas V. Campana, 175–250. Philadelphia, PA: National Park Service, 1991.

———. *The Munsee Indians: A History*. Norman: Univ. of Oklahoma Press, 2009.

———. "Strangely Decreast by the Hand of God: A Documentary Appearance-Disappearance Model for Munsee Demography, 1630–1801." *Journal of Middle Atlantic Archaeology* 5 (1989): 129–45.

———. "Taphow: The Forgotten 'Sakemau and Commander in Chief of All Those Indians Inhabiting Northern New Jersey.'" *Bulletin of the Archaeological Society of New Jersey*, no. 43 (1988): 23–28.

———. "That Their Issue Be Not Spurious: An Inquiry into Munsee Matriliny." *Bulletin of the Archaeological Society of New Jersey*, no. 45 (1990): 19–24.

Grumet, Robert S., and Herbert C. Kraft. "Munsee." In *The Encyclopedia of New York State*, edited by Peter Eisenstadt, 1023–25. Syracuse, NY: Syracuse Univ. Press, 2005.

Hazard, Samuel, ed. *Minutes of the Provincial Council of Pennsylvania, from the Organization to the Termination of the Proprietary Government, 10 March 1683 to 27 September 1775*. 16 vols. Harrisburg, PA: Theophilus Fenn and Co., 1838–52.

Historical Records Survey, New York State. *Minutes of the Board of Supervisors of Ulster County, 1711–1731. Transcriptions of Early County Records of New York State*. Prepared by the New York State Historical Records Survey Project, Division of Professional and Service Projects, Works Project Administration Historical Records Survey I. New York (State). Albany: New York State, 1939.

Hoes, Roswell Randall, trans. and ed. *Baptismal and Marriage Registers of the Old Dutch Church of Kingston, Ulster County, New York, 1660–1809*. New York: De Vinne Press, 1891. Reprint, Baltimore, MD: Genealogical Publishing Co., 1980.

Hollister, Joan. "Account Books and Economic Life in Early New Paltz." *Symposium on Early New Paltz History, Nov. 15, 2003*. New Paltz, NY: Huguenot Historical Society, www.hhs-newpaltz.org/library_archives/exhibits_research/early_newpaltz_history/hollister.html). Accessed May 25, 2007.

Hollister, Joan, and Sally M. Schultz. "From Emancipation to Representation: John Hasbrouck and His Account Books." *Hudson Valley Historical Review* 20 (Spring 2004): 1–24.

Hunter, William A. "Documented Subdivisions of the Delaware Indians." *Bulletin of the Archaeological Society of New Jersey*, no. 35 (1978): 20–40.

Kip, Frederic E. *History of the Kip Family in America*. Montclair, NJ: privately published, 1928.

Kraft, Herbert C. *The Lenape-Delaware Indian Heritage: 10,000 BC to AD 2000*. Stanhope, NJ: Lenape Books, 2001.

Lenik, Edward J. *Indians in the Ramapo: Survival, Persistence and Presence*. Ringwood, NJ: North Jersey Highlands Historical Society, 1999.

Lincoln, Charles H. *Manuscript Records of the French and Indian War in the Library of the American Antiquarian Society*. Reprint, Westminster, MD: Heritage Books, 2007.

McDermott, William P., and Clifford Buck. *Eighteenth Century Documents of the Nine Partners Patent, Dutchess County, New York*. Dutchess County Historical Society (DCHS) *Collections*. Baltimore, MD: DCHS, 1979.

Megapolensis, Johannes. "Kort ontwerp van de Mahakuase Indianen in Nieuw-Nederlandt, haer landt, statuere, dracht, manieren en magistraten, beschreven in 't jaer 1644." In *Beschryvinge van Virginia, Nieuw-Nederlandt, Nieuw Engelandt en d'Eylanden Bermudes, Berbados en S. Christoffel*, edited by J. Hartgers, 42–49. Amsterdam: N.p., 1651.

Merrell, James H. *Into the American Woods: Negotiators on the Pennsylvania Frontier.* New York: W. W. Norton and Co., 1999.

O'Callaghan, Edmund B., ed. *Documentary History of the State of New York*. 4 vols. Albany, NY: Weed, Parsons and Co., 1849–51.

O'Callaghan, Edmund B., and Berthold Fernow, eds. *Documents Relative to the Colonial History of the State of New York*. 15 vols. Albany, NY: Weed, Parsons and Co., 1856–87.

Olde Ulster Magazine. Kingston, NY: Benjamin Myer Brink, 1905–14.

Otto, Paul. *The Dutch-Munsee Encounter in America: The Struggle for Sovereignty in the Hudson Valley*. New York: Berghahn Books, 2006.

Pearson, Jonathan, and A. J. F. van Laer, trans. and eds. *Early Records of the City and County of Albany and Colony of Rensselaerswijck*. 4 vols. Vols. 2–4 revised by A. J. F. van Laer. Albany: Univ. of the State of New York, 1869–1919.

Philhower, Charles A. "The Indians of the Morris County Area." New Jersey Historical Society *Proceedings* 54, no. 4 (1939): 249–58.

Ramsey, William L. "'Something Cloudy in Their Looks': The Origins of the Yamasee War Reconsidered." *Journal of American History* 91 (2003): 44–75.

Reynolds, Cuyler, ed. *Hudson-Mohawk Genealogical and Family Memoirs*. 4 vols. New York: Lewis Historical Publishing Co., 1911.

Schultz, Sally M., and Joan Hollister. "Jean Cottin, Eighteenth-Century Huguenot Merchant." *New York History* 86 (Spring 2005): 133–67.

Schutt, Amy C. *Peoples of the River Valleys: The Odyssey of the Delaware Indians*. Philadelphia: Univ. of Pennsylvania Press, 2007.

Scott, Kenneth, and Charles E. Baker. "Renewals of Governor Nicolls' Treaty of 1665 with the Esopus Indians at Kingston, N.Y." *New-York Historical Society Quarterly* 37 (1953): 251–72.

Smith, J. Michael. "The Highland King Nimhammaw and the Native Indian Proprietors of Land in Dutchess County, New York: 1712–1765." In *The Continuance:*

An Algonquian Peoples Seminar, edited by Shirley W. Dunn, 39–76. *New York State Museum Bulletin* 501. Albany: Univ. of the State of New York, 2004.

———. "The Seventeenth Century Sachems of the Wapping Country: Ethnic Identity and Interaction in the Hudson River Valley." In *Mohican Seminar 3, The Journey: An Algonquian Peoples Seminar, Selected Research Papers, 2003–2004,* edited by Shirley W. Dunn, 39–67. *New York State Museum Bulletin* 511. Albany: Univ. of the State of New York, 2009.

———. "Wappinger Kinship Associations: Daniel Nimham's Family Tree." *Hudson River Valley Review* 26 (Spring 2010): 69–98.

Sullivan, James, et al., eds. *The Papers of Sir William Johnson.* 14 vols. Albany: Univ. of the State of New York, 1921–65.

Trelease, Allen W. *Indian Affairs in Colonial New York: The Seventeenth Century.* Ithaca, NY: Cornell Univ. Press, 1960. Reprint, with an introduction by William A. Starna. Lincoln: Univ. of Nebraska Press, 1997.

Vassar Brothers Institute. *Book of the Supervisors of Dutchess County, NY.* Poughkeepsie, NY: Vassar Brothers Institute, 1911.

Waterman, Kees-Jan, trans. and ed. *"To Do Justice to Him and Myself": Evert Wendell's Account Book of the Fur Trade with Indians in Albany, New York (1695–1726).* Lightning Rod Press Vol. 4. Philadelphia, PA: American Philosophical Society, 2008.

Waterman, Kees-Jan, and J. Michael Smith. "An Account Book of the Indian Trade in Ulster County, New York, 1712–1732." *Hudson River Valley Review* 24 (Autumn 2007): 59–83.

Waterman, Kees-Jan, Jaap Jacobs, and Charles Gehring, eds. *Indianenverhalen: De eerste beschrijvingen van Indianen langs de Hudsonrivier, 1609–1680.* Zutphen, the Netherlands: Walburg Pers, 2009.

Wermuth, Thomas S. *Rip Van Winkle's Neighbors: The Transformation of a Rural Society in the Hudson River Valley, 1720–1850.* Albany: State University of New York Press, 2001.

Wheeler, Rachel M. "Living Upon Hope: Mahicans and Missionaries, 1730–1760." PhD diss., Yale Univ., 1999.

Whitehead, William A., ed. *The Papers of Lewis Morris, Governor of the Province of New Jersey from 1738 to 1746.* New Jersey Historical Society *Collections* 4. Newark: New Jersey Historical Society, 1852.

Winchell, Debra. "The Impact of John Van Gelder: Mohican, Husbandman and Historical Figure." In *Mohican Seminar 3, The Journey: An Algonquian Peoples*

Seminar, Selected Research Papers, 2003–2004, edited by Shirley W. Dunn, 127–44. *New York State Museum Bulletin* 511. Albany: Univ. of the State of New York, 2009.

Wright, Henry A., ed. *Indian Deeds of Hampden County: Being Copies of All Land Transfers from the Indians Recorded in the County of Hampden*. Springfield, MA: N.p., 1905.

Index

Note: Information presented in figures and tables is represented by *f* and *t*. Entries from the profiles are marked with *p*. Information in notes is indicated by n following the page number. The index provides no entries for the transcription.

rum, 49*t*, 80–87, 90–97, 99, 100, 102–3, 105,
107–8, 110–12, 114–17, 119–24, 126–35,
137–39, 141–49, 151–56, 159–60, 162, 164,
167–68, 170–71, 173–78, 180–82, 184–85,
187–92, 194–95, 198–204; for burial of
Mannonck, 165; as grave gift, 8
rum beer, 136
Rumbout Precinct, 40n36
Runup, Quick's son-in-law. *See*
Noundawagaeron
Rutgers, Jacob, 237*p*
Rutgersen, Jacob, 237*p*, 239–40*p*, 246*p*
Rutsen, 119

sachems (principal leaders), 7, 293*p*; complaint to Kingston authorities, 9–10;
Kingston court minutes identification of, 32–34; listed in Ulster County
account book, 8; Van der Donck on,
45n114. *See also throughout appendix*
Sackoenemack. *See* Nimham
saddle, 125
sallon, 107
Salomon, 45n113
Sammetie, 45n113, 206nn16–17; son, 82
Sancoolakheekhing (Wappinger), 296*p*
Sander (also Nachnawachena) (Esopus
sachem), Lendert's and William's
brother, 8*f*, 9, 16, 20, 24–25, 28, 43n91,
45n113, 58–59*t*, 64*t*, 71*f*, 93–94, 113,
209n52, 209n60, 210n68, 236*p*, 274–78*p*;
wages for traveling, 59*t*
Sanders, Robert, 290*p*
Sansis Rennos, small fellow, 31, 61*t*, 172–73
Sar, 161, 208n48, 222n289, 250*p*, 283*p*
Sar, Hendreck Hekan's wife, 6, 45n113,
56*t*, 90, 161, 177, 208n48
Sar, Jurewen's sister, 96

savage from across the river, the, 119
Sawagonck/Sawagoneck Hendreck,
Kobes's father, 32, 45n112; as escort,
60*t*; sons, 24, 32, 45n112, 62–63*t*, 65*t*,
119, 141, 147, 148, 167, 169, 188, 218n218,
220n246, 220n254, 220–21n258,
222n289, 227n360, 227n364, 227n370,
230n437, 236*p*, 250*p*, 251*p*, 283*p*, 285*p*
Sawanagh. *See* Schawenackie
Sawanossie/Sawanos/Sawannes/Sawa-
nnos, 22–23, 33, 46n117, 57*t*, 60*t*, 62*t*,
136–37, 143, 178, 219n230
Sawenakies. *See* Schawenackie
Sawis. *See* Achpalawamin
Schawenackie/Shawanachkie/Sawena-
kies/Sawanagh/Sawanaghki (also
Jepthah) (Esopus sachem), 8*f*, 37n14,
43n91, 94, 209n61, 229n415, 251–52*p*,
265*p*; son, 94, 97, 209n61; wife, 94,
209n61
Schoonmaker, Elisabeth, 209n62
Schoonmaker, Frederick, 298*p*
schulp (shell), 225n321
Schut, Johannes, 293*p*
Schuyler, Philip John, 3
Schuyler, Pieter, 290*p*, 292*p*
scissors, 92, 105
securities, provided by Indians, 22–23,
61*t*, 103, 106, 121, 123, 141, 164; wampum, 121, 174, 191, 263–67*p*
Sekomeck, 291*p*
Senecas/Sinni, 265*p*
services, to pay debts, 52–53*t*, 100–102,
110, 115, 132, 135, 139, 147, 152, 161, 172,
175, 180, 188, 196, 203; Mannonck's, 73*f*
Sett, 45n113
seyette stockings, 92, 209n53
Shamokin village, Susquehanna River,
41n60